D1229462

USAopoly Inc. is a leading developer and manufacturer of board g[...] [...] producing the world's most beloved games "with a twist," under license from Hasbro, since 1994. Our partners include marquee brands and licensors such as Disney, Nintendo, Warner Bros., Cartoon Network, HBO, FOX and CBS. With the 2009 release of Telestrations®, named the #1 Party Game by Board Game Geek, we launched our original game business. Our portfolio of original games is constantly growing and now includes the award-winning games: Telestrations After Dark®, Harry Potter™ HOGWARTS BATTLE™, Tapple®, Rollers®, Nefarious™ The Mad Scientist Game, and many more.

GET READY FOR OVERSTREET® #48

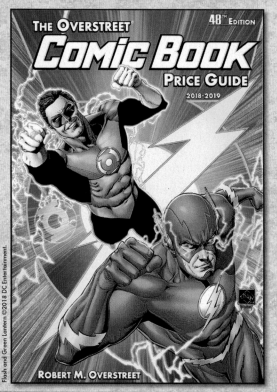

Flash and Green Lantern ©2018 DC Entertainment.

THE OVERSTREET®
Comic Book
PRICE GUIDE
48TH EDITION
2018-2019
ROBERT M. OVERSTREET

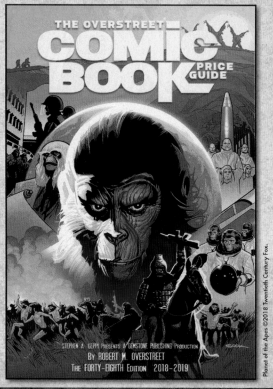

Planet of the Apes ©2018 Twentieth Century Fox.

THE OVERSTREET
COMIC BOOK
PRICE GUIDE
STEPHEN A. GEPPI Presents A GEMSTONE PUBLISHING Production
By ROBERT M. OVERSTREET
The FORTY-EIGHTH EDITION 2018-2019

COVER BY ETHAN VAN SCIVER!

HC • APR181581   SC • APR181580

All New Pricing Data   All New Market Reports
New and Updated Listings   All New Feature Articles

COVER BY RYAN SOOK!

HC • APR181583   SC • APR181582

New Record Prices   Key Anniversaries
Top Comics   and so much more!

Buffy The Vampire Slayer ©2018 Twentieth Century Fox.

Big! Big!
OVERSTREET
COMIC BOOK
PRICE GUIDE
48th EDITION
2018 2019
ROBERT M. OVERSTREET

$35.00 HC $29.95 SC

The Overstreet® Comic Book Price Guide
has been the definitive guide for
collectors and dealers alike since 1970!

Don't forget
The "Big Big" Edition!
Larger Print
Square Bound $47.50

**ALL THIS
PRICING GOODNESS
ON SALE
JULY 18, 2018**

WWW.GEMSTONEPUB.COM

GEMSTONE
PUBLISHING

THE OVERSTREET GUIDE TO COLLECTING TABLETOP GAMES

BY CARRIE WOOD & RICHARD ANKNEY

ALEX CARRA, ROBERT M. OVERSTREET,
AND J.C. VAUGHN
CONTRIBUTING WRITERS

MARK HUESMAN
LAYOUT & DESIGN

BRAELYNN BOWERSOX
MARK HUESMAN
AMANDA SHERIFF
J.C. VAUGHN
EDITORS

TOM GAREY, KATHY WEAVER, BRETT CANBY AND
ANGELA PHILLIPS-MILLS
ACCOUNTING SERVICES

SPECIAL THANKS TO
PETER ADKISON, LARRY ELMORE, SEAN EWING,
ERIC MENGE, SCOTT GAETA, HERITAGE AUCTIONS,
JAMES HUDSON, MATT MERCER, ALAN NANES,
BILLY SACCARDI, DAVE TAYLOR, ELISA TEAGUE,
BRAD VANVUGT, GAVIN VERHEY, AND DANIEL ZAYAS

GEMSTONE PUBLISHING • HUNT VALLEY, MARYLAND
WWW.GEMSTONEPUB.COM

From the Publisher

For many comic shop owners, comic books and tabletop games have long gone hand-in-hand. So it's perhaps overdue that tabletop gaming and all it has to offer is officially being brought into the Overstreet lineup of books with this very volume. Though at the same time, it might be arriving at exactly the right moment for this industry – one that has been enjoying a renaissance within the last few years thanks to a number of factors, all of which you'll learn about in this book.

You may be surprised to learn how valuable some classic board games are worth these days. But beyond the board games we all grew up with – *The Game of Life*, *Monopoly*, *Scrabble*, and so on – the industry has far more to be explored. Collectible card games may still seem "new" to many, but the original *Magic: The Gathering* arrived two and a half decades ago and many of the cards from those early sets are worth a simply astonishing amount. And on the role-playing end of things, certainly *Dungeons & Dragons* is still the top name in the business, but is hardly the only one worth paying attention to.

Carrie Wood and Richard Ankney worked together on this project, marking an exciting collaboration between Gemstone Publishing and Game Trade Media. Carrie, our assistant editor at Gemstone, previously brought her passion for gaming to our lineup of books with *The Overstreet Guide to Collecting Video Games*. Rick, Game Trade Media's production manager, is an absolute wealth of knowledge when it comes to tabletop gaming in general.

Together, these two and the team that's brought this book to life have done an incredible job at shining a spotlight on this exciting hobby. By providing historical context to many games, they've highlighted why they're valued as collectibles. And most importantly, they've done so in a way that can still fascinate veterans while also grabbing the attention of newcomers.

As always, let us know what you think.

Robert M. Overstreet
Publisher

GEMSTONE PUBLISHING

STEPHEN A. GEPPI
PRESIDENT AND CHIEF EXECUTIVE OFFICER

ROBERT M. OVERSTREET
PUBLISHER

J.C. VAUGHN
VICE-PRESIDENT OF PUBLISHING

MARK HUESMAN
CREATIVE DIRECTOR

AMANDA SHERIFF
ASSOCIATE EDITOR

CARRIE WOOD
ASSISTANT EDITOR

BRAELYNN BOWERSOX
STAFF WRITER

WWW.GEMSTONEPUB.COM

THE OVERSTREET GUIDE TO COLLECTING TABLETOP GAMES. JUNE 2018.
ISBN: 978-1-60360-216-7
PUBLISHED BY GEMSTONE PUBLISHING, INC., 10150 YORK RD., SUITE 300, HUNT VALLEY, MD 21030.

TABLETOPICS

INTRODUCTION

What can I say about tabletop gaming? Hopefully a lot, as that's why we wrote this book! Not only has gaming been an activity I could enjoy with my friends and family, but it also provided a place where I could escape.

I began my trek in the realm of board gaming during Sunday dinners at my grandparents' house, when my family would play the classics: *Monopoly*, cribbage, backgammon, chess, *The Game of Life*. Later, I would find a love for a much more intense game – and it would literally change my life.

In the early '80s, while I was at my cousin's house for the weekend, I watched as he and his friends played a game in which they rolled dice and declared actions against unseen foes. I hovered around them just wondering what was going on. I was only about 10 at the time and I idolized my cousin (who was three years older than me), so I was excited when he asked if I wanted to play. I asked him what the game was, and he told me – *Dungeons & Dragons*, a game of embarking on adventures and fighting bad guys. I never took a seat at a table so fast! They helped me create my very first character, a ranger, named Orion Fraust – I still have him to this day!

Once I began playing *D&D*, it opened up a new world to me as far as what we call "gaming." I sought out others to play, and I've had the pleasure of playing with many around the world. My time spent in the U.S. Navy gave me lots of opportunities in that regard. But I didn't limit myself to *D&D* – I started playing other games too, like *Axis & Allies, Fortress America, Risk,* and *Stratego*. These were some early additions to my collection, and I knew then that this would be something I'd be collecting for a long time.

Speaking of collecting, it's without a doubt one of the things about the tabletop industry that I truly enjoy. I've found over the years that I subconsciously started to seek out obscure gaming material, from art, to rare tokens, and more. I find the collecting aspect just as enjoyable as the gameplay!

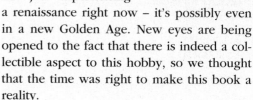

With so many limited items available, the hunt is part of why I thought the idea of this book would be so interesting.

Tabletop gaming is not just experiencing a renaissance right now – it's possibly even in a new Golden Age. New eyes are being opened to the fact that there is indeed a collectible aspect to this hobby, so we thought that the time was right to make this book a reality.

As I said, a new Golden Age is among us, and, with more games being published than ever before, there's literally a game for everyone. With so many new games and mechanics and themes, there is some amazing collectability being spawned as well. So, for both the gamer and the collector in me, I am over the top excited for the present and for the future of tabletop gaming!

I hope that this book opens your eyes to the love so many of us have for this hobby and all of the facets that it encompasses. It has been a joy to be a part of its creation. I'd like to thank, first and foremost, Carrie Wood for shouldering the project. You are truly an amazing spirit and I am better for knowing you. To J.C. Vaughn, thank you for taking an idea and allowing it to come to fruition, especially under the *Overstreet* name. To Josh Geppi, I'd like to say that I can never repay you for the opportunities you have blessed me with – I never in my wildest dreams thought I would be where I am now. To all of the people who I've worked with, interviewed, played games with, or just shared a laugh with – thank you for those memories! I'd list all of you if I could, but I feel like that would require another book. To my family, I love you. And finally, thanks to Steve Geppi, for being not just a fan of pop culture but for providing a space for a guy like me to have his dreams realized.

Richard "Rick" Ankney

Like a lot of people, many of my earliest childhood memories are of playing board games with my family and friends. My mom indulged my kid sensibilities on many rounds of *Candy Land* when I was real young and, meanwhile, my dad was absolutely savage at *Monopoly* and *Scrabble* (I don't recall ever once beating him... I was seven years old, dad, give me a break!).

Later into my childhood, *Pokémon* invaded, and I was instantly hooked on the card game. I remember going to my local mall and buying my first booster pack – I still have the exact Pikachu that came in that pack. I enjoyed the game so much that I joined the official League, which was hosted at the Wizards of the Coast store at that same mall. Three times a week my extremely patient parents dropped me off so I could play against friends and get badges. For years this continued; on more than a few occasions I irritated my parents quite a bit by being too sick to go to school... but not too sick to play *Pokémon* cards at the mall.

It was at that Wizards store that I had my first exposure to a slightly bigger and more involved game: *Dungeons & Dragons*. I was about 10 when I stayed a little later after a *Pokémon* League session because a group of people slightly older than I was were setting up for *D&D* and I thought it looked cool. They invited me to play, and I was handed a pre-made character – a druid with a raven companion. I don't recall much about how that session went, but I had enough fun that it stuck with me.

My *D&D* story truly began in high school, when the guy I was dating at the time invited me to play. His whole family was into it, and we got a couple other kids from band class to come play with us, and generally had a good time. That is, until the DM made the mistake of letting me play the antagonist, and, well, long story short, I blew everyone up with a Fireball spell and then had to endure some awkward tension in jazz band the next day. Sorry, guys.

I still play *D&D* today, thanks to a good group of friends who enjoy getting together to do so. While I don't actively play the game anymore, I still have all of my old *Pokémon* cards. And though the mall I used to play these games at is now a crater in Owings Mills, MD waiting to be redeveloped, I somehow managed to get my hands on the old signs from that Wizards store. All forms of gaming were a part of my formative years and I cherish those memories so sincerely. It seems as though, as I've matured, so have the games I've been playing. Where I used to figure out who the culprit was in *Clue*, I'm now becoming the traitor in *Betrayal at House on the Hill*; where my previous card games involved battling monsters with *Pokémon* and *Yu-Gi-Oh!* they now involve drinking and gambling with *Red Dragon Inn*.

The aim of this book, *The Overstreet Guide to Collecting Tabletop Games*, was to provide a snapshot of the tabletop industry – where it came from, and where it's going. By looking at the history of various games and companies as well as at why games like *The Game of Life, Pathfinder* and *Magic: The Gathering* are valued as collectibles, we looked to shine a light on the industry at large. Like many hobbies, tabletop gaming is constantly evolving, but providing the context for why these games remain so popular and so collectible is important to keep in mind even as it moves ever forward.

I'd like to thank all of our interview subjects for granting us a little bit of their time and a lot of their knowledge for this project. I'd also like to express my gratitude towards Lex Carra, our reliable freelancer, and towards the entire staff of Gemstone Publishing for believing in this project. I also have to thank my cohort on this book, Rick Ankney, for wishing this book into existence and facilitating its production. And finally, to my parents – thank you for not throwing away my *Pokémon* cards when I know you wanted to. Look how valuable they are now!!

Carrie Wood

GET YOUR GAME ON!

THE HISTORY OF GAMING
- The earliest computers and games
- Early dominance of arcades
- The 1980s industry crash
- Console dominance of today

HOW TO COLLECT
- By company
- By creator
- By character
- By series

CARE & PRESERVATION
- Storing
- Displaying
- Grading
...and more!

MORE THAN JUST GAMES
- Tying gaming into different collections
- Adding promotional materials
- Arcade cabinets and other relics
...and much more!

The Overstreet® Guide To Collecting Video Games

brings our "How To" series inside this exciting hobby, in full color, with so many levels to explore.

FOREWORD

Scott Gaeta
Renegade Game Studios

Books like this should come with a warning label. In this case: "Danger! Reading this book may lead you to an increased love of games!" I know that may sound a bit cheesy, but every time I pick up a book like this I tend to fall deeper in love with the subject matter. I figured we should get that out of the way first. I would hate to mislead you in any way.

I know that was my experience back when I read my first *Overstreet Guide to Collecting Comics*. It opened up a world of possibilities: titles and characters that I didn't even know existed, but there it was, in black and white. I felt like a treasure hunter, and still do to this day. So now that Overstreet has published a guide to tabletop games, I know I'm in for more of the same. Maybe my warning applies to me as much as it does you.

For tabletop games, my love affair started like most people, as a child. We all played games such as *Monopoly, Connect Four, Candy Land* and others growing up. Those games provided us with a common experience where, to this day, you would be hard pressed to find someone who hasn't had a similar experience. It really is amazing how tabletop games are ingrained in our culture, and as children we all share in that common thread. The sad version of this story is that for many people, for many years, that's where the story would end. You would play some board games as a child and that would be the end of it. If you were lucky you may have been exposed to something more. I was one of those lucky few back in my day.

Like most kids my age I outgrew board games, but then in middle school I experienced this thing called *Dungeons and Dragons*.

You mean there is a game that takes make believe and puts it on a table? We get to experience an adventure? I get cool little toy soldiers to play with, but instead of little army men they are miniatures of adventurers with swords and monsters? My mind was blown.

This wasn't like any other game I had ever experienced at that point in my life. You could even create your own adventures and run the game for your friends. Just like that, my perception of what a *game* was had changed. Little did I know that was just the tip of the iceberg.

That time in my life was a turning point of sorts. It later led to games like *Blood Bowl* and *Warhammer 40K*, *Magic the Gathering* and the *Star Wars Customizable Card Game*. These games weren't like the games of my childhood. They were smart, challenging, and - most of all - very fun! There was always some new world to explore or challenge to overcome. There was always some figure to paint, even if my painting skills were pretty terrible. Sometimes the challenge was beating the game itself, and other times it was beating your friends!

Tabletop games have evolved. Where modern board games first started out being tied to a literal board and rolling dice, we now have so many more options. Role-playing used the tabletop setting in new ways and brought immersive stories and vast narratives to it. Modern miniature games built on their wargame roots and took us to strange new worlds. WizKids then took miniatures and put all the stats on this newfangled dial and gave those of us that are painting-challenged cool minis that are pre-painted. *Magic the Gathering* invented a whole new genre of tabletop game with cards and then *Dominion* continued in a similar fashion but in a whole new way.

We now live in a Golden Age of tabletop games. The choices are endless and the experiences are vast. Tabletop has become a platform for shared experiences across generations, not simply in childhood. Families can get together and go on an adventure. Adults can play games with their kids and have fun too. Gone are the days of suffering through a game just to make your kids happy. Lifelong friendships are made just

sitting down at a table and playing a game. The game designers and publishers continue to innovate, and we are all the beneficiaries of their passion and hard work. The possibilities are as endless as the selection.

But, most importantly, there is always a great sense of community in whatever game you were involved in. I think that's one of the greatest things that games do. They bring people together. It's no wonder tabletop is growing at such a tremendous rate and so many people are so passionate about it.

But be warned, dear reader... a book like this will only fuel that passion further. You are likely to make new friends and have more fun in your life. You are bound to crack these pages and discover something you never knew before. There is treasure in these pages! And speaking from experience, you *will* be compelled to play more games.

Personally, I wouldn't want it any other way.

A HISTORY OF BOARD GAMES

For as long as humans have been on this planet, they have sought out ways to entertain themselves. So the fact that the roots of contemporary board games can be traced back several thousands of years should hardly come as a surprise.

Evidence of dice games dating back to about 5,000 B.C. have been found in Turkey, Syria, Iraq and the items found generally point to these games originating in the Fertile Crescent region. Ancient dice have been discovered throughout the region, with many dice made out of carved bone, wood, or stone. Dice from ancient Rome bear a close resemblance to the standard six-sided die used in many board games today.

Senet is one of the oldest known board games, with a hieroglyph from ancient Egypt depicting the game dating to about 3,100 B.C. The rules to *Senet* are based on pieces of text that were written over the course of roughly a thousand years or so, so the exact nature of how the game is supposed to be played today is still subject to a lot of debate. *Senet* boards were prized possessions and were often buried with the dead so that they could take the game with them into the afterlife. *Mehen* was another game played in ancient Egypt; named for the snake god Mehen, the board appropriately resembles a coiled snake, whose body is divided into individual spaces. Archeological evidence has uncovered playing pieces for the game, though the rules of play are still unknown.

The *Royal Game of Ur*, also sometimes referred to as the "Game of Twenty Squares," was discovered in the Royal Tombs of Ur in Iraq in the 1920s. Two boards were found in the tombs, though similar boards have been found elsewhere in the world (including in King Tut's tomb). A tablet that describes some of the rules was also found, which allows the game to still be played today – though as the tablet only described but so much, there's been a wide variety of play styles.

More games began springing up in other regions around the same time, such as chess and pachisi in India, liubo and go in China, bao in Africa, backgammon in Persia, and many others. Many of these games are still played today. Chess in particular is still enjoyed by millions of people around the world and is played by roughly the same rules and with the same goal as when it first appeared as "chaturanga" in 6th century India. It became popular after arriving in Persia, where learning how to play the game was actually a part of higher-class education. In Persia, it became common to call out "Shah Mat!" – "The King is helpless!" – which today is known simply as "checkmate." Chess made its way around the rest of the world, and though there have been several regional variants on how the game is played, the core elements remained the same. Chess today is played as a competitive sport, with tournaments regularly held worldwide.

By the time the colonial period began in America, the general lifestyle didn't leave much time for socializing and playing games. Though checkers and other simple card games were played on occasion, the overall puritanical attitude meant that game-playing was generally shunned. Dice in general were viewed as demonic and sinful – Thomas Jefferson actually once wrote that games, "... produce nothing, and endanger the well-being of the individuals engaged in them or of others depending on them." It wouldn't be until the cultural shift away from agricultural living and into the more urban lifestyle of the 19th century that board gaming resumed a spot as a normal leisurely activity.

That being said, the popular board games at the time still valued puritanical Christian morals and themes, and games like *The Mansion of Happiness* – in which players travel along a virtuous path, trying to avoid various sinful acts in order to reach heaven – remained popular well into the 1800s. After *The Checkered Game of Life*, a game that focused on more measurable success like getting a job or getting married, took off in

popularity, attitudes in games soon followed suit. Rags-to-riches stories were popular around this time, and board games emulated this with *Game of the District Messenger Boy* and, more notably, *Monopoly*.

With mass production of games becoming possible, companies such as Milton Bradley and Parker Brothers were able to spring into existence and find success. Throughout the 20th century, both companies saw significant popularity with the likes of *Sorry!*, *Trouble*, *The Game of Life*, *Trivial Pursuit*, *Twister*, *Candy Land*, *Risk*, *Battleship*, and many others.

Contemporary Eurogames also began springing up in the mid-20th century, with *Acquire* setting the standard when the 3M series arrived in the 1960s. The style of game development that followed – in which players were not in conflict to eliminate each other but in competition to establish a single winner – remained somewhat exclusive to Europe, until *The Settlers of Catan* picked up steam in the U.S. in the 1990s.

The market at large has experienced a huge surge in growth since the beginning of the 21st century. Year-over-year, the industry has grown as much as 40 percent annually since 2010 according to some studies (though the exact number varies depending on what the study considers a "board game" to be). The rise of crowdfunding sites online has given birth to a whole new generation of developers and publishers who are now able to appeal directly to their audience thanks to the power of the internet. Conventions dedicated entirely to tabletop games, while certainly not new, are more plentiful and larger than they ever have been.

Board gaming is one of the world's greatest pastimes and for centuries now it's a hobby that's brought generations together. With several thousand years' worth of history in the rear-view mirror, it's pretty clear to see that it's not going anywhere – and, if anything, is only just now getting started.

BATTLESHIP

War has long served as an inspiration for tabletop games, and perhaps one of the best-known mass-market success stories in the genre is *Battleship*. Though known today as a successful plastic board game, the original iteration of *Battleship* dates back to World War I, when it was played as a pencil-and-paper game.

The original *Battleship*'s origins are somewhat muddled – some believe it took inspiration from the French game *L'Attaque* (a title which would eventually go onto influence another widely-known board game, *Stratego*), while others insist it evolved from the 1890 game by E.I. Horseman, called *Baslinda*. The paper-based version

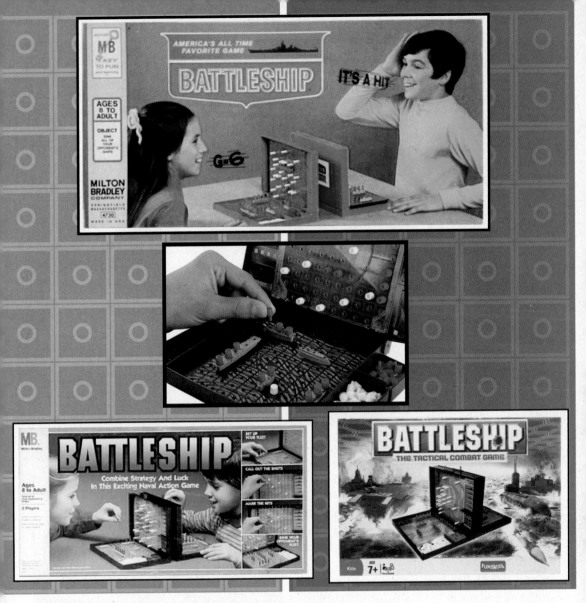

of *Battleship* was first published in 1931 by Starex, when it was called *Salvo*; other companies would publish variants on the concept throughout the '30s and '40s. These companies included the Strathmore Company (*Combat, The Battleship Game*), Milton Bradley (*Broadsides, The Game of Naval Strategy*), L.R. Gebert Company (*Sink It*), and the Maurice L. Freedman Company (*Warfare Naval Combat*).

The mass-market success story for *Battleship* came in 1967, when Milton Bradley introduced the plastic board-and-peg version of the game to great success. In both the paper and plastic versions of the game, players work off of two 10-by-10 grids, which are labeled with numbers vertically and letters horizontally. The primary grid,

usually larger, tracks a player's own ships, while the tracking grid records their shot attempts on their opponent. Before the rounds of play begin, each player arranges their ships (out of view of their opponent) on their primary grid. There are generally five ships, which occupy two to five spaces on a grid depending on what kind of ship they are. Ships are accordingly sank when they are hit enough times. Players typically announce what type of ship has been sunk when it happens – leading to the game's trademark line, "you sunk my battleship!" When all of a player's ships have sank, they lose the game.

There are some popular rule variants for play, notably a modern interpretation of the original *Salvo* rules. This variant has players

calling shots for all of their unsunk ships all on one turn, and as they lose ships, they lose the ability to call those shots. This is considered a variant for more experienced players, as the game becomes far more difficult as players lose more ships. Another popular style of play is to not have players announce when a ship is actually sunk, which forces the opponent to continue to shoot in a given area on the grid to confirm they cleared it.

Milton Bradley's success with the game has continued on through the decades since the original plastic version release, particularly with 1977's *Electronic Battleship* and 1989's *Electronic Talking Battleship*, which added sound effects to make play more exciting. The company released an updated version of the game in 2008, currently referred to as *Battleship Islands*; the game accordingly added several islands to each player's board which ships must be placed around, and "captured man" pieces can be found on the islands.

Battleship has found significant success out of the board game realm, too – it was one of the first games converted into

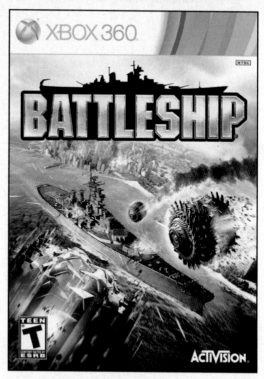

a video game, with the first digital version of *Battleship* releasing for the Z80 Compucolor in 1979. Dozens of other video games based on *Battleship* have released in the years since, for consoles including the Commodore 64, Amiga, Nintendo

Entertainment System, Game Gear, Game Boy, Super Nintendo, Sega Genesis, Xbox 360, PlayStation 3, and Wii – to name a few. Some of these alter the playing field a bit, by changing the size of the grid or by adding four-player gameplay.

In 2012 the game was infamously turned into a live-action feature film, directed by Peter Berg and starring Taylor Kitsch, Alexander Skarsgård, and Rihanna. *Battleship* as a film was an attempt by Universal Pictures to capitalize on their Hasbro licensing, which had previously brought them great success with the *Transformers* franchise. Unfortunately for them, the film was largely blasted by critics and underperformed at the box office. The plot of the film focused on a fight against an invading alien force; accordingly, a new version of the board game released that year in which one player controlled aliens instead of an opposing naval force.

The game is pretty easy to include in a collection of classic board game titles, as even vintage iterations of the game only go for about $15-20 online. Some licensed editions of the game have been made, themed to properties such as *Pirates of the Caribbean* and *Star Wars* – these tend to go for a little bit more, but can still be found in the $30-50 range.

Thanks likely due to the fact that it's translated so well into video games, the contemporary form of *Battleship* has established itself as one of the most popular board games out there today. Even after 50 years, kids and kids-at-heart still seem to enjoy hearing "you sunk my battleship!"

CANDY LAND

For many children over the last several generations, one of their first exposures to the concept of a board game was with one colorful classic – *Candy Land*. Despite the fact that (or perhaps because) there is no strategy involved in the play, the simple game has managed to remain a family favorite since its conception in the 1940s.

Candy Land was created in 1948 by Eleanor Abbott, a schoolteacher who, at the time, was in a California hospital recovering from polio. Perhaps in part due to her career, Abbott understood what her fellow patients – many of whom were young children – would seek in a fantasy world. *Candy Land* was developed with those children in mind, and the kids at the hospital helped to test the game while Abbott was working on it. They'd eventually encourage Abbott to submit the game for publication by Milton Bradley; she did just that, and Milton Bradley published *Candy Land* beginning in 1949, billing it as "a sweet little game for sweet little folks."

The first edition of *Candy Land* almost immediately became Milton Bradley's best-selling game, quickly surpassing the company's previous top game, *Uncle Wiggly*. This edition has some unique features

The Legend of the Lost Candy Castle

 nce upon a time, King Kandy, the Imperial Head Bonbon and Grand Jujube of Candy Land disappeared.

It was a bright, sunny morning and to everyone's surprise, the King and his fabulous Candy Castle simply were no longer where they should be...

"A lost King is so distressing," says Plumpy, The Last Of The PlumpaTrolls, as he shoves a juicy Gingerbread Plum into his mouth. Plumpy is the Caretaker of the Gingerbread Plum Trees and his job is to gather up all of the ripe plums that fall from the trees. But ever since the King's disappearance, Plumpy does more eating than gathering ...growing more plump and more glum with every bite of a plum.

Mr. Mint, the Peppermint Lumberjack and Keeper of the Royal Peppermint Forest, also thinks the situation is somewhat sticky.

 Mr. Mint cuts down big red and white peppermint trees into bite-sized whistles and flutes, creating the sweetest-sounding musical instruments ever. "My peppermint piccolos have been rather off-key ever since the King left," says Mr. Mint..."I certainly hope he returns soon."

 "And what of my Gumdrop Mountains," moans Jolly, the Official Gumdrop Mountain Greeter..."they just don't glisten and glow the way they used to." Indeed, the pastel-colored, sugar-crested range does grow paler and paler every day the King's away!

"Oh, do cheer up," says the ever-hopeful Gramma Nutt, who lives in the Peanut Brittle House. Gramma believes that a very special little girl and boy can find the missing King and his Castle right at the end of the Candy Land path...if they look hard enough! "But whoever can these very special children be?", she asks.

 "I know just the twosome to find my father, the missing King," says Princess Lolly, of the Lollipop Woods. In a voice as light and airy as the fluffiest marshmallow, she says, "They're the Candy Land Kids... courageous, clever, and ever so determined."

"They'll never find the King or his Castle," Lord Licorice says sourly..."for I have hidden them from sight so all of Candy Land will be mine!" His heart is as hard as rock candy. Always gloomy, ever grim, Lord Licorice lives very much alone, except for a few Bitter Chocolate Bats to keep him company!

 "Utter nonsense," Queen Frostine says of Lord Licorice's evil plan. Peacefully adrift on an Ice Cream Float in an Ice Cream Sea, warm-hearted Frostine thinks the Candy Land Kids will surely find the King. "And no matter how many times Lord Licorice plots and plans," she adds, "Candy Land will sparkle once again."

"When the Kids pass my Molasses Swamp, the King and His Castle will soon be found," oozes Gloppy, the kindly Molasses Monster who is definitely more "goosome" than gruesome...

All of Candy Land is ready to help the Candy Land Kids find the King. Even the Gingerbread Men from the Cookie Patrol have offered to act as guides along the path.

You can help, too, by moving the Gingerbread Men cautiously and cleverly along the path, all the way to its end. If you do, you'll find the King and his Lost Castle and everyone in Candy Land will live happily ever after!

about it that are worth noting – for example, the player pieces are made of wood (rather than plastic, as they have been since 1967), the track layout itself is a little different, and there are only marked locations instead of individual character spaces on the board.

Most editions of the game that have been published throughout the years focus on a simple story revolving around the missing king of the titular land, King Kandy. Players each choose a pawn to represent themselves and take turns drawing cards to advance on the multi-colored track. The track is primarily made up of spaces colored red, blue, yellow, green, orange, and purple; there are a handful of pink spaces that are named with either locations (such as Candy Cane Forest) or characters (such as Queen Frostine). When a player draws a card, that card is usually marked with a single colored square indicating what color space to next advance their pawn to. Some cards have two marks, allowing them to move ahead two spaces of that color.

Other cards show a picture of a character or location, which will warp them immediately to the corresponding space. Most editions of *Candy Land* also have three spaces marked with a dot, which represent either "cherry pitfalls" or the Molasses Swamp – in these cases, players who land on such a space are stuck and cannot advance until a card of the same color as the dotted space is drawn. As of 2006, dotted spaces were replaced with "licorice spaces" that simply lose the player's next turn rather than keeping them stuck there for several rounds.

Because of how players advance linearly through the game's track based on card draws, there's no strategy or problem-solving skills necessary to win. The winner, determined by whoever reaches the end of the track first, is left entirely to the whim of a shuffled deck of cards. As of 2013, the cards were replaced by a spinner, though the spinner's potential outcomes are the same as the cards.

Several editions of the game have been published since the inaugural version from the '40s. Hasbro has been *Candy Land*'s publisher since 1984, when they purchased Milton Bradley outright. Besides changing the deck of cards to a spinner, some other minor changes have occurred with some recent reissues of *Candy Land*, such as changing character names (Queen Frostine to Princess Frostine) and location names (Molasses Swamp to Chocolate Swamp). Due to its primary demographic being small children, some themed editions

of *Candy Land* have also been produced with other kid-friendly characters, such as Winnie the Pooh and Dora the Explorer.

Candy Land has also seen success outside of the board game realm, with an animated film having released in 2005 (which in turn spawned a "DVD game" edition of the game itself) and some video game adaptations having been released as well.

Most contemporary editions of *Candy Land* can be found at just about any toy store for about $10-15. For the sake of collectability, vintage editions of the game from the 1950s through the 1980s have a tendency to fetch a higher price, particularly if the game is still complete and in good condition, but even still can be found for about $25-50 in online auctions.

Though extremely simple, *Candy Land* has solidified its place of importance when it comes to board games thanks to the fact that it's almost always a young kid's first exposure to board gaming. In 2005, *Candy Land* was inducted into the National Toy Hall of Fame at The Strong in New York. With Hasbro showing no sign of slowing down the print runs on the game, it's clear *Candy Land* will be on store shelves for years to come.

Clue

Was it Colonel Mustard in the kitchen with the candlestick? Or perhaps Mrs. Peacock in the conservatory with the rope? Whatever the outcome may be, deductive skills and reasoning are at the heart of the classic board game *Clue* (or *Cluedo*, depending on what part of the world you happen to live in). Originally manufactured by Waddingtons in the United Kingdom in the late 1940s, *Clue* has become far more than just a clever murder mystery board game in the decades since.

The original game was developed by a musician, Anthony E. Pratt. During his time playing small concerts at hotels, Pratt gleaned the idea for a murder mystery board game from the trend at the time of including murder mystery games as part of the evening entertainment. The fact that detective and mystery fiction by the likes of authors such as Raymond Chandler and

Agatha Christie were also wildly popular at the time also fed into the desire to turn the genre into a board game. By 1943, Pratt and his wife Elva began designing the game; the original version was called "Murder!"

Pratt already had a strong connection to the board game industry at the time – his friend Geoffrey Bull, who had created the game *Buccaneer*. Bull introduced Pratt to the managing director at Waddington's, and the company, after making some tweaks to the game and renaming it *Cluedo* (a combination of "clue" and "ludo," the Latin word for "play"), signed on to manufacture it. But due to shortages of materials during the aftermath of World War II in Britain, the game didn't actually get produced for the first time until 1949. Parker Brothers would license the game from Waddingtons and publish it as *Clue* in North America starting the same year.

The game begins by drawing three cards, one from each of the three decks – suspects, rooms and weapons – at random, and placing them in an envelope without anyone seeing them. The cards in the envelope represent the crime that happened (who murdered the victim, where, and with what), and the rest of the cards are distributed amongst the players, who keep them hidden from each other until necessary to show them. With six suspect characters, six murder weapons and nine rooms, it makes for 324 possibilities for the crime.

The board is laid out with nine rooms – the kitchen, the ballroom, the conservatory, the dining room, the billiard room, the library, the lounge, the hall, and the study – making up the majority of the mansion. These are the possible rooms in which the murder could have happened. Hallways make up the spaces between the rooms and are used to navigate between them. The center room is where the envelope containing the three selected cards is placed and is usually called the cellar; players cannot access this area. The four rooms in the corners each have a secret passageway that can be used to navigate diagonally across the board

from each other (the conservatory and the lounge have a passage between them, and the kitchen and study have one between them as well).

The player pieces representing the six different suspects are placed at their marked starting points on the board. Suspect characters in most versions of Clue consist of Miss Scarlet, Professor Plum, Mr. Green (Reverend Green in UK editions), Mrs. Peacock, Colonel Mustard, and Mrs. White. Generally, players are instructed to assume the role of whatever character is closest to them at the start of the game, though some people will pick their character at will. Earlier editions of the game had Miss Scarlet always being the first character to move, and going around clockwise from there; more contemporary versions have players roll the dice, with the first move going to whoever rolled the highest. Each player is also given a "Detective's Notes" notepad for the sake of keeping track of information throughout the game.

The object of the game is to figure out who committed the crime – that being, of course, the murder of the victim (named

either Mr. Boddy or Dr. Black, depending on the edition being played). Players each take turns rolling the dice to move however many spaces through the hallways and into rooms. Once in a room, a player can make a suggestion as to the crime that occurred. Players must be in the room that they're suggesting the crime happened in (they cannot suggest the crime happened in the kitchen if they are currently in the billiard room, for example), and players cannot suggest the crime from a hallway space. An example of a suggestion is: "I suggest it was Colonel Mustard, in the kitchen, with the knife."

After a player makes a suggestion, the other players must try to disprove that suggestion by showing one of the cards in their hand privately to the suggesting player. So, for the example just provided, that suggestion would be disproved by another player showing the Colonel Mustard card in their hand to the person making the suggestion. Generally, that person would then make a note on their Detective Notes pad in order to keep track of what elements cannot possibly be in the envelope. If no players are able to disprove the suggestion, the player can immediately make an accusation.

An accusation can include any room, not just the one the player's character happens to be standing in at that given moment. The accusing player privately checks the three cards in the envelope, and if they match the accusation, that player shows them to the others and wins the game. If not, the cards are returned to the envelope and the player loses, as they are no longer able to make any suggestions or accusations. However, they must still continue to be present during play, as they have to continue to privately show cards to others in order to disprove suggestions being made by the remaining players.

Throughout the game's history, Parker Brothers and Waddington's both individually produced new editions of *Clue/Cluedo* between 1949 and 1992; both of these companies were bought out by Hasbro in the 1990s. While *Clue* was regularly updated with new editions over that time, only three editions of *Cluedo* were manufactured in the UK. Most of these editions simply changed the look of the art style or updated the player pieces without any actual gameplay changes.

Hasbro reinvented the game somewhat in 2008 with their release of *Clue: Discover the Secrets*, which changed up the gameplay and added to the characters' stories. *Discover the Secrets* added additional weapons and made the center of the board a playable area, as well as adding an additional deck of cards called Intrigue Cards. These were divided into Keepers and Clocks. Keeper cards give the player holding them special abilities. Clocks initially do nothing for the first seven cards; however, whoever draws the eighth Clock card is killed by the murderer and is knocked out of the game.

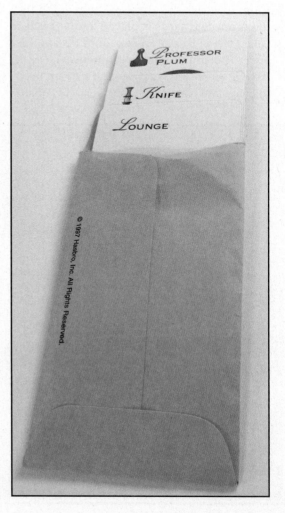

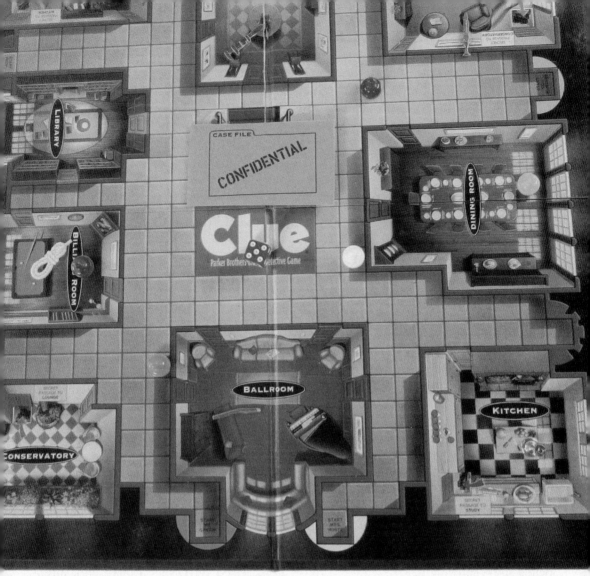

Interestingly, despite the fact that the story of the game bore no connection to the Sir Arthur Conan Doyle stories, Sherlock Holmes was often used in marketing for *Clue*. Advertising for early editions of the game called it "The Great New Sherlock Holmes Game," and commercials as late as the 1970s featured Sherlock playing the game against Watson.

Like many other long-running board games, *Clue* has seen a number of spinoffs and other licensed editions over the years. These have included *Super Cluedo Challenge* (which added characters and weapons), *Travel Clue* (a simplified, miniature edition), *Master Detective* (also added characters as well as weapons and rooms), *Clue Jr.: Case of the Missing Pet* (a variant aimed at young children), and many more. In 1985 there was also a *Clue VCR Mystery*

Game, which accordingly used a VCR tape containing scenes of suspects interacting with each other rather than a board, and players used cards containing clues to what's happening on the screen.

Dozens of *Clue/Cluedo*-based video games have also released over the years, for systems ranging from the Commodore 64 to the Xbox 360 and mobile devices, and everything in between. Some of these, such as the Super Nintendo game, allowed for up to six people to play like the original board game by simply passing around the controller between them.

Clue has been one of the few games to make the leap from board game to multimedia franchise in a successful fashion. The 1985 film *Clue* is easily the best-known film based on a board game; though it initially

performed poorly at the box office (making just $14.6 million against a $15 million budget) it's since attained a strong cult following, likely due in part to its comedically talented cast. The film starred Tim Curry as Wadsworth, Lesley Ann Warren as Ms. Scarlet, Martin Mull as Colonel Mustard, Madeline Kahn as Mrs. White, Christopher Lloyd as Professor Plum, Eileen Brennan as Mrs. Peacock, and Michael McKean as Mr. Green. Staying true to the nature of the board game, the film had three possible endings, depending on which theater happened to be showing it.

Other adaptations of the game have included a television miniseries, an off-Broadway comedic musical, a stage play, and game shows. There have also been several books (primarily aimed at children) based off of *Clue*, and IDW Publishing ran a six-issue *Clue* comic book miniseries in 2017.

Licensed editions of *Clue* have included versions based on numerous television shows, such as *The Office, Family Guy, Supernatural, Big Bang Theory, 24, Seinfeld, Scooby-Doo, SpongeBob SquarePants* and *The Simpsons,* and films such as *Star Wars* and *Harry Potter*. There have also been editions based on Disney theme park attractions, those being The Haunted Mansion and *The Twilight Zone* Tower of Terror. There's even been an edition based off

another tabletop game – *Dungeons and Dragons*.

Most editions of *Clue* are remarkably easy to find due to the widespread popularity of the game leading to huge print runs. Contemporary editions of *Clue* can be found for usually around $15-20, while even vintage editions can be found online for $30-40 (depending on condition). Certain editions run a little more; the 50th Anniversary edition typically runs $30-50. The two versions based on Disney attractions are also a little pricier, with the Haunted Mansion version fetching $30-50 and the Tower of Terror version seeing prices go as high as $100. The *Dungeons and Dragons* variant also regularly demands prices of $70-100 in online auctions.

Between the dozens of variants on the basic board game, the books, the comics, and the film, *Clue* has permeated pop culture around the world for decades. Thanks to its narrative gameplay that relies on skill moreso than simple chance, it's been a mainstay of the board game scene since its inception and has appealed to generations of gamers – and likely will continue to do so for years to come.

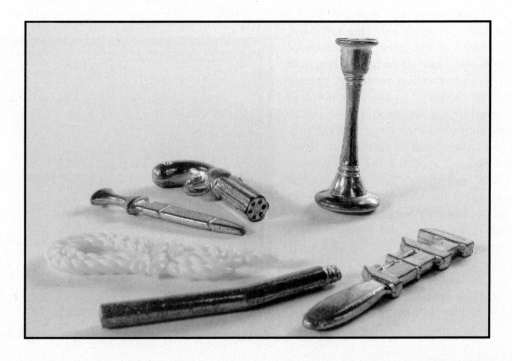

THE GAME OF LIFE

One of the best-known board games of all time also happens to be one of the first, having debuted as a "parlor game" in the 19th century. *The Game of Life* – perhaps known better as just *Life* – first arrived in 1860 and was created by none other than Milton Bradley himself.

The original version of the game was known as *The Checkered Game of Life* and, true to that name, was built on what was essentially a modified checkerboard. The object of the game was to move around the game board, avoiding bad spaces and traveling from the starting point of "infancy" to the end point of "happy old age," collecting 100 points along the way. The "good spaces" promoted values such as "influence" while "bad spaces" involved the concepts of "prison" and "ruin." This version of the game didn't use dice at all – as it didn't want to have any connection to gambling of any sort – and instead used a six-sided top known as a teetotum. By the end of its first year in circulation, *The Checkered Game of Life* had sold more than 45,000 copies, helping to establish The Milton Bradley Company as a go-to name for gaming and leisure.

The Game of Life that we know today was created in 1960 in celebration of the 100th anniversary of the original. Rather than a checkerboard, it focuses on a track that's traveled by players, who are represented by small plastic cars that are filled with pegs (with the pegs representing a family expanding over the course of the game). Players move their pieces ahead on the track by spinning a multi-colored wheel located in the center of the board. Also

The collectability of *The Game of Life* is fairly good, especially given the number of different licensed versions of the game that have come out more recently. There are many different editions of *Life* based on a variety of popular films and other media franchises, ranging from classics like *Star Wars, Indiana Jones* and *The Wizard of Oz* to more recently popular shows including *Yo-Kai Watch, SpongeBob SquarePants* and *My Little Pony*. Interestingly, there are two licensed *Life* games that were only ever available in Japan, focusing on *Sailor Moon* and *Pokémon*. These licensed editions may be more appealing to collectors focusing on those specific franchises involved.

included in this version of the game is the bank as well as insurance policies, stock certificates, and other tangibles.

The first "modernized" *Game of Life* was released in 1963 and featured television personality Art Linkletter as its spokesperson. Linkletter, who was known for hosting *House Party, People Are Funny* and *Kids Say the Darndest Things*, appeared on the game's $100,000 bills as well as on the game box itself. The game would be reissued several times throughout the 20th century with a number of small changes each time, such as changing the model of car used as the player pieces, updating the dollar amounts on bank bills, and adding rewards for good behavior such as recycling. The most recent update to the game arrived in 2005, which reduced the reliance on chance for how it plays out.

Most recent editions of the game can be found in the $15-20 range, though reproductions of the 1960s version have also surfaced as of late; those tend to run $30 or more. Older editions of the modern game can typically be found for around that price as well, largely depending on the condition of the box and if the game is still considered "complete." Finding the original *Checkered Game of Life*, though, is a little trickier – finding a 150-year-old board game in good condition will likely run buyers $200-300 or more.

MONOPOLY

Having been published in more than 100 countries around the world, *Monopoly* has long been firmly established as one of the go-to names in board gaming. The property management game, which blends elements of pure chance with actual strategic thinking and problem-solving skills, is one of the most recognizable brands in gaming history.

Though *Monopoly* was first published by Parker Brothers in 1935, the game can trace its roots to nearly three decades earlier, to a similar title called *The Landlord's Game*. This original game was developed by Elizabeth Magie, an ardent supporter of the economic ideas of Henry George. She designed *The Landlord's Game* to illustrate Georgist ideas in a simple format – to highlight the downfalls of land monopolism and how it can be fixed by way of the land value tax. The goal of the game was really to be an instructional tool to explain why the vast income inequality at the time was a negative thing. Her original patent on the game was granted in the U.S. in early

1904; she soon formed the Economic Game Company with like-minded individuals, and started publishing *The Landlord's Game* in 1906. She also took her game to Parker Brothers in 1909 in an attempt to get more wide publication – however, they dismissed it as being too complicated at the time.

Magie would make some changes and updates to her original game in the '20s, such as adding named streets and eliminating the second round that focused on the land value tax. This version was called *Auction Monopoly,* and added a rule that auctioned unowned property to all game players when it was first landed on.

Another predecessor to *Monopoly* was *The Fascinating Game of Finance* (also known as simply *Finance,* or *Finance and Fortune*). This game was first published in 1932 and itself was based on *The Landlord's Game*; it notably added railroads to the board. Both *Finance* and *The Landlord's Game* proved to be popular, particularly among a college-age crowd, in the '20s and early '30s.

The *Monopoly* we know today was pitched to Parker Brothers in 1934 by Charles Darrow, an American salesman. Darrow had been familiar with both *The Landlord's Game* and *Finance*, having been introduced to their game mechanics by a family friend, Charles Todd. The version of the game that Todd had taught Darrow was that played by a specific group of Quakers in Atlantic City; the game board was modified with street names and locales around Atlantic City. The version of the game that Darrow would then go on to pitch to Parker Brothers – where he claimed it was an original invention of his – was nearly identical to the variation Todd taught him in the first place, right down to the misspelling of Marven Gardens as "Marvin Gardens."

Parker Brothers bought the rights to *Monopoly* and began producing it on a mass scale in 1935. Incidentally enough, that same year Parker Brothers bought the rights to *The Landlord's Game* from Magie for $500. The company only really printed

enough copies of Magie's original game to secure their copyright claims; surviving copies of a Parker Brothers-produced *Landlord's Game* are among the rarest board games ever made.

Monopoly was being produced in excess of 20,000 copies per week within just a year, making it easily the bestselling board game in the U.S. These kinds of numbers made Darrow the first millionaire game designer in history – despite the fact that the product he claimed was his original invention was simply a derivative work. Parker Brothers (and later Hasbro) would long promote Darrow as the sole inventor, though research in the early 21st century proved that Magie, among many others, had contributed to the final game's design via their earlier games.

While there are variations in the naming of spaces – based on what region the game is being produced in or if the version played is based on a licensed property – the basic board layout is essentially the same today as it was when it was produced in the '30s. The square board features 40 spaces, 10 on each side, with four larger spaces in the corners. The 40 spaces are divided into 28 properties (which are subdivided further into 22 streets, four railroads, and two utilities), three Community Chest spaces, three Chance spaces, a Luxury Tax space, and an Income Tax space. The four large corner spaces are GO, In Jail/Just Visiting, Free Parking, and Go to Jail. The center of the board itself has designated areas for the Chance and Community Chest cards.

Each player is represented on the board by a small token (made out of metal or plastic, depending on the edition) that they move around when it's their turn. The original tokens were the Battleship, the Boot, the Cannon, the Iron, the Lantern, the Purse, the Racecar, the Rocking Horse, the Thimble, and the Top Hat. All of these, save for the Battleship, Racecar, and Top Hat, have been replaced with updated or otherwise different pieces over the years. Other tokens over the years have included a Scottie Dog, a Sack of Money, a Horse and Rider, a Cat, and a T-Rex. Since the 1990s, Hasbro has held several contests encouraging fans to vote on new tokens to be added to the game (or, in some cases, to save their favorite existing token from being retired).

Each player is provided $1,500 in the game's currency at the outset of the game. It starts with all players beginning on the GO space; players roll a pair of dice and advance their representative token around the board in clockwise fashion. Rolling doubles allows that player to roll and advance again – however, rolling doubles three times in a row causes that person to be "caught speeding" and go to Jail.

The outcome of a turn depends on what kind of space that person lands on. If they land on an unowned property, they are allowed to buy it for the listed price and receive the deed for that space. Opting out of buying it puts that property up for auction to the highest bidder (the person who chose not to buy it is allowed to bid). If a person lands on a property space already owned by another player, they have to pay that player rent; rent level depends on what the space's level of development is. A player who lands on either the Income Tax or Luxury Tax space has to pay that respective tax to the bank (the exact tax amount depends on what edition is being played). Landing on a Chance or Community Chest space requires the player to draw the top card from that respective deck and then

follow the instructions accordingly. Some cards will either reward the player by giving them money from the bank, while others will force them to pay the bank or another player – others still will either provide the famous "Get Out of Jail Free" card, or send them instead directly to Jail.

Players are knocked out of the game by going bankrupt. Bankruptcy happens when a player can no longer pay what they owe, either to another player or to the bank. Players are not allowed to choose bankruptcy – if they can avoid it by selling, trading or mortgaging properties, they are forced to do that rather than simply leave the game. The win condition for *Monopoly* is simply to be the last person left after all others have gone bankrupt. One of the leading criticisms of the game is the length of time that it often takes to reach the end of the game; while there's easy-to-understand win conditions, the amount of players involved and their know-how of the game can turn a single play session into a several-hour ordeal.

Monopoly has been able to reign supreme as one of the biggest names in board gaming due to its gameplay style that perfectly blends the element of chance (via the roll of the dice and the various card-pulls) with legitimate strategy (via determining what properties to aim for and develop). The popularity of the game not only spurred updated editions to the original version, but a remarkable amount of special editions and variants.

Outside of board games, *Monopoly* has become a recognizable brand, thanks largely in part to its mascot – Rich Uncle Pennybags. Also known colloquially as "Mr. Monopoly" or simply "The Monopoly Man," Uncle Pennybags first appeared on the game's Chance and Community Chest cards. He later appeared in other Parker Brothers games such as *Dig*, and in *Monopoly*-related spinoff titles like *Advance to Boardwalk, Free Parking, Don't Go To Jail*, and more. Pennybags' image has culturally been associated with unchecked greed or simply a ludicrous amount of

money. In 2017, during the Senate Banking Committee hearing on the Equifax data breach, a young man dressed as Pennybags – complete with monocle, top hat and white mustache – and sat in the audience to draw more attention to forced arbitration and to protest Equifax's behavior in the wake of the breach. Far more than just a game mascot, Pennybags has become a cultural icon in the decades since he first appeared in the game.

Video games based on *Monopoly* have been around for quite some time, though the earliest were unlicensed projects distributed in the late 1970s. Officially-licensed *Monopoly* games first started appearing in 1985, and some version of the game has appeared on nearly every system, from the Commodore 64 to the Nintendo Switch and just about everything in between. Most games have been praised as faithful adaptations of the source material. One standout was the PC game, *Monopoly Star Wars*, which released in 1997; it featured characters from the franchise and full-motion video cutscenes lifted from the films.

A television game show based on the game was also developed, running briefly on ABC in 1990. The show was created by Merv Griffin and featured three contestants, who each tried to take control of properties in a similar fashion to how the board game functioned. Whoever had the highest amount of money after two rounds was deemed the champion and advanced to a bonus round, in which they tried to advance all the way around the board within five turns (while also staying out of Jail). A *Monopoly* film has also been in discussion since at least 2008; Hasbro's Allspark Pictures division will be involved with the project.

At this point, hundreds of variants of *Monopoly*, based on different regions around the world and on specific licensed properties, have been produced. The first license for *Monopoly* was awarded in 1994 to USAopoly, who have gone on to produce regional themed editions (beginning with San Diego) and have also produced

official corporate editions of the game for organizations including the Boy Scouts of America and FedEx. Winning Moves Games received the second license for *Monopoly* variants in 1995, and have produced localized editions primarily based on European and Australian locales. In 2000, Winning Solutions received the third such license; the company focuses on deluxe special editions sold through specialty stores.

There's variants based on cartoons: *Adventure Time, Doraemon, Family Guy, Phineas and Ferb, Pokémon, Scooby-Doo,* and more. There's versions based on both sports leagues (MLB, NHL, NBA, and college leagues) and specific teams within those leagues (Boston Celtics, Seattle Mariners, Tennessee Volunteers, Chicago Cubs). There's a Beatles *Monopoly*, a Batman *Monopoly*, a Doctor Who *Monopoly*, a Marvel Comics *Monopoly* – there's a *Monopoly* edition out there to suit your specific taste no matter what that taste may be. Collectors of any of these various other kinds of properties – sports, music, movies, television, comics – could easily incorporate a *Monopoly* edition (or even several!) into their lineup.

There have been a handful of high-dollar editions of *Monopoly* made over the years. Perhaps the strangest of these was a set exclusive to Neiman Marcus through its

1978 Christmas Wish Book. This particular set had the game board, money, tokens and every other piece made entirely out of edible chocolate, buttercream and butterscotch. At the time, it retailed for $600. The catalog advertisement for it simply read: "Pass GO and you'll collect 200 calories."

The FAO Schwarz in New York sold a custom, "One-Of-A-Kind" *Monopoly* for $100,000 back in 2000. It featured a suede-lined case, 18-carat gold tokens, street names written in gold leaf, as well as emeralds, sapphires and rubies embedded into the game board itself. The over-the-top set was made complete by using actual U.S. currency as the game money, rather than the colorful paper *Monopoly* money.

In 2011, The Strong National Museum of Play acquired one of the earliest handmade editions of *Monopoly*: one handmade by Darrow and his family on a circular oilcloth before they sold the game to Parker Brothers. One of maybe only 5,000 Darrow had made in the early 1930s, the copy of the game – which featured hand-drawn spaces on the game board – sold at Sotheby's to the museum for $146,500. The Strong features a number of different edi-

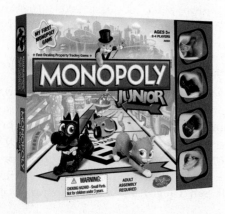

tions of *Monopoly* in their museum, which is fitting, seeing as the game itself was inducted into the museum's National Toy Hall of Fame in 1998.

However, none of those compare to the single most expensive *Monopoly* set ever produced: one worth roughly $2 million. The set's extreme value was verified by the Guinness Book of World Records, and the set itself was put on display at the Museum of American Finance. It features dice with 42 full-cut diamonds to signify the numbers, which alone are worth more than $10,000. The board itself, the cards, and all of the tokens are made out of gold. The game was originally made in 1988 by jeweler Sidney Mobell, who also made sure to incorporate a fair amount of precious gems into the set.

For those not looking to go into actual bankruptcy for the sake of owning one of those extreme deluxe editions, there's plenty of ways to incorporate *Monopoly* into a classic board game collection. Vintage editions, even those dating to the 1930s, are fairly easy to find in online auctions for pretty reasonable prices. Depending on the exact condition of the game (and if it's a complete set with the box), vintage *Monopoly* editions can be found for about $50-$100 at most. The amount of people who sell just portions of the game – such as just the board, the cards or the tokens – on sites such as eBay also make it easy to complete a vintage set for less than you might expect.

Most contemporary releases of the game, including those based on specific licenses, can be found fairly easily either in toy stores or online for usually no more than $20 or so. Certain licensed editions demand more – *Star Wars* editions, depending on what exact release, can range from $25 up to $100 or more. *Doctor Who, Game of Thrones* and most Disney-related editions can usually be found for between $25-50; interestingly, the *Power Rangers* 20th Anniversary Edition seems to be one of the more difficult releases to find, with prices regularly up over $100.

Monopoly has become far more than just a board game that aimed to teach a lesson about economics – it's a huge, instantly-recognizable part of pop culture. Phrases such as "Do not pass GO, do not collect $200" and "Get out of Jail free card" have long been a part of the American lexicon. Uncle Pennybags has maintained his status as one of the most instantly-recognizable mascots across any brand out there. Regardless of how one's real-world finances are going, a round of *Monopoly* can surely make anyone feel rich for a day.

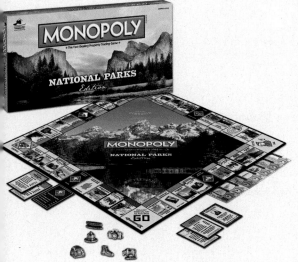

PROJECT RAYGUN™

Project Raygun is a revolutionary boutique board game, puzzle, and collectibles brand. The company's launch of *The Thing: Infection at Outpost 31* with Mondo Tees in 2017 delivered an innovative tabletop gaming experience with cutting edge nostalgia, the finest pop art, and a contemporary retro style—all signature qualities of Project Raygun creations. Project Raygun products celebrate pop culture of past and present, while paying homage to the artists that bring them to life. Partnering with fellow pioneers in the creative and collectibles space, Project Raygun aims to deliver unparalleled experiences to their audience.

FUSING EXCEPTIONAL ART AND ENTERTAINMENT

LOOKING FOR A COMIC SHOP NEAR YOU?

COMIC SHOP LOCATOR SERVICE

comicshoplocator.com

 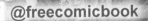

SETTLERS OF CATAN

Though there have been many European-style board games that have proved themselves successful in the American market and elsewhere around the world, few have been quite as significant as *The Settlers of Catan*. Arriving in the mid-1990s, *Catan* broke the mold of what a board game could be and introduced concepts to an international audience that many had not yet seen before. Much of the success of the contemporary board game industry can be credited to the accessibility and popularity of *Catan*.

The game was first published in 1995 in Germany as *Die Siedler von Catan*, and was a creation of Klaus Teuber. *Catan* is a game that puts its players in the role of settlers, who each try to establish the most successful colony on the island of Catan itself. Each settler must build up towns into cities, eventually connecting them by roads, and can do

so by gathering and spending resources. The ultimate goal of the game is to end up with a total of 10 Victory points.

When setting up the game, the first things set are the terrain pieces. These are hex pieces that are usually placed in a random manner, though more recent editions have included a fixed layout in the manual that is meant for new players. Another popular variant on standard play with the hexboard is to have each individual hex placed face-down in a random manner, only turning them face-up when someone wants to place a settlement or road on that piece. After the hexes are set, the rubber tokens are placed around the board; each token has both a number and a letter on it, and are placed in alphabetical order in a clockwise manner until the last token is on the board. These represent resources that can be gleaned from the terrain, and the only hex that gets skipped over when placing these tokens is the desert. Instead, the Robber, represented by a standing grey piece, begins on the desert tile. The Robber blocks any resources from being taken from the hex it happens to be on, and is moved by use of the Knight card or when the die roll happens to be a seven.

After this, the Resource and Development cards are placed. Resource cards should be separated by what specifically they are (bricks, lumber, rocks, sheep, and wheat) into five smaller piles, facing up. Development cards should be shuffled and then faced down.

The turn order is determined by rolling the dice, with the player who has the highest roll selecting their respective color and taking the first turn. The game then moves around clockwise from there. Players set their settlements at an intersection – where three hexes meet. This placement involves a good deal of

strategic thinking, as the three hexes adjoining the settlement will provide the resources for that player, so it's important to give consideration as to where settlements are put.

After a settlement is placed, a player can create a road. Roads have to be placed at one of three possible places next to the settlement, along the side of the hexes. After all players have laid down their initial settlement and road, the player who went last then places another settlement and road and, counter-clockwise, all players do the same until it goes back to the first player (when all participants have two settlements and two roads on the board). Players then gather their initial resource cards, which involve taking a resource card for each hex tile that's adjacent to each settlement for each player.

From here, the dice are rolled. The players then gather an extra resource card for the hex tile corresponding to the number

rolled, if they happen to have a settlement on the corner of that terrain tile.

Players then begin the game in earnest. On each person's turn, they can either build  structures, play a Development card, or trade resources. They can do all of these on any turn or opt to do none of them, depending on how things have played out so far.

To build structures, players must have the necessary resources to do so. For example, to build a road, a player would need one lumber and one brick, but to upgrade a settlement to a city, players need three rocks and two sheep. Players can also use resources to buy a Development card.

Once players have a Development card, they can play it on their turn. Each type of card does something different. The Victory Point card automatically gives the player one additional victory point to get them closer to the 10 needed to win. The Monopoly card allows the player to take one specific type of resource  from every other player. The Knight card allows the player to move the Robber to any other spot on the board, and also allows that player to take a card from any other player that has a settlement on the blocked hex.

Players can also trade as needed, either with other players or with the bank. To trade with the bank, players must give four of the same resource card for one resource card out of the bank of their choosing. Players can also trade resources between them at their whim.

The game ends when one player has accrued 10 Victory Points and announces as such to the rest of the participants. Victory Points can be gained by the previously-mentioned Development card, by building up settlements (worth one point each) or cities (worth two), or by fulfilling Special Cards, such as "Longest Road" or "Largest Army," which are worth two points each.

The unique balance of resource management, strategy, and occasionally cooperative gameplay struck a chord with audiences worldwide, and *Settlers of Catan* was an instant hit. The game picked up the 1995 Spiel des Jahres (Game of the Year), and a year later won the Origins Award for Best Fantasy or Science Fiction Board Game.

The base game of *Catan* supported 3-4 players, and a year later, an extension was released to accommodate up to six players for the original release. Klaus Teuber immediately got to work on a proper expansion for the game, which arrived in 1997: *Seafarers of Catan*, which introduced a new scenario, a new resource (gold), and ships to the gameplay. A year later, *Cities and Knights of Catan* arrived, which added battles between knights and barbarians and commodities (paper, cloth and coin) in addition to the base resources. Further expansions have  included *Oil Springs, Explorers and Pirates,* and *Frenemies of Catan.* Each of these have added variations on the basic gameplay and additional components to consider.

There have also been some historical scenarios that use the *Catan* system to reenact everything from the building of the pyramids of Egypt to the Trojan War;

these packs were released between 1998 and 2001. In addition to that, there's been licensed adaptations of the original game (such as the *Travel Edition*), as well as space-themed spinoffs (*Starfarers of Catan* and *Starship Catan*), and multiple card games (*Catan Card Game* and *The Rivals for Catan*).

Teuber, the creator of *Catan*, also released two games that many consider to be "sister titles" to *Settlers of Catan* – *Entdecker*, released in 1996, and *Domaine* (or *Lowenherz*), released in 1997. These games were born of the same idea that Teuber originally had for Catan and were both received well. *Domaine* in particular was critically acclaimed, picking up the Deutscher Spielpreis (German Game Prize) much like *Settlers* had done before it.

The base *Catan* has also seen upgraded editions, which have included improvements to the board and hex tiles, updated artwork, and slight rule changes. All in all, there have so far been dozens of *Catan* and *Catan*-related games released since the original game's inception in 1995, with no sign of slowing down.

Catan's base game is fairly easy to find due to its popularity, and the most recent edition can generally be bought for only $30 or so; the expansion to add compatibility for up to six players would be another $15-$20 on top of that. Most variations of the game will fall within this range, though given how many of those variations there are, it still ends up being a fairly hefty investment for a collector looking to get their hands on everything *Catan*.

There are some standouts within the larger *Catan* catalog though when it comes to prices, such as the *15th Anniversary Edition*, which featured higher-quality playing pieces and came in a special wood box. This edition typically goes for anywhere between $300 and $500 in online auctions, due to its limited nature.

Star Trek Catan, which themed the board game to the legendary sci-fi series, is also in higher demand, and has a tendency to achieve prices from $100 to $200 or so, depending on the condition. The *Federation Space* expansion, which added map tiles to the game, usually sees prices of $30-$40 – not exorbitant, but still higher than the base game's standard expansions.

Game of Thrones Catan: Brotherhood of the Watch, based on the HBO series as well as on the *A Song of Ice and Fire* books, sees prices slightly higher than the normal, unlicensed editions – usually about $50-$70 – but not nearly as high as *Star Trek*.

Settlers of Catan paved the way for other Eurogames to make their way stateside thanks to its challenging but balanced gameplay and easy learning curve. Though it's only been available for a few decades, its impact on the market is absolutely clear, and it's certainly one to include in any collection of board game classics.

SORRY!

When it comes to classic, straightforward, fun-for-the-whole-family kinds of board games, *Sorry!* is certainly a top choice. The game, taking many cues from other old cross-and-circle games like *Parcheesi*, has a pretty easy to understand goal: get your pieces around the board faster than your opponents can.

The earliest version of *Sorry!* was first trademarked on May 21, 1929 by William Henry Storey, in England; Storey would also patent the game in the U.S. the following year. The U.K. version of the game would eventually be sold to Waddingtons (the gaming company otherwise known for *Monopoly* and *Clue*), who began selling it in Great Britain in 1934, while the U.S. patent was bought out by Parker Brothers that same year.

Sorry! has each player picking a certain color of pawn, of which they have (usually) four; the goal is to move the pawns around the board in a clockwise fashion, from the starting point to the "home" goal space. The board itself is a square, with 16 spaces on each side. Each player has color-coded start

and home areas, plus a five-square path in that color designated as a "safety zone" leading from the outer square into the goal space. There are also colored "slides" around the board – if a player's pawn lands at the start of a slide, it accordingly slides to the last square in that color, and all pawns sitting on any other space of the slide is knocked back to their respective start.

Unlike many other games of this style, which used dice to designate how many spaces a player could move, *Sorry!* instead used numbered cards. The game begins with participating players having all four of their pawns on the start area. They are only allowed to move pawns out from that area if they draw a 1 or a 2 card, which places one pawn on the space just outside the start. Players can then move around the board in the attempt to get back around to the finish. Pawns can jump over any other pawn during its turn; however, as two pawns are not allowed to occupy the same space, if a pawn lands on a square already taken, the active pawn bumps the other pawn back to its own start space. Whoever

three pawns instead of four (allowing for quicker games), and "fire" and "ice" cards were added as well. These elemental cards change how a pawn is allowed to move – fire cards speed up pawns, while ice cards stop them completely.

Contemporary versions of *Sorry!* can be found for just about $10 or so at most toy retailers or online, and even vintage copies of the game range from about $25-$50, depending on the exact year of publication. Typical to most mass-market board games, there's also been a number of themed editions, such as *Spider-Man, Pokémon, Star Wars, SpongeBob SquarePants* and more. This makes *Sorry!* a pretty easy game to collect, whether on its own or adding to a collection of a different property. One of the more unique editions of the game is probably the version themed to Disney's Splash Mountain attraction. The *Splash Mountain Sorry!* is usually only available in the Disney theme parks and is therefore harder to find on the open market, driving the price up to usually $40-$50 when someone does decide to sell it online.

Though simple in both form and execution, its longevity on the market goes to show that *Sorry!* has nothing to apologize for.

is able to get all of their pawns around the board and back home successfully first wins the game.

Some cards in the set had certain rules attached to them. For instance, a 7 card would allow for one pawn to move seven spaces *or* for the allotted seven spaces to be split between two pawns however the player chooses. A 10 card allows for either 10 spaces moved forward or one space backwards, and an 11 card can mean either moving 11 spaces forward or outright swapping a player's own pawn with one of their opponents. Then there's the *Sorry!* card, which allows the player to take any one of their pawns from the start and move it directly to a square occupied by one of their opponents, sending that pawn back to their start.

The 2013 edition of the game instituted some rule changes – players now have

TICKET TO RIDE

When someone hears the phrase "Ticket to Ride," it's entirely possible that the first thing that will pop into their head is the jingly guitar riff from the 1965 Beatles song bearing that name. It's also equally as possible at this point that someone would instead think of the strategy board game, *Ticket to Ride*, which has been at the forefront of the industry boom.

Ticket to Ride was created by Alan R. Moon, one of the leading designers of German-style board games, or "Eurogames." What tends to differentiate Eurogames from American-style board games is a greater reliance on strategy and themes that generally rely on economics; to contrast, American-style games have a far greater emphasis on chance or luck and themes that focus on conflict and drama between players. Eurogames typically don't feature

much in the way of randomness and also strive to keep all players involved in the game until a win condition is met, whereas American-style board games have a tendency to eliminate players until one winner is left standing. Moon's previous successful board games included the award-winning *San Marco* and *Capitol*, both of which released in 2001, and *Elfenland*, which was published in 1998. Moon has designed or co-designed dozens of other games over the course of his career.

The game is designed for two to five players, with each player being designated on the board by a specific color (red, blue, yellow, green, or black). Each player places their appropriately-colored scoring marker at the corner of the board marked "100," and the players all begin the game with 45 train pieces of that same color. The

Train Card deck is shuffled and each player begins with a hand of four cards. Five more cards are then placed face-up along the board, with the rest of the deck next to the face-up cards to act as a draw pile.

The Train Cards are used to claim the routes necessary to fulfill Destination Tickets. Three Destination Ticket cards are dealt to each player at the start of the game after a shuffle of that deck, and the rest are placed alongside the train cards to create two different draw piles. Each Destination Ticket, once completed, awards a set number of points to be awarded – however, if they are not fulfilled by the end of the game, they will count against the player's final score. Players are encouraged to wait until the game's completion to announce the fulfillment of the Destination Tickets, which adds a greater level of strategy as they try to figure out what routes each other player is trying to complete. There is also a "longest path" Destination Ticket card, which can grant a significant point bonus if it is completed.

On a player's turn, they may do one of three things: draw Train Cards, claim a route between two cities, or draw Destination Tickets.

If they choose to draw Train Cards, they may either pull two blindly from the deck, pull two of the five face-up cards, or one

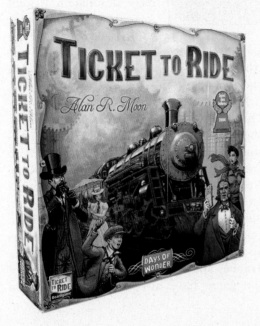

of each; any face-up card picked must be immediately replaced with a pull from the deck so that there are always five Train Cards face-up next to the board. An exception to this is if the player chooses to pull a Locomotive card from one of the five face-up cards – as this is the most versatile and important of the Train Cards, if the player specifically picks that from the five face-up cards, that becomes the *only* card they are allowed to draw that turn.

Another note on Locomotives: if three of the five face-up Train Cards end up as locomotives at any time, all five are immediately discarded and five brand-new cards are blindly pulled from the draw deck to replace them instead.

If the player chooses to claim a route, they must play a set of Train Cards that match the color and amount of train cars along that route on the game board. For example, just two pink Train Cards are needed to take the route between Kansas City and St. Louis, but six blue Train Cards are needed to do the same between Portland and Salt Lake City. There are many grey-colored routes along the board – these can be claimed by any set of the Train Cards that are of the same color and match the number of grey spaces on the board. Many available routes have two different possibilities of different colors running side-by-side, which allow for two different players to potentially claim the same route.

Points are awarded based on the length of the route claimed, and the players then must move their score marker around the border of the game board accordingly.

If the player chooses to draw Destination Tickets, they draw the top three cards from the Destination Ticket draw pile. The player must keep at least one card of those three, but can keep two or all three if they so choose. Any cards not kept out of the three drawn are put back into the deck at the bottom of the draw pile.

The game is brought to a close when any of the players are left with two or less train pieces left to be put on the board. Everyone then takes their last turn, including the player who initiated the ending of the game. The final point tally is then determined – the points for completed routes should already be on the board at the end of the game, and additional points are added when players reveal the Destination Ticket cards in their hand. The point values on the Destination Ticket cards are added to the total based on completed routes, or subtracted if those routes were not fulfilled. A further 10 bonus points are added to the total of the player who had the longest continuous path on the board. If there is a tie, a winner is determined by whoever had the most Train Cards left in their hand.

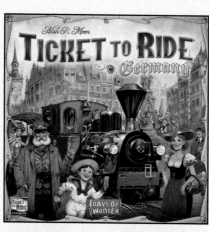

The original *Ticket to Ride* was published in 2004 by Days of Wonder, and the game was an immediate success. After the initial release, *Ticket to Ride* picked up the 2004 Spiel des Jahres (Game of the Year) award in Germany, as well as Best Board Game at that year's Origins Awards –

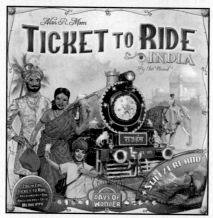

among dozens of other accolades around the world. The Spiel des Jahres win made Days of Wonder the youngest ever board game publisher to win the award, as the company had only been founded two years earlier.

Several additional standalone *Ticket to Ride* games have released since then: *Ticket to Ride: Europe, Ticket to Ride: Märklin, Ticket to Ride: Germany, Ticket to Ride: Nordic Countries, Ticket to Ride: 10th Anniversary, Ticket to Ride: Rails and Sails,* and *Ticket to Ride: First Journey*. The initial four in that list feature different regions of the world,

while the *10th Anniversary* edition features the original USA-focused game with nicer metal train pieces replacing the original plastic ones, and a larger board space.

Rails and Sails features the largest board used in any *Ticket to Ride* game, as well as one that's double-sided; one side of the board is "The World" while the other is "The Great Lakes." This edition of the game introduces Ship Cards in addition to the Train Cards, which are used to accordingly claim routes along the water. Finally, *First Journey* is an edition of the game specifically designed for younger children, with a smaller board and easier route connections. Rather than racking up points, the players instead try to be the first to fulfill six Destination Tickets.

In addition to the board games, there has also been *Ticket to Ride: The Card Game*, published in 2008, which features a train-building scenario in a "rail yard" to complete Destination Tickets. A number of electronic editions of the game, for mobile platforms as well as for PC and Xbox Live, have also been released over the years.

Outside of the additional standalone entries, the *Ticket to Ride* franchise has also introduced a number of smaller expansions to the main games that introduce everything from a dice-rolling mechanic to additional Destination Tickets to an invasion by an alien and a dinosaur. There have also been board expansions to include new regions such as Asia, India, Switzerland, Africa, France, and the United Kingdom. Fans of the game have also often taken it upon

themselves to create unofficial fanmade boards to be used with the game, many of which can be printed for home play by finding them online.

Though it's only been around for a decade and a half now, *Ticket to Ride* has established itself as a must-have for any board game collector. Most editions of the game are fairly easy to find either online or in a toy or gaming shop, and can usually be found for $30 or so. The one big outlier for collectors is the *10th Anniversary* edition, which regularly sees prices of $150 in online auctions – sometimes $200 or more, depending on if it's still factory-sealed, and those prices are likely to continue to rise due to the nature of this edition. *Rails and Sails* is also going to be pricier than one of the standard editions of the game, likely due to its larger nature; it usually demands prices of about $70 or more, roughly twice what the standard game costs.

With more than 3 million copies of the games sold worldwide – or roughly $150 million in retail sales – it's clear that *Ticket to Ride* has broken the Eurogame barrier for the rest of the world and is bound to remain at the forefront of the board game renaissance for years to come.

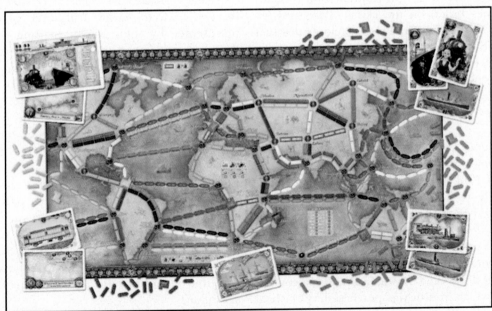

TROUBLE

There are a lot of contemporary board games based on the classic *Parcheesi* (or *Pachisi*) – cross-and-circle-style games that have been made more simple and easy to understand for younger players. One of the most successful of these has been *Trouble*, known elsewhere around the world as *Frustration* or as *Kimble*.

Trouble was originally developed by the Kohner Brothers Company, run by Frank and Paul Kohner. The brothers had previously worked in toy making in the post-World War II era, ranging from simplistic wooden string toys to push-button puppets of licensed properties such as *Howdy Doody*. *Trouble* was first launched in 1965; it was later distributed by Milton Bradley, a company which in turn was purchased by Hasbro.

Extremely similar to *Sorry!*, *Trouble* is for two to four players with each player represented by color pawns. Starting with their color pawns in the Home area, players must roll a six on the die located in the center of the board to begin moving around the track. All of the pawns must travel the entire way around the board via die rolls and reach the Finish lane in order for a player to win.

Players can bump another player's pawn by landing on them. Bumped pawns are sent back to their Home area on the board (however, a variant of this rule places the bumped pawn back at the Start area outside of Home in order to bypass the time it would take to try and roll a six again).

What made *Trouble* a standout when it released (and popular among younger players) was the Pop-O-Matic die container. The clear plastic bubble contains the die and is used to quicken the pace of play by keeping the die in a small enclosed space as well as ensuring that all rolls are fair; for younger players, it also helps to make sure that the small die itself never gets lost and is always contained with the game. The Pop-O-Matic bubble also produces the trademark satisfying pop noise each time it's pressed.

Like many board games aimed at children, *Trouble* has seen a number of variations released over the years, all themed to different films and other properties. These have included a number of Disney properties, such as *Frozen, Cars* and *Toy Story*, as well as other series such as *Despicable Me* and *SpongeBob SquarePants*. There have also been a couple of *Star Wars*-themed releas-

es: one themed to the *Clone Wars* animated series (which featured an R2-D2 figure in the Pop-O-Matic and a sound chip that would appropriately beep when pushed) and another themed to *The Force Awakens*. Both feature a detailed game board with themed character pawn pieces.

Most editions of *Trouble* can be found for about $10-15. Themed editions usually run a little more, usually ranging between $20-30, though some particularly popular properties (such as *Star Wars*) can garner prices upwards of $50 or more. *Trouble*, thanks to the satisfying click of the Pop-O-Matic die roller, has endured as a childhood favorite board game for many generations. Simple in its premise, it lends itself well to themed releases, making it a solid addition to any collection focusing on those properties – though it's just as well found as part of a general board game lineup.

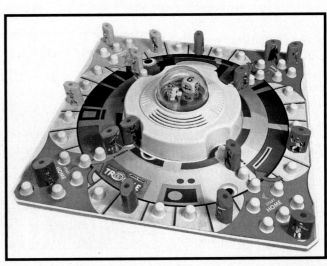

ALAN NANES
THE COLLECTOR

Alan Nanes is a senior game designer with Bethesda Studios, and has worked on such smash hits as Fallout 4 *and* The Elder Scrolls V: Skyrim. *Nanes also happens to be a longtime tabletop RPG and board game collector and discussed how these experiences helped to shape his current career.*

Overstreet: What got you into actually collecting board games instead of just playing them as a hobby?

Alan Nanes (AN): I think what happened was, for me, I think it was *Risk 2210*, I was realizing that it was a gateway into more board games. I come from an RPG background. I played tons of pen-and-paper when I was kid, so that was already appealing to me. But when I would play RPGs, I would always be the [Dungeon Master] – and that's got a lot of work involved. So it's nice to have a game that I can play where I don't have to run it or be responsible for how things play out. When I saw [*Risk 2210*] I figured that there had to be more games out there like that, and I already went to a lot of gaming stores where they were there, but I was a little bit blind to it. So I slowly graduated up from there.

As far as collecting

goes, I collected a lot of RPG stuff anyway, so it was very natural. It just kind of happened. I know that's not a great explanation! But eventually you end up going into a store and going – oh, I don't have that yet, I don't have this yet – and suddenly you have a collection. Now, there's a huge renaissance for board games and you can get them at Target and whatnot, and then people can explore different stores and find more.

Overstreet: You mentioned a renaissance in board games. Why do you think that's happening?

AN: I think it's because there's this stigma of being so social on social media, but you're really just kind of anonymous on there. I think people miss and crave enjoying time with other people actually in-person rather than on Skype or Facebook. It's more fun. When I have my game nights people have fun and can just laugh and relax – well, sometimes we get frustrated because of the game, but that's how it goes – but I think it's a social gathering conduit.

All of a sudden there's this rise in popularity of bars where you can go and borrow a board game and get a beer and a burger and hang with your friends. These board game parlors are getting big! It's such a social experience, and I think that this shows that people really miss that.

Overstreet: So you already collected RPGs before getting into board games, so let's talk about that. What would you say is the most-coveted piece in your collection?

AN: Not the wood-grain box, but the white box for *Dungeons & Dragons*. It's super cool to look back at everything that was hand-typed back then and whatnot. They were hobbits instead of halflings, and so on. The history there is really neat. That's where it all started.

Overstreet: When you think of TTRPGs, what do you think there has influenced your path as far as being a game creator in your career?

AN: When you're playing RPGs, you're coming up with stories and ideas. So for me, personally, as I said, I was always the DM. And that helped to sharpen and focus my creativity and my imagination of creating an experience and passing it on to the player – making it vivid, making it come alive. With video games, that translated somewhat. I'm lucky that with video games you get an actual visual; I'm not just talking to you and hoping you get the idea. In a way, *D&D* was harder, because you had to make sure that you weren't boring your player to death.

I don't know that it translates as well from board games. It does for theming, that's for sure. Board games are basically just a mechanic with a theme attached to it. Sometimes, if the theming is done right, it can make a mechanic and the game way better than it would've been. If I did a board game, I don't think I'd ever be good at the mechanics or the number crunch on that, but I think I'd be pretty good at the theming on that.

At my job, we always talk about player expectation. As a designer, that's something that I have to be aware of. We always do the best we can, though we always get questions from players of "well why can't I do this?" And the problem is that if every-

one got their wish, the game would never get done. It doesn't invalidate your wish to have that, though – and a lot of the things the players wish for, we want to make happen. Eventually one of the producers has to decide what stays and what goes as far as sticking to the schedule.

We want to create a story in your mind that goes with our story. And all that came from an RPG past for me – player expectation, what do people want to do, what can I really get done in this one RPG session tonight. But there's more freedom with a video game. If I hadn't been a DM I don't know that I'd be as good at being a game designer.

Overstreet: Can you think of any specific *D&D* plays that may have translated directly into a sidequest or a character in one of the *Elder Scrolls* games?

AN: Not directly, no, but the general archetype of certain characters. So maybe someone's really greedy but in a pinch they've got your back. That sort of thing. Just formulating characters in a *D&D* session and taking that idea and turning it into a video game character.

One of the things we really worked on in *Fallout 4* was the companion system. A couple of us worked on that, and I was lucky enough to work on that. We gave each of them sort of an archetype and that influenced how they reacted to certain things. We would have liked for the player to get to romance all of them! But we had certain constraints to work within, or maybe that wouldn't have really made sense for the character. So you have to work within that.

Overstreet: As a collector with a lifetime worth of collecting, what are your thoughts on Kickstarter? How do you think that system affects collectability? Do you back anything yourself?

AN: I may be a super backer... don't tell my wife! What attracts me to Kickstarter games is usually going to be the theming first. To take a quick aside here, bear with me, there's a pretty hard split between Euro games and then what people tend to call "Ameritrash," but I like to call it

"Amerithrash." So, I prefer Amerithrash. There's only so many goddamn cubes I can look at all day – and I know there's some fantastic Euros out there, I don't want to diss on them – but the thing is, I've played several Euros. Their mechanics are great, but I just was bored. So even though the mechanics are great there, I can't get into that. I need theming. So then I look at Amerithrash first, and those are often on Kickstarter.

As far as collectability is concerned, Kickstarter is a little different. I think what happens is that they get more popular than the creator expected sometimes, and then they're an instant collectible. An example of one is *Glory to Rome*, where the person lost money on it but the game is fantastic. I don't know exactly what happened, but he just wasn't able to find a publisher for it. And now if you find that in the black box edition still sealed, that's a $250 game or more. But that was total happenstance. I don't look at a Kickstarter and go "this will be collectible." I've never thought of it that way before.

Overstreet: With Kickstarter "stretch goals" often including exclusive miniatures and the like, do you think that people are starting to look at Kickstarter in that collector mindset?
AN: For me, I back because I'm a fan. I've seen a really big split on the stretch goals. Some people think they're weird and unfair and the game should just come with them, which is funny, because that's exactly what a lot of people say about DLC for video games. The whole "it's cool, but it should come with it, it shouldn't cost extra" idea. You can also just wait until a game goes to retail and maybe get some of the stretch goal items included, but probably not. Obviously these people making the games want people to hit those stretch goals, because they make the most money selling directly to the consumer through Kickstarter. For me, personally, I don't mind. I back games because I think they're cool games, and then if they hit all these stretch goals then they can make more cool games, right? Me paying extra money to help hit a stretch goal is just me giving a little extra to ensure that more good games will come out.

Overstreet: For someone who is tangentially interested or maybe just plays casually, what kind of resources would you suggest they look into to expand that interest?
AN: One that springs to mind would either be to go to a site like Geek & Sundry. I recommend them over BoardGameGeek just because BoardGameGeek isn't really user-friendly if you're new to board games – much as I love that site. But when you go to that page, there's all these boxes of info all over the place. If I was just an average person trying to figure out a board game, that would be a little too much. Geek & Sundry is almost like a news site. So I would go with something like that.

Or just walk into a friendly local game shop! You can go in and say "Look, I've played *Ticket to Ride*, give me a recommendation of what to play next" and they'll be able to help you. I've never been to a shop where the people working there weren't gamers themselves. There's no way they don't know. That's probably the number-one best resource.

Overstreet: How would you describe the board game community at large?
AN: I would say they're very welcoming. I went to a BoardGameGeek convention I guess in 2015 – I haven't been able to go since then because it doesn't gel with work – and I went with a friend. There were two of us, so we could obviously go and pick up two-player games, but I can do that at home. So we wanted to play with other people and it was never a problem. And people are willing to teach you and make suggestions and are just so friendly. It's a good environment. When I go to these conventions I never feel left out or bored and it never feels clique-ish. Maybe I've been lucky, but I feel like that's how it is for everyone.

Overstreet: To steer back to RPGs for a bit, what within the *D&D* or *Pathfinder* or other tabletop RPGs would you consider to be the most collectible?
AN: Probably older editions of *Dungeons & Dragons*. *Pathfinder* is newer, though it

is becoming somewhat collectible because of how many resources there are out there. There's a lot of cool stuff out there now. But with older books, even now I'll go and pull one out and just page through it for nostalgia's sake. That, to me, is the most collectible stuff out there.

Overstreet: As an RPG collector and for a board game collector, what would you consider to be the end-all-and-be-all kind of collectible to have for your own collection?
AN: The one that I do have on the RPG end is the white box. I have a lot of old modules, too, and much like comic books I have them bagged and boarded – and you gotta do that because otherwise they'll just disintegrate. And I gotta keep them away from the kids.

Board games I'm not as good at because I'm newer to that. I recall there being a little bit of a ruckus when the guy who did *Diplomacy* put up his own first copy of the game up for auction. The most valuable thing I have – I think, because there's no price guide for these things – would be the *Star Wars* edition of *Gambit* from Avalon

Hill? I've had a lot of inquiries on that one from people wanting to purchase it from me. I've seen that go as high as $500. And I have that *Glory of Rome* that I was talking about, sealed in the black box, so that's $250 or so. I have nothing that's like thousands of dollars or anything like that, and I'm not well-versed enough to really even say what that would be. But I'm sure there's a "Holy Grail" out there for collectors. But usually what drives the price up is that a game goes out of print but becomes popular and doesn't get a second printing.

Overstreet: Do you have a sort of sentimental favorite within your collection?
AN: Probably my copy of *Risk 2210*. I haven't touched it in a long time, but that was my gateway. It's not super advanced or rare or anything – it's just another version of *Risk* – but I still have it and I don't think I'd ever get rid of it. My kids are also now old enough to play some games, and we like to play *King of Tokyo* together, because they can get into it and play it well. The sentimentality there is because my kids play it with me, so that's nice.

THE
MILTON BRADLEY
COMPANY

One of the most recognizable names in board gaming history has long been that of Milton Bradley, a man responsible for founding his eponymous company as well as for developing many of the best-known games of all time. Bradley was born in Maine in 1836, and spent his childhood in various other areas of New England while growing up with his family. As a young man he opted to learn lithography, eventually setting up the first color lithograph shop in Springfield, Massachusetts.

However, it was a failure with that business that spurred the young Bradley to pursue gaming as a way of life instead – he had printed a lithograph of then-nominee Abraham Lincoln, who at the time was clean-shaven. But when Lincoln grew his distinctive beard, those prints ended up totally worthless, and Bradley burned the remaining stock. Bradley then took inspiration from a European board game shown to him by his friend George Tapley, and developed *The Checkered Game of Life*.

His game proved to be wildly popular right out of the gate, selling more than 45,000 copies within its first year. *The Checkered Game of Life* stood out from other similar board games of the time by defining success via secular or business-oriented values; other games, such as *Mansion of Happiness* (another extremely popular board game of the same era) focused on religious, puritanical or moral values. By appealing to America's ambition for material wealth, Bradley was able to increase his own.

Though the company paused game production during the outbreak of the Civil War in 1861, it quickly resumed after Bradley observed how bored many of the Union soldiers were at their stations. This led to the Milton Bradley company's production of many

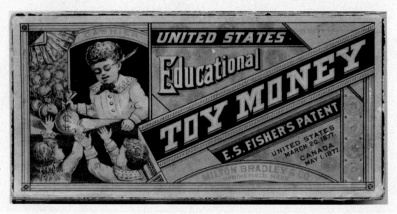

of the first "travel" games for the soldiers to take with them and play on their downtime, such as small versions of checkers, chess, and even *The Checkered Game of Life* itself.

The company diversified in the late 1860s when the Kindergarten movement headed by Friedrich Froebel gained steam in the States; Bradley and his family not only became some of the earliest Kindergarten teachers and students in Massachusetts, but the Milton Bradley Company began creating educational materials specifically for Kindergarteners. The company produced various wooden playthings meant to enhance creative development and would continue to do so for years. As the company entered the turn of the 20th century, it continued to produce various toys meant for grade school teachers to use in classes with young children, such as toy clocks and toy money. The company also began producing jigsaw puzzles as well as educational games aimed at children, such as *Bradley's Sentence Builder*.

The company also entered the realm of art materials around this same time, introducing the first standardized watercolor sets for children as well as crayons of the same colors. Bradley wrote four books on colors and teaching them to children between 1890 and 1900: *Color in the Schoolroom, Color in the Kindergarten, Elementary Color*, and *Water Colors in the Schoolroom*.

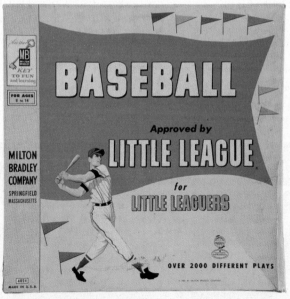

Milton Bradley himself was so dedicated to the idea of Kindergarten that he had his company produce and sell two different publications, *Kindergarten Review* and *Work and Play*. Though neither of them ever turned a profit, he continued to produce them on his own until his passing in 1911.

Following Bradley's death, the company was passed through a few of his family members and friends, and eventually was headed by George Tapley's son, William. A few years later, in 1920, the company bought out McLoughlin Bros., which had been a competitor for Milton Bradley for several years, having produced a variety of puzzles, games, and other toys for small children. However, during the '20s and into the '30s, largely due to the effects of the Great Depression, the Milton Bradley Company was unable to turn a profit, as fewer people were spending money on games. By 1940, the banks were starting to demand payment on the loans, and the company was faced with the threat of bankruptcy.

To avoid going out of business, the company hired businessman James J. Shea as the new president. One of his first acts was to simply burn old games and other inventory that had been sitting around for nearly 40 years at that point. As the country entered World War II, the company began producing a joint meant for use on fighter planes that had been developed by Shea – though they hardly ceased production on board games. The company reproduced some of the travel games that had proved popular during the Civil War, which proved to be profitable. While the overall game lineup was slimmed from more than 400 titles down to about 150, some of the company's best-known games were introduced during this period, such as *Candy Land* and *Chutes and Ladders*.

With the arrival of televisions in homes throughout the country in the 1950s, the company was able to secure rights to one of the more popular TV game shows of the time,

Concentration. The first board game based on the show released in 1959 and proved to be so successful that Milton Bradley was able to release new editions annually until 1982 – which was nine years after the television show itself was cancelled.

The company celebrated its centennial anniversary in 1960 and rebooted their original game success, *The Checkered Game of Life*, as simply *The Game of Life*; it featured a brand-new board style and way to play while still maintaining the values of success and failure

in life that Milton Bradley himself had promoted. During this decade, *Twister* also made its debut. "The Game that Ties You Up in Knots" took off as a popular party game after Johnny Carson and Eva Gabor (somewhat suggestively) played it together on Carson's May 3, 1966 show. Within the following year, 3 million copies of *Twister* were sold.

Throughout the '70s and '80s, traditional analog board gaming gave way to the rise of various electronic games. Milton Bradley's *Simon* arrived in 1978 and was an immedi-

ate success. The four brightly-colored buttons and the electronic tones were a simple but addicting entry point for electronic games. *Simon* was actually pitched to the company by Ralph Baer, who was already a groundbreaker in the realm of electronic gaming with his "Brown Box" console that eventually became the first home video game console in the form of the Magnavox Odyssey.

The Milton Bradley Company had their own groundbreaking moment when it came to video games, though – the Microvision, which arrived in November 1979. It was the first handheld game console ever, and was a moderate success, though it suffered from some significant issues such as "screen rot" on the primitive LCD screen as well as the keypad falling apart. Though it only ever had 12 games produced for it, the Microvision would later be credited by Nintendo as having inspired their Game & Watch lineup of handhelds (which in turn later gave birth to the Game Boy).

In 1984, Milton Bradley was bought out by Hasbro, ending more than a century of family ownership. The company continued producing new games throughout the '80s and '90s, including updated versions of classic titles as well as new ones like *1313 Dead End Drive, Battlemasters, Fireball Island, Knockout*, and many more. In 1998, Hasbro merged both Milton Bradley and longtime rival Parker Brothers (which had been acquired by Hasbro in 1991) to form Hasbro Games; both companies operated simply as brands of Hasbro at large before they were both dropped in 2009 in favor of the singular Hasbro company name.

Though it's now been several years since a game was released with the Milton Bradley name, the legacy of the man himself clearly lives on in the products his company produced for nearly 150 years. Without Milton Bradley – both the man and the company – the landscape of board gaming would likely be hugely different to what it is today.

PARKER BROTHERS

As the home of more than 1,500 different tabletop games in its history that dates back more than a century, Parker Brothers has long been one of the most iconic names in gaming. Initially founded by George S. Parker in 1883, the company has published some of the most popular board games of all time, including *Monopoly, Clue, Risk* and many more.

George S. Parker was born in Salem, Massachusetts, and got his start in the realm of gaming at just 16 years old, when he published a card game called *Banking*. The game had players borrowing money from a bank and attempting to generate more wealth by guessing on how well they could possibly do. George's brother Charles encouraged him to seek wider publication of *Banking*, and after George had been shot down by other publishers in the Boston area he opted to self-publish. He made 500 copies of the game and ended up having just a dozen left over.

It was from there that George founded his game company, first called Geo. S. Parker & Company. He soon published two more games: a card game called *Famous Men* and a board game called *Baker's Dozen*. Charles officially joined the business in 1888, and the company was henceforth renamed as Parker Brothers. A decade later, Edward H. Parker joined the company as well.

Besides games, Parker Brothers produced various other toys, some of the most notable being puzzles, which they introduced around the turn of the 20th century. The most notable of these consisted of the Parker Pastime line, a wooden puzzle line featuring handcut pieces. At one point, Parker Brothers employed 225 puzzle cutters and cranked out nearly 15,000 puzzles per week. The images depicted in the Pastime line were color portraits consisting of everything from cute animals to military scenes and even scenes from popular literature. The line of puzzles was discontinued

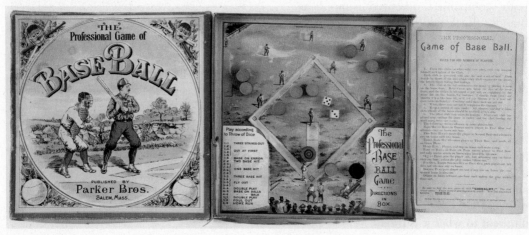

in the mid-1950s. Parker Pastime puzzles are still highly sought-after today and regularly fetch upwards of $200 or more in online auctions.

George remained the primary game designer for Parker Brothers, releasing games based on then-current events, such as *War in Cuba* (based on the Spanish-American War). He also released the card game, *Rook*, in 1906. George and his wife, Grace, designed the cards in *Rook* so that it would be marketable to those of certain religious affiliations (such as those within the Mennonite culture) who had objections to the face cards in a standard deck. The Ace was replaced with a 1 card, and the Jack, Queen and King were replaced with 11, 12, and 13, respectively; a 14 card was also added. The four suits of hearts, clubs, spades and diamonds were also replaced with colors – red, green, yellow and black. There was also the Rook card itself, which served as the Joker equivalent. Though jokingly referred to by many as "missionary poker," *Rook* was significantly successful for Parker Brothers, becoming the best-selling game in the country, and is still played today.

As the country entered the Great Depression, Parker Brothers managed to keep afloat while others around them floundered due to a little game called *Monopoly*, which they published in 1934. The game was derived from *The Landlord's Game* and sold to Parker Brothers by Charles Darrow after Darrow experienced significant success with self-publishing the title. *Monopoly* has gone on to become a part of pop culture

around the world, having been translated into roughly 40 different languages and locally licensed in more than 100 different countries.

Another success around this same time was *Sorry!*, which was first published in the U.K. by Waddingtons in the late '20s before being licensed and sold by Parker Brothers in 1934. A cross-and-circle game based on *Pachisi, Sorry!* simplified the gameplay so that it could be played by children of all ages. Dozens of editions of *Sorry!* have been sold around the world in the years since, and the game remains a popular choice for younger players due to its simplicity.

In the 1950s, Parker Brothers published two key games in their lineup: *Clue* and *Risk*. The former, known as *Cluedo* in England (where it was invented by Anthony E. Pratt and originally published by Waddingtons) is a murder mystery board game where the players take on the roles of one of several house guests. The players must use powers of deduction in order to solve the questions of who committed the crime, in which room, and with what weapon. *Clue* remains popular around the world, having seen multiple different editions over the years and even a Hollywood feature film, but the core problem-solving gameplay has remained the same.

Risk was published by Parker Brothers in 1959 as *Risk: The Continental Game*; it was originally invented by Albert Lamorisse, a French filmmaker, as *La Conquete du Monde* (*The Conquest of the World*). Accordingly, the game's objective for the players is to control as many territories as possible and eliminate the other players in order to take additional land. Like many other popular board games, other editions of *Risk* have been produced and sold over the years, including *Castle Risk* and *Secret Mission Risk*; there have also been various releases of the games themed to popular media such as *Mass Effect, Star Wars* and *Lord of the Rings*.

In 1968, Parker Brothers was bought out by General Mills. The company would then diversify beyond board games in the '60s and '70s with the introduction of Nerf, which hit the market in 1969 as a simple foam ball. The material was designed to avoid causing any harm if thrown indoors, something the marketing was particularly focused on. The original Nerf ball has since become part of the Nerf Sports line, while the most popular products today are the Nerf Blasters.

In 1977, Parker Brothers introduced their first electronic action figure, Rom the Spaceknight, in an attempt to break into the burgeoning action figure market. Though the toy itself was somewhat of a failure (the allure of glowing eyes couldn't overcome the overall lack of articulation in the figure), the *Rom* comic book by Marvel managed to keep interest in the character himself at a high level, and would run for several years after the company ceased production of the toy.

The 1980s was an interesting time for Parker Brothers, as they began to expand into the home video game market that was rapidly growing at the time. Parker Brothers produced home ports of already-popular arcade titles like *Q*bert* and *Frogger*, but perhaps more notably they were responsible for some of the first video games based on *Star Wars*. These were *Star Wars: The Empire Strikes Back* for the Atari 2600 (1982), *Star Wars: Jedi Arena*, also for the 2600 (1983), and *Return of the Jedi: Death Star Battle* for the 2600, the Atari 5200 and the ZX Spectrum (1983-84).

Parker Brothers also established a book publishing branch in 1983, with books featuring popular characters like the Care Bears and Strawberry Shortcake. This proved to be lucrative for the company, with more than 3.5 million books sold within the first couple of years.

In 1985, Parker Brothers was merged with General Mills' other subsidiary, Kenner, to form Kenner Parker Toys Inc. Just two years later, they would be acquired by Tonka. And, just a few years after that, in 1991, Hasbro bought out Tonka for more than a half a billion dollars (Hasbro had already acquired longtime Parker Brothers competitor Milton Bradley by this time as well). Parker Brothers would eventually be merged with Milton Bradley in 1998 to form Hasbro Games. Games would continue to be published under the name Parker Brothers as a brand of Hasbro, but that stopped in 2009 when the company elected to publish all board games under the Hasbro name instead.

Though no longer truly in existence as a company, the Parker Brothers legacy continues on via the continued popularity of many of its titles today.

AVALON HILL

Wargames and military-themed board games have long been a popular genre within tabletop gaming, with a rich history that dates to centuries ago. But one of the great innovators in wargaming established themselves in the middle of the 20th century – Avalon Hill.

The company was founded by Charles S. Roberts in 1954, who started Avalon Hill as a mail-order business out of his garage in Avalon, Maryland. Two years prior, Roberts had created *Tactics*, one of the earliest board wargames designed for mass-market production. *Tactics* featured several game mechanics which have since become standard for board wargames, such as variable movement costs and a combat results table.

In 1958, *Tactics II* was released, providing a slightly revised version of the original game.

Roberts also released *Gettysburg* that same year. Not only was *Gettysburg* the first board game to be based on an actual historical battle, but the second edition of the game, released in 1961, introduced the hex map. Hex maps, or hex grids, have since become commonly used in all types of games, ranging from wargames to board games to role-playing games and even many different types of video games.

The advantage of the hex grid over a traditional square grid map is that the distance between the center of each individual cell is exactly the same in a hex grid. On a square grid, moving diagonally is a greater distance to traverse. Hex grid cells also always share an edge with their neighbors and never connect to another cell at only a point.

Avalon Hill moved out of a garage and into a proper office building in Baltimore in 1959, and the company started publishing games from other designers as well, such as *Verdict*, and the various sports-themed *Baseball Strategy*, *Football Strategy*, and *Basketball Strategy*.

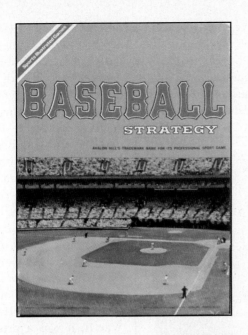

In the early 1960s, the economy hit a recession, and Avalon Hill was faced with a large amount of debt. Roberts had planned on filing bankruptcy at the end of 1963, but instead, Monarch Office Services and J.E. Smith & Co., his creditors, took over the company. The company retained just one original staff member, Thomas N. Shaw (responsible for designing the sports *Strategy* games), appointed J.E. Sparling as the president, and adopted a twice-per-year game release schedule.

Though Roberts left the gaming industry at this time and never really returned to it, the Charles S. Roberts Award was created in his name at the first Origins Game Convention in 1975, and has been given out in recog-

nition of excellence in historical wargaming. Roberts himself went on to form a small book publishing company – Barnard, Roberts and Company, Inc. – where he wrote several books about railroad history. He passed away in 2010.

Following Roberts' departure, Avalon Hill continued publishing games in much the same fashion as it had before, with the release of *Blitzkrieg* in 1965, followed by more real-life battle recreations via *Midway* and *The Battle of the Bulge*.

The General, a magazine, also began publication in the 1960s, and would be published up until the company's final sale in 1998. The periodical ran bi-monthly and covered a variety of wargaming topics, ranging from industry news to different types of game tactics its readers could adapt. It also, of course, promoted various Avalon Hill wargaming products.

Monarch would buy out J.E. Smith & Co. by the end of 1971, and Avalon became a subsidiary of the renamed Monarch Avalon company.

It was in this decade that the company would make a long series of acquisitions: the purchase of 3M games in 1976 (which gave Avalon Hill the rights to the already-successful *TwixT* and *Acquire*), the acquisition of the *Sports Illustrated* lineup of games in December of that year, and the purchase of the Aladdin Industries lineup in 1977. This rapid expansion greatly increased Avalon Hill's presence in the market, and successful games from this era included *Squad Leader, Outdoor Survival* and the popular *Statis Pro* line of sports games.

As Avalon Hill entered the 1980s, it diversified beyond just board games and entered the realm of role-playing market, publishing *Powers and Perils* in '83 and *Lords of Creation* in '84. The former ended up being a significant failure for the company, as not only did it feature plagiarized drawings from fantasy and comic book artist Frank Frazetta, but it also faced stiff competition from the first edition of none other than *Dungeons & Dragons*; the *Powers and Perils* line was put to rest in 1984. *Lords of Creation* fared a bit better, having been written by Tom Moldvay (who also worked on *Dungeons & Dragons*) and being more malleable in its setting. A handful of adventure modules were released (*The Horn of Roland, The Yeti Sanction* and *Omegakron*), and though two more were announced, they never came to fruition.

The rights to *RuneQuest* were bought from Chaosium around this time as well, and Avalon Hill published the 3rd Edition of the game in 1984. The agreement allowed for *RuneQuest* to be distributed to a wider audience, while Chaosium retained the approval rights for the content itself. Unfortunately, due to the extreme popularity of *Dungeons & Dragons*, it was difficult for any other role-playing system to compete. However, Avalon Hill did their best with what they had, publishing the role-playing magazine *HEROES* from 1984-1986. The publication promoted *Powers and Perils*, *RuneQuest* and the company's other role-playing games.

Avalon Hill also started publishing video games through its Microcomputer Games division in the early '80s. Many of these games were adaptations of their already-successful board games, and were published on a variety of computer platforms, such as the Apple II and the Commodore 64. The only big success sales-wise came towards the end of company history, which was *Achtung Spitfire!*, published in 1997. It focuses on turn-based air combat and is set during the first half of World War II; it was a prequel to 1996's *Over the Reich*, which has similar gameplay and focuses on the latter half of the war. *Achtung Spitfire!* was the runner-up for *Computer Gaming World*'s "Wargame of the Year" award in 1997, and was called the "best Battle of Britain game ever" by the publication.

The company faced a downturn in the 1990s, and Monarch Avalon closed its New York office and began to reduce inventory. In 1998, Monarch sold Avalon Hill to Hasbro for $6 million; Avalon Hill was later transferred to Wizards of the Coast, another subsidiary of Hasbro. Unlike Milton Bradley and Parker Brothers, there continue to be games made with the Avalon Hill name today. Some of the more successful titles have included *Axis and Allies, RoboRally* and *Betrayal at House on the Hill*. Though a far cry from the humble, garage-based beginnings, Avalon Hill continues to be a name worth paying attention to when it comes to gaming.

Few companies have been quite as synonymous with toys and games over the years as Hasbro has been. Thanks to the enormous success of several key franchises such as *My Little Pony* and *Transformers*, Hasbro has become one of the largest and most influential toy makers in the entire world. But they, like many, started from humble beginnings.

What few people probably realize is that Hasbro is actually short for Hassenfeld Brothers. The company began in the early 1920s, when Henry, Herman and Hilal Hassenfeld – three brothers that had recently moved to the U.S. from Poland – began their business. The trio entered the textile market, first selling just remnants but soon moving on to making small items like hat liners and pencil boxes. Hassenfeld Brothers, Inc. was formally incorporated in 1926 with just a handful of employees, all members of the Hassenfeld family.

The company soon expanded to more than 150 employees and managed to survive the Great Depression in the 1930s by making school supplies and pencil boxes, even moving on to making the pencils themselves after their supplier raised

prices. It was also during this decade that the company introduced its first toys, primarily consisting of modeling clay and nurse kits. As the country entered World War II, Hassenfeld Brothers also began making a junior air-raid kit, which came with toy gas masks and flashlights. In 1943, Hilal passed away, and Henry took over as CEO with his son, Merrill, becoming the company's president.

Under Merrill, the company began entering the growing plastics field to support the toy lines, which were also growing at a rapid pace (though school supplies were still a large part of the company's business at large). Mr. Potato Head hit the market in 1952, having been purchased from George Lerner, and was an instant success; notably, the toy was the first to be advertised on television and also marked the first time a commercial was specifically aimed at children, rather than at their parents. More than 1 million Mr. Potato Head kits were sold in just the first year.

Between Mr. Potato Head's success and the fact that the company acquired the Disney license in 1954, Hassenfeld Brothers headed into the swingin' sixties with their heads held high, with revenues in excess of $12 million.

In 1964, the company introduced what would quickly become one of their most successful products: G.I. Joe. The 12-inch figure was the first toy on the market to be dubbed an "action figure," as Hassenfeld believed that boys would not be interested in anything called a "doll." G.I. Joe actually evolved out of a meeting that the company had with a licensing agent the year prior, who had suggested that Hassenfeld do a toy tie-in to a show called *The Lieutenant*. The company turned down the offer for the license as they didn't want to tie a toy's success to a show they didn't have faith would last particularly long (which they'd be right about, as *The Lieutenant* only ever aired 29 episodes). Within two years, G.I. Joe accounted for roughly two-thirds of Hassenfeld Brothers' total sales.

In 1968 the company officially renamed itself to Hasbro Industries, and by the end of the decade it started to diversify into other areas – it bought out Burt Claster Enterprises, producer of the *Romper Room* show, in 1969. Unfortunately, at the end of '69, Hasbro posted a $1 million loss due to supplier troubles and strikes.

Some ill-fated decisions were made in the early 1970s, not the least of which was the Romper Room Nursery School chain, which was opened to take advantage of President Nixon's Family Assistance Plan (which subsidized daycare for working parents). Within just five years the entire chain was shut down. Hasbro also introduced cookware based on the *Galloping Gourmet* in an attempt to capitalize on the popular show, but the line quite literally fell apart when termites ate bowls that had been left in a warehouse. Then there was the one-two punch public relations fiasco of Javelin Darts and the Hypo-Squirt. The former, colloquially known as simply

"lawn darts," proved to be extremely hazardous since they were sharp projectiles with metal points that were meant to be thrown across the yard for fun – leading to serious injuries. And then the latter, which was a needle-shaped water gun, was quickly deemed a "junior junkie kit" by the media. Both ended up being recalled.

Even G.I. Joe faced problems due to the controversy surrounding the Vietnam War, and Hasbro had to reframe the character as being more adventurous instead of simply a soldier. Hasbro actually discontinued the G.I. Joe line entirely in 1975 due to the rising cost of plastic. By '77, the company was not only under a large amount of debt but also was posting losses of $2.5 million.

In the early 1980s, the school supply division was spun off into an entirely separate company, Empire Pencil, and the toy line was cut by a third (with new products being reduced by half). Hasbro refocused onto simple, low-cost products, like Mr. Potato Head, and stayed out of the tumultuous electronics industry entirely, in order to become profitable again. G.I. Joe was revived in '82 with help from Marvel Comics, *My Little Pony* saw success that same year, and *Transformers* debuted in '84, succeeding both as a toy and as a cartoon.

The '80s saw a series of significant acquisitions for Hasbro. In 1983, the company bought out GLENCO, known for their infant items, and also picked up Knickerbocker Toy Company, known as the producer of the Raggedy Ann lineup of dolls. In 1984, Hasbro acquired Milton Bradley, bringing long-running popular board games such as *The Game of Life* and *Candyland* under the Hasbro umbrella. By the middle of the decade, the company renamed themselves to simply Hasbro (from Hasbro Industries) and became the largest toy company in the world, moving past Mattel for the first time.

Further acquisitions by the end of that decade included Coleco Industries and Tonka; the latter of these also included game maker Parker Brothers and action figure producer Kenner Products. Parker Brothers and Milton Bradley, which had been competitors up until that point, were then merged into one division.

By the 1990s the company was continuing to compete with Mattel, with the two fighting for the top spot in the business. Hasbro established the video game development division Hasbro Interactive in 1995, which would go on to produce a number of CD-ROM titles based on various Hasbro-owned properties (*Monopoly, The Game of Life, Candy Land, Clue, Sorry!, RISK,* and *Mr. Potato Head,* to name a few). Hasbro Interactive was eventually sold off to Infogrames for $100 million in 2001. In '98, Hasbro bought the Avalon Hill game company (home to a variety of board wargames) and the following year purchased Wizards of the Coast (home to *Magic: The Gathering*). Wizards is now a subsidiary of Hasbro, with Avalon Hill as a division of Wizards.

Hasbro has continued to diversify into other forms of media, particularly with the formation of Hasbro Films (which contains Allspark Pictures and Allspark Animation). Hasbro Films has produced the hugely-successful *Transformers* movie franchise, but is also responsible for some less-popular films based on Hasbro products, such as the *G.I. Joe, Battleship* and *Jem and the Holograms* movies.

By 2008, Hasbro had acquired another game maker, Cranium, Inc., and absorbed it into the Hasbro Games brand. As a result of the various acquisitions, Hasbro is now the largest producer of board games in the world, and is responsible for publishing *Cranium, Clue, The Game of Life, Monopoly, Risk, Trivial Pursuit* and dozens of other classic board games. Via Wizards of the Coast, it also publishes *Magic: The Gathering* and *Dungeons & Dragons.*

To have a single company controlling such a strong majority of the board game market – particularly the mass-market games that are available in any department store – is certainly something that has caused some serious debates. But regardless of how the consumers feel about it, it's become clear that Hasbro still isn't going anywhere but up. Whether they hit a ceiling or not is yet to be determined, but at the very least, Hasbro continues to put board games and tabletop merchandise in the hands of the next generation of gamers.

OTHER BOARD GAMES

Board games might be the single largest aspect of the ever-expanding tabletop gaming industry – it really goes to show that this book only had room for so many that people consider "classic" games! There's far more that could have been talked about within the discussion of all-time greats and the kinds of games that even the most casual player would have on their shelf: *Trivial Pursuit, Scrabble, Risk, Chutes and Ladders, Uno, Yahtzee, Stratego...* the list goes on seemingly forever.

There are also a significant number of games that have made a splash in the industry within the last decade or so and will likely eventually find themselves being called a "classic." These are the games to start collecting (and, of course, playing) right now.

Cooperative board gaming has become hugely popular within the last several years. While competitive player-versus-player gaming is still popular, player-versus-board games have shot up in notoriety (and there are many games that now use elements of both). The idea of a truly cooperative board game isn't new, but early examples of the subgenre were mainly used in education-focused settings in order to teach young children what cooperation actually was. One of the earliest successful examples of a co-op board game for entertainment's sake was 1987's *Arkham Horror*, published by

Chaosium. The board game is set in the same world of Chaosium's role-playing setting of *Call of Cthulhu* and was immediately popular, with the original run selling out quickly. And while Chaosium had announced reprints, none ever actually happened.

Arkham Horror was revised and reprinted by Fantasy Flight Games in 2005, and the game has seen a number of expansions (*Curse of the Dark Pharaoh, Dunwich Horror, The King in Yellow, Black Goat of the Woods*, among others) in the years since. Contemporary releases of the base game are fairly easy to find for $30 or less, though copies of the original 1987 edition tend to command prices of at least $100 in online auctions.

Contemporary cooperative gaming was popularized largely by 2007's *Pandemic*, designed by Matt Leacock and published by Z-Man games. The game put players in the roles of a particular disease specialist as those playing worked together in order to prevent four deadly diseases from wiping out the world's population. While one of the long-time criticisms of *Arkham Horror* has been the length of time it takes to play (usually a few hours), a session of *Pandemic* can be finished in usually an hour or less, making it far more appealing to mass market audiences.

Pandemic has seen a handful of expansions – *On the Brink, In the Lab,* and *State of Emergency* – and the publisher has also released additional free-to-download scenarios that change up the basic game. In 2013, a second edition of the game released, adding new characters. A dice game, *Pandemic: The Cure*, released in 2014; that year also saw the card-based *Pandemic: Contagion*, in which players attempt to spread infections rather than cure them. *Pandemic: Reign of Cthulhu* changes up the setting quite a bit, having players trying to prevent the titular monster from being summoned.

The biggest change-up to *Pandemic* was 2015's *Pandemic Legacy*. As a "legacy" game, each session with the game permanently changes how the story and game will play out in further sessions, including permanent rule changes and other variables that arrive in the form of sealed packages included in the game's pieces that are not opened until certain things have happened.

Pandemic Legacy received massive critical acclaim for its game design and is one of the highest-rated board games of all time. A second "season" of *Legacy* released in late 2017.

Most versions of *Pandemic* and related releases can be found for about $50 or less – though that can obviously add up quickly for collectors looking to own every edition and expansion for this popular title.

An example of a game that's managed to blend both competitive and cooperative elements is *Betrayal at House on the Hill*, a horror exploration game published by Avalon Hill since 2004. The game begins with all participating players – up to six people – playing as allies as they explore the titular haunted house on the hill. Each player controls a different character that has unique stats in four categories: Might, Knowledge, Speed and Sanity. If any of the four stats drop to zero – something that can occur based on combat or other in-game events triggered by card draws – that character dies and the player is out of the game.

Eventually, a "haunt" is triggered in the game, and one player ends up "betraying" the others in order to side with whatever nasty creature has entered the building. With 50 possible haunts (chosen based on the card that triggered the haunt) the game has a significant replay value. The game ends when one side – either the traitor or the remaining players – achieves their goal as listed in the in-game materials.

ISAAC CHILDRES

Betrayal at House on the Hill saw a second edition release in 2010, followed by an expansion, Widow's Walk, in 2016. A Dungeons & Dragons-themed spinoff title, Betrayal at Baldur's Gate, arrived in 2017, using most of the same rules of the original release. A legacy edition of the game entered development in late 2017.

Most materials related to Betrayal are easy enough to find, with the game being popular enough on the mass market to be found in just about any store that sells board games. Both Betrayal at House on the Hill and Betrayal at Baldur's Gate can be found for about $50, at most, brand-new, while the Widow's Walk expansion usually runs about $25. The original, out-of-print release of the base game is the most difficult to find, and can usually garner about $75 or more online accordingly.

Straddling the line between a board game and a tabletop RPG is Gloomhaven, a 2017 release known as much for the depth of the

gameplay as it is for the literal physical size of the game itself. Containing more than 1,500 cards, 95 different playable scenarios, 17 different playable classes and more, the game's box itself weighs more than 20 pounds.

Gloomhaven is a cooperative role-playing board game that plays out via card draws rather than by stat sheets and dice. The game's world is explored by the players, who can choose to fight their way through dungeons together or make any other kind of narrative decision that impacts how the world evolves. Sessions can be lengthy, running upwards of several hours for a single playthrough, but it's still a slightly more contained role-playing experience compared to that of a true tabletop RPG, and has appealed to longtime fans of both board games and RPGs.

Due to the sheer size of the game, Gloomhaven's retail release runs about $150 – not a small investment by any means. However, the original release of the game was funded through Kickstarter, and the Kickstarter releases command even higher prices, sometimes going for $350 or more in online auctions (particularly if the game remained unopened). Given the immediate popularity of *Gloomhaven*, it will likely remain one worth paying close attention to as additional materials and editions release in the years to follow.

A number of card-based board games have also hit the scene as of late, not the least of which has been *Dominion*, which first released in 2008. The game introduced the concept of "deck-building" to gaming, in which players compete to have the most valuable deck; it's a similar idea to "drafting" in collectible card games. In *Dominion*, players all begin with the same starting stack of cards and compete, via their Action and Buy phases, to try and earn Victory cards and avoid gaining Curse cards. The deck-building idea has since been applied to numerous other games in the decade-plus since *Dominion*'s original release.

Several expansions have released for *Dominion* as well, including *Intrigue, Seaside, Alchemy, Prosperity, Cornucopia, Hinterlands, Dark Ages, Guilds, Adventures, Empires,* and *Nocturne*; a second edition of the base game has also been published. Many of the expansions add various other gameplay elements, such as different kinds of cards, additional phases of player turns, and so on.

Due to the widespread popularity of the game, *Dominion* and its expansions are fairly easy to find for about $30 to $50 per set, depending on the set itself. There are also "Big Box" releases which contain the base set as well as additional expansions, which tend to run for $75 or more. In addition to that, there have been several promotional mini-expansions, but for the most part those can be found for $15-$20.

Other card-based board games that have seen significant success have included *Red Dragon Inn, Codenames, Ascension* and many more. Despite having cards as the main mechanic, these games are not collectible card games in the same ballpark as a *Magic: The Gathering* or *Yu-Gi-Oh!* since, while they use cards, they are not built by use of blind card packs and do not have a collectible focus to them.

Thanks to crowdfunding websites, it seems as though there's a new hot board game hitting the market everywhere you look. It can be hard to keep up with everything new coming out. New mechanics have been introduced, unique themes have been explored, and the board game industry accordingly has absolutely exploded. Paying attention to what's worth playing and collecting can be difficult, but you can never go wrong with simply buying what you like! And, who knows? Maybe the niche board game you backed online will become the next big thing.

TABLETOP FOR TWO
WITH BRAD VANVUGT

Brad VanVugt is a gamer and podcaster who resides in Baltimore, Maryland. Together with his wife, Emily, he hosts Tabletop for Two, a podcast that examines whether or not some of the hottest board games on the market that are described as "for 2-4 players" can actually be played with just a pair. Overstreet talked with Brad about his gaming hobby, his collection, and what's next for the podcast.

Overstreet: Tell us a little bit about yourself.
Brad VanVugt (BV): Gaming in all forms has been a hugely important part of my life. My current career is focused around video games, and I also host two gaming themed podcasts: Dense Pixels (video games) and The Tabletop for Two Podcast (a tabletop gaming podcast that is co-hosted by my wife, Emily).

Overstreet: What first sparked your interest in board gaming in general? How has that transitioned into your hobby today?
BV: I used to play several mass market board games as a kid. My childhood friend and I would play board games frequently, even heavier stuff like *Hero Quest* and *Magic: The Gathering*, which he introduced me to. Emily also had a love of board games as a kid, and that led us to getting back into gaming as a hobby we could do with one another. That mutual love for games, especially playing together, has persisted today for us to the point where we decided to produce a podcast specifically catering to gamers who primarily play with just two.

Overstreet: How or why did you start collecting board games?

BV: My first entry into the hobby side of gaming was *Magic: The Gathering* when I was a teen. I never ventured much deeper than that, but Emily and I still played and collected a lot of mass market games, but they grew stale for us. We wanted to find games that would hold our interest so, after a brief attempt to get back into *Magic,* I started researching games that were of similar style but weren't collectable as *Magic* is. I found a game called *Ascension: Chronicle of the Godslayer* (that happened to be designed by former *Magic* professional players) which was described as a "self-contained *Magic*" game. We were hooked, often playing three or four games of *Ascension* in a row a night! *Ascension* opened me up to a whole world of games that I never even knew existed, and we were quickly down the rabbit hole.

Overstreet: Board games have seen a real boom in popularity over the last few years. Why do you think that is?

BV: The "hobby" market (a term generally attributed to more strategic board games, i.e.: not your *Monopoly*'s and *Sorry!*'s) has been something that has flourished in mainly European markets for a few decades. The US never saw these, as there weren't publishers willing to bring those games over here outside of small circles. One that did break through was *The Settlers of Catan,* which steadily gained popularity to the point that you could find it in Target and Barnes & Noble. Eventually a lot of the folks who played *Catan* started looking for some-

thing more, and US publishers began bringing more games from the European market to the US. The Wil Wheaton YouTube show "Tabletop" has also been hugely influential to exposing people to games that are fun to play and generally very accessible. The industry is still very much a cottage industry, but it has grown exponentially in the past decade in particular.

I'd also be remiss if I didn't mention the impact Kickstarter has had, especially in the last five years in particular. The argument can be made that tabletop gaming has been the industry that has benefitting the most from the emergence of crowdfunding. Kickstarter has allowed many games, for better or worse, to see distribution that probably wouldn't have seen the light of day under traditional publishing models. Without Kickstarter, it's possible many game publishers that have put out some great games, like Tasty Minstrel Games and CMON for example, wouldn't exist.

Overstreet: Kickstarter has seemed to be a huge boon for the board game industry. Why do you think that is?

BV: I think the biggest reason is because it's given many games a chance to be published that might not have been under traditional publishing models. Some would argue there's been a detrimental effect because of this. One of the benefits of traditional publishers is game development: the process where a developer works with the designer of a game to help polish the rough edges. Several games have come from Kickstarter that would have strongly benefited from having a developer work with the game before it gets published. Also, anything with cool miniatures often gets funded even if the game itself is pretty weak.

I feel like Kickstarter has been a net positive though. Many games in our collection were a product of crowdfunding, and we've found that our personal retention of Kickstarter games is only slightly lower than traditionally published games. Some projects will also reward their backers in the form of including expansions that will be sold separately at retail or exclusives like promotional items and upgraded components. Many equate it to nothing more than a pre-order system, and there's an argument to be made for that from some publishers, but it's a service I plan on continuing to use where it makes sense to.

Overstreet: Have you backed a Kickstarter for a board game simply out of wanting to get a Kickstarter-exclusive reward for that game?
BV: Absolutely! Most Kickstarter games that get funded usually get released in the regular channels eventually, so really anytime I back a project that's already funded, it's to get whatever bonuses or exclusives that are included with it.

Overstreet: Do you have a standout game in your collection as far as value/collectability is concerned?
BV: From a value standpoint, surprisingly not! As much as I spend on games, I tend to have a very strict valuation of individual games and tend not to overpay for a hard-to-find game, especially as many rare games are getting reprinted nowadays – the same demand that drives their value up also inspires publishers to want to sell them again. I may have a few worth money down the road, but that's entirely dependent on maintained demand and availability for those titles which is difficult to forecast. I guess if I could point to one, it would be the 10th Anniversary edition of the venerable *Ticket to Ride*. It sells today for a decent amount over its $100 retail price as it was a very limited print.

Overstreet: Are there any "holy grail" kind of games that you'd want to have in your collection but haven't had the chance to pick up yet?
BV: *Glory to Rome* is a very popular "grail" title that many gamers strive after because the game is very good, and its English language rights are in somewhat of a purgatory, making it unlikely that it will ever be reprinted. Funnily enough, you can get it for very cheap in foreign language versions, but making it playable for English speakers would take a lot of work.

Overstreet: Do you have anything in your collection that you picked up just for collectable value instead of play/entertainment value?
BV: There are a few games I've purchased that I've been on the fence on from a game-play standpoint, a recent example is the *Mechs vs Minions* game from Riot Games (the *League of Legends* folks), that I only took a chance on because I knew the game could probably be flipped for at least it's MSRP if we didn't like it. We have so little space for storage, though, that we're hard pressed to keep anything that we don't enjoy playing.

Overstreet: Do you have a sentimental favorite in your collection – something that maybe isn't worth a whole lot monetarily but you never plan on getting rid of?
BV: *Carcassonne* was a game that we played almost nightly when we acquired it, and was probably the single game that Emily really fell in love with. It doesn't hit the table as much anymore as it doesn't provide the challenge that Em and I typically seek out, but I could never see us parting with it, especially as it is also a great gateway title to teach new players.

Overstreet: You run a podcast called Tabletop for Two – where did the idea for that come from?
BV: As I started listening to more board game podcasts and reading reviews for various games, I felt like the two-player part of the hobby was woefully underserved. Many reviews you would hear would discuss playing a game with three or four

players and, as someone who plays with two players 90 percent of the time, that can give me an unclear view of a game as many games play drastically different with two players than at the other player counts.

We began the channel by doing video reviews of games where we would specifically discuss the feel of playing with two. With the birth of our son it became much more difficult to film reviews, so we shifted instead into a podcast, which was much easier to record. We've now been at it for over two years at this point and are considering even more ways to expand the channel, like doing live plays.

Overstreet: Have you learned anything about the industry from playing board games with just two people?
BV: I think there are many games out there that shouldn't have a "2" in that player count box! Many games, whether or not they were designed with two players in mind, will still concoct a two-player variant or just allow for the game to be played with two players because having a wider player count range usually leads to more sales as you're widening the audience for that game. We've played several games where it was apparent that you needed three or more players to have the experience the designer intended, and I wish sometimes

that discretion would be practiced more in this area. Put out the game in its best form, even if that means fewer games supporting two players in the market.

Overstreet: For people looking to get into board gaming these days, where would you suggest they go to look for games?
BV: The biggest benefit to the board game boom these past few years has been that major retailers have been wanting to get in on the act. Barnes & Noble has a game section equivalent to that of specialty game shops these days, and even Target has a respectable selection now as well.

Still, I'm an advocate of shopping your local specialty game stores as much as possible, as they provide expertise, play space, and community that you can't find at a big box store. I've met many good friends at my local store, Canton Games in Baltimore, MD, and have bought several games that remain in my collection today based on recommendations received there.

If you don't have a local place nearby, there are several online retailers with great service as well. BoardGameGeek is the online resource I use the most to gain information on games. It's also an invaluable resource for rules questions and the like, as you'll often be able to get responses from the game's designer themselves!

A History of Role Playing Games

Role-playing as a genre has proved popular over multiple forms of media, from video games to live-action and, of course, on a tabletop. While tabletop RPGs gained a massive amount of traction and popularity since the mid-20th century, its origins extend far beyond that.

Role-playing for the sake of entertainment goes back several hundreds of years, to the origins of historical reenactment. The idea of recreating or reenacting a historical battle has been around since at least the Middle Ages, when tournaments would take themes from ancient Rome and have its participants act out known stories. By the 1800s, interest in recreating battles from medieval times soared, as it began to be seen as a more romantic, simpler time when compared to the ongoing industrial revolution. Historical reenactment continues to be practiced today around the world, with many groups using it as an educational tool to show how people lived or how soldiers fought hundreds of years ago.

A fantastical twist to historical role-play didn't really take shape until the 1960s,

Chainmail
rules for medieval miniatures
by
Gary Gygax & Jeff Perren

GUIDON GAMES
"WARGAMING WITH MINIATURES"

when mild fantasy elements were introduced to medieval reenactment. This eventually gave rise to live-action role-playing, or LARPing, an activity that's still popular today – and one that often uses rules inspired by tabletop RPGs.

When it comes to tabletop RPGs, though, they largely evolved out of wargaming and other board games. Many parlour games that were popular during the Victorian era included role-playing elements, with participants taking on the role of a given character (particularly murder mystery games such as *Jury Box* or "Wink Murder" games). Wargames, such as *Diplomacy*, began to introduce social skills as a core part of the gameplay by the 1950s. While many wargames put their focus on actual military units, fantasy elements began to be introduced to these games by the late 1960s.

In 1969, an informal wargaming session held by Dave Wesely took place, focusing on a town called "Braunstein." Players were assigned civilian roles in addition to military roles, and many of the rules of the game were being improvised on the spot; much of the game was taking inspiration from how *Diplomacy* was played, but the results were considered chaotic by those involved. A second "Braunstein" was later run by both Wesely and Dave Arneson. Arneson later reworked the game to include fantastical elements and created the fantasy world of "Blackmoor."

Chainmail, a medieval fantasy wargame, was created by Gary Gygax and Jeff Perren and released in 1971 by Guiddon Games. Taking a heap of influence from the J.R.R. Tolkien-written world of Middle Earth as well as from Robert E. Howard's *Conan the Barbarian*, *Chainmail* was one of the first commercially available fantasy wargames on the market. The Fantasy Supplement for *Chainmail* added various things such as magical weapons and spells like "Fireball" and "Lightning Bolt."

Incidentally, the *Chainmail* rules would be used to resolve combat in Arneson's "Blackmoor" scenarios. Arneson worked in elements to "Blackmoor" that have since become standard in RPGs, such as trackable hit points and experience points, character levels, and so on.

Arneson and Gygax would later collaborate to create the defining game of the tabletop role-playing game genre – *Dungeons & Dragons*, which arrived in 1974. (The two had actually previously worked

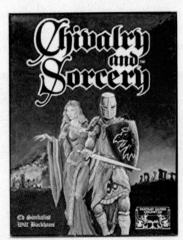

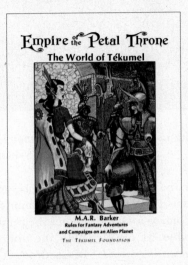

together on *Don't Give Up the Ship*, a set of rules for Napoleonic wargaming, in 1972.) A quaint set of three booklets, the original *D&D* release relied heavily on knowledge of wargames – but despite that, proved to be popular, establishing a fanbase around the world. That original set went through several printings and would be later supplemented with additional material – including an official *Blackmoor* supplement.

The instant success of *D&D* caused a number of other fantasy tabletop RPGs to suddenly spring into publication by the end of the '70s, including *Tunnels and Trolls* (1975), *Chivalry & Sorcery* (1977), and *RuneQuest* (1978). Most fell by the wayside, simply unable to compete with the overall popularity of *D&D,* but some stuck it out and are still around today. Today, *Tunnels and Trolls* is still framed as a more accessible alternative for newbie RPers who haven't played a game like *D&D* before, and has gone through eight different editions. *Chivalry & Sorcery* instead took inspiration from *D&D* to create something more focused on a realistic medieval setting, rather than a fantastical one, and notably was the game to coin the term "game master."

Empire of the Petal Throne also arrived in 1974, designed and self-published by M.A.R. Barker. The game was based on Barker's *Tekumel* universe, which would later be the basis for the 1975 board game *War of Wizards* as well as a number of novels. The RPG would later see republication by TSR, as the staff there was impressed by Barker's stories – and more importantly, by the mechanic of "critical hits" that would later see introduction into *D&D* – but *Empire of the Petal Throne* never achieved much in terms of popularity.

new areas and battle deadly foes. A number of editions have been published over the years, with some of the more recent being 2013's *Traveller5* and 2016's *Mongoose Traveller* 2nd Edition.

Tabletop RPGs picked up steam and saw more widespread popularity throughout the 1980s, with a number of new games seeing success and introducing new mechanics, such as *Call of Cthulhu* (1981), *Champions* (1981), and *Ars Magica* (1988). Meanwhile, already-successful games experienced changes to and rebalancing of gameplay in newer editions. Many publishers tried to create a unified role-playing system that could be used across multiple genres of role-playing, giving rise to the likes of systems like GURPS (Generic Universal Role-Playing System), created by Steve Jackson Games in 1986. The decade also marked the rise of role-playing in international markets, with already-successful games being translated into a number of different languages and localized for different countries, and new games – such as *Warhammer Fantasy Roleplay* – beginning to pop up overseas.

But tabletop RPGs were hardly limited to just classic fantasy realms, as science-fiction games also started to pop up by the late '70s. The first was *Metamorphosis Alpha*, created by James M. Ward and published by TSR (the original publisher of *D&D*). The game allowed players to control a human or a mutated creature of some sort in order to complete missions on a starship, the *Warden*, that had been affected by an unknown event. The combat played similar to how the original *D&D* played out. *Gamma World*, also designed by Ward alongside Gary Jaquet, first released in 1978; it borrowed a number of things from *Metamorphosis Alpha* and has since seen seven editions.

Traveller, another sci-fi RPG, also arrived around the same time, with the first edition being published by Game Designers' Workshop in 1977. Players control a character they create and are able to travel throughout a star system in order to explore

Role-playing was adapted for the digital age beginning in the 1990s, with video games beginning to dominate the genre. With the ability to play solo, video game RPGs drove a lot of attention away from the tabletop industry. However, many successful video games were taking direct inspiration from their pen-and-paper counterparts, such as *The Elder Scrolls*; 1998's *Baldur's Gate* used *Advanced D&D* rules and the *Forgotten Realm* campaign setting as the basis for its story.

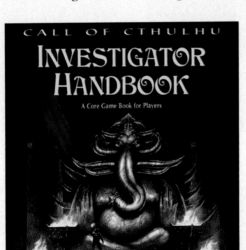

By 2000, *D&D*'s Open Game License (OGL) had launched, allowing other companies to publish materials compatible with the game. This, along with the new *D&D* rules being dubbed the "d20 system," helped to give rise to a boom in the industry. Many new games have released since then making use of the d20 system, the most notable of which has been *Pathfinder* (2009). The popularity of *Pathfinder* actually eclipsed that of *D&D* between 2011 and 2013, and – while the 5th Edition of *D&D* has been huge – *Pathfinder* has proven to be a suitable alternative for many gamers.

The advent of the internet and of crowd-funding websites has brought tabletop RPGs back to the forefront and allowed for more varied genres than ever to be highlighted via role-playing. However, the fact that role-playing has been brought out of basements and into the spotlight via popular web series like *The Adventure Zone* and *Critical Role* has perhaps been the biggest boon to tabletop gaming. Role-playing games were long considered an extremely niche activity, and the shift in culture has allowed them to become more normalized than ever before. The benefit of that culture shift cannot be quantified, but it's certainly visible given the huge uptick in role-players and in new games hitting store shelves. Whether this rise is set to continue or if it will plateau is yet to be determined, but the industry's renaissance is one that fans of all ages have been able to enjoy.

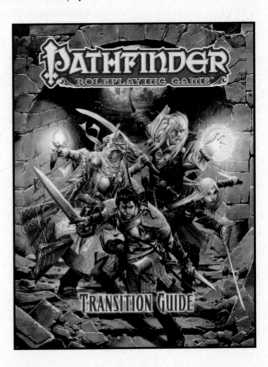

DUNGEONS & DRAGONS ®

No single game has been as synony-mous with the idea of tabletop gaming as *Dungeons & Dragons*. Since its 1974 debut, *D&D* has been inspiring gamers, writers and fans of all ages through a system that encourages problem-solving and coopera-tion as much as it does combat.

THE HISTORY

The earliest predecessor to *D&D* came in the form of a ruleset created for medieval-themed wargames, originally written by Jeff Perren. Perren worked alongside Gary Gygax, a fellow wargamer, to expand the rules and together they published them as *Chainmail* in 1971. *Chainmail* itself would later be expanded upon by Dave Arneson in order to help resolve combat in other game experiments. Arneson and Gygax, who had previously worked together on *Don't Give Up the Ship!* (a 1972 set of rules for Napoleonic naval wargames), eventu-ally went to work together on what would become *Dungeons & Dragons*.

The high fantasy theming of *D&D* took a lot of inspiration from popular fantasy novels of the time; the original *Dungeon Masters Guide* listed immediate influences as the works of H.P. Lovecraft, Fritz Leiber, Fletcher Pratt, Edgar Rice Burroughs, and many others. *The Lord of the Rings* also had an impact on the game's world, with "Halfling" having been changed from "Hobbit" (among other name changes) in order to avoid a copyright lawsuit.

The original *D&D* set was published by Tactical Studies Rules (TSR) in 1974, and contained three booklets – *Men & Magic, Monsters & Treasure*, and *Underworld & Wilderness Adventures* – as well as a handful of reference sheets and charts. These books shipped in a woodgrain-colored cardboard box, which was limited to just 1,000 copies, and the boxes themselves were assembled by hand. Within the first year, the entire run sold out, and TSR went back to print on another run of 1,000 in '75, which too sold out quickly, in less than six months. A third printing of 2,000 was made and also sold out In 1976, TSR published a fourth run of the game, running 5,000 copies, in a white box that would be used for all future printings of the game.

Being an initial release, the original launch of *D&D* contained a lot of the basic elements that would later be expanded upon in further additions, such as races (humans, elves, halflings), character classes (fighters, clerics, and so on), monsters, armor, treasure and magic, as well as rules for how to travel throughout the lands and towns. However, the books largely assumed that the people playing the game had previous experience with wargaming, particularly

with *Chainmail*; a lot of the original *D&D* rules rely on *Chainmail* rules for both movement and combat.

Supplements made for the first edition of *D&D* included *Greyhawk* and *Blackmoor* in 1975 and *Eldritch Wizardry, Swords & Spells* and *Gods, Demi-Gods & Heroes* in 1976. Also in 1975, the first major convention tournament was held at the inaugural Origins, and would later be published as the *Tomb of Horrors* adventure module. *The Dragon*, an early professional publication focused on fantasy gaming, entered publication in June 1976 as well.

Beginning in 1977, TSR took a dual approach to *D&D*, dividing the game into the *Basic* and *Advanced* versions. This strategy followed the game for more than two decades.

The initial *Dungeons & Dragons Basic Set* was developed by outside writer John Eric Holmes in order to provide a basic, introductory iteration of the game for mass market consumption. The original *Basic Set* was available either as a standalone rulebook or in a larger box set (aimed specifically at toy stores) that included dice and other materials. In 1981, the *Basic Set* saw a significant revision, handled by Tom Moldvay, that took the game further away from its *Advanced* counterpart. In addition to the *Basic Set*, which focused on early adventuring and leveling, the first *Expert Set* was also released, intended for players to pick up once they had exhausted what could be done with the *Basic Set*.

The best-known version of the *Basic Set* is the 1983 edition, which is also colloquially known simply as "The Red Box" due to its packaging and recognizable cover art from Larry Elmore. This release, handled by designer Frank Mentzer, was retitled *Dungeons & Dragons Set 1: Basic Rules*, and contained a *Players Manual*, a *Dungeon Masters Guide*, and a pack of dice. This set later saw expansions to include the *Expert Rules, Companion Rules, Master Rules,* and *Immortal Rules.*

In 1991, a further revision of the set was released, renamed as *The New Easy-to-Master Dungeons & Dragons Game,* also known by many as "The Black Box." Where previous *Basic* releases had only included materials covering characters up to third level, this release covered up to fifth level. This edition was primarily designed by Troy Denning and contained an interesting presentation of the rules themselves – rather than only being presented in book form, they were also printed in card format, with each card containing information on a specific rule itself.

The *D&D Rules Cyclopedia* also released in 1991, and compiled everything from the *Basic Rules, Expert Rules, Companion Rules*

and *Master Rules* boxes – but was intended to "be a reference volume for those who already play the *D&D* game," according to the book's own introduction. It was considered a comprehensive addition to the available lineup of materials especially for those already familiar with earlier releases of the game.

A final revision was released in 1994, called *The Classic Dungeons & Dragons Game.* This removed the cards from the Black Box and instead reincorporated them into sidebars in the main rulebook itself.

On the other side of the coin was *Advanced D&D*, which was primarily aimed at the hobby market – folks who had already been playing wargames and similar games. The initial *AD&D* release consisted of three hardcover rulebooks released in the late '70s: *Monster Manual* (1977), *Player's Handbook* (1978), and *Dungeon Master's Guide* (1979). Significant additions to these books were made, pulling from supplemental materials from the original 1974 release as well as from *Dragon* magazine articles. These included additional classes (assassin, bard, druid, illusionist, monk, paladin, ranger, and thief) and other rules and guidelines.

AD&D saw a handful of supplements into the 1980s, including *Deities & Demigods* (1980), *Fiend Folio* (1981), *Monster Manual II* (1983), *Oriental Adventures* (1985) and *Unearthed Arcana* (1985), among many others. TSR was publishing dozens upon dozens of supplements and adventure modules at the time, many of which are highly collectible today.

A true second edition of *AD&D* was released in 1989, appropriately called *Advanced Dungeons & Dragons 2nd Edition*. It aimed to do a number of things, including consolidating a lot of the material that had spanned the several books of the original *AD&D* release, as well as maintaining some compatibility with the first edition. Some of the most notable changes with the *2nd Edition* release were the attempt to scrub the game of things that had caused some negative public reception – specifically, devils and other demons, as well as the assassin class and half-orc race options. The focus was placed on truly heroic storytelling, and the target age for the game was also adjusted to be teens, rather than adult gamers.

In 1995, *2nd Edition* saw a rerelease as well as the addition of the *Player's Option* books, which allowed for more variety in gameplay and character creation. These included *Player's Option: Combat & Tactics, Player's Option: Skills & Powers,* and *Player's Option: Spells & Magic*, as well as the *Dungeon Master's Option: High-Level Campaigns* for higher levels of gameplay.

By the start of the 21st century, both the *Basic* and *Advanced* rulebooks had been discontinued in favor of a unified edition, simply referred to as *3rd Edition*, which arrived in 2000. This followed TSR being bought out by Wizards of the Coast in 1997, due to how close the company was to complete bankruptcy. The *3rd Edition* of the game reconciled the two separate *D&D* brands to unite the game under a single banner – and Wizards also settled some ongoing disputed between Dave Arneson and *D&D* around that time as well.

This also marked the introduction of the contemporary d20 system, allowing for a wider breadth of role-playing options designed around a 20-sided die. The d20 system is easy to learn for both RPG veterans as well as newcomers, as basically every action is resolved by rolling a d20 and then applying whatever modifiers are necessary to determine the final number.

D&D 3rd Edition was designed by Monte Cook, Jonathan Tweet and Skip Williams, all of whom collaborated on the main books (*Player's Handbook, Dungeon Master's Guide, Monster Manual*). This edition changed up some key things from earlier additions, such as renaming "thief" to "rogue" and adding the sorcerer class. It also eliminated restrictions on class-race combinations, meaning any race could be used to play any class of character – though there are still some combinations that are favorable over others.

The *3rd Edition* also marked the end of the boxed sets of games that had been popular during the *Basic* and *AD&D* era, with Wizards opting to instead switch to hardcover books.

Notably, the d20 system was presented under Wizards of the Coast's Open Game License (OGL), which allowed any third-party developer or publisher to create compatible material without needing to seek approval from Wizards. Quick adaptation of the d20 system and OGL by the community meant that the available content compatible with *D&D* expanded quickly. The system has also been adapted to create other games, the most significant being *Pathfinder*.

D&D 3rd Edition saw some tweaks and changes, leading to a "half edition" update with *Dungeons & Dragons v. 3.5*, which released in July 2003. This edition of the game addressed a lot of the common complaints players had with *3rd Edition*, particularly regarding spells (many of which were changed or outright removed) and feats (with new feats added and existing feats changed). A number of small updates were also made to the *Dungeon Master's Guide* and *Monster Manual*, both of which saw expansions with this release. However, the base of the game was essentially the same, and many materials from both *3rd* and *3.5* are still compatible with each other.

The *4th Edition* of *D&D* saw a preview book, *Wizards Presents: Races and Classes*, arrive at the end of 2007. A second preview, *Wizards Presents: Worlds and Monsters*, debuted in January 2008. But *D&D 4th Edition* wouldn't arrive in earnest until June 2008, with the release of the new *Player's Handbook, Monster Manual* and *Dungeon Master's Guide*. Wizards of the Coast took a different approach to the *4th Edition*: the core rulebooks were updated with new volumes annually, adding additional classes, monsters and so on to the game with each new book. Certain elements of the gameplay, such as resource and spell management, skills, and "epic level" gameplay, were also added and updated for this edition.

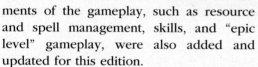

Though not quite the same as *D&D Basic*, a separate iteration of the game released in 2010 in much of the same spirit – *Dungeons & Dragons Essentials*. This version was aimed at newcomers to the game, via its relative simplicity compared to *4th Edition,* as well as at old-school fans of earlier editions, due to how it lined up better with earlier releases. The *Essentials* lineup included the *Starter Set, Dungeon Master's Kit, Rules Compendium* and *Monster Vault.*

The *Player's Option* books also returned to the game in 2011, adding various new classes, races, powers and more to the game. These included *Heroes of the Feywild,* which was themed to the Feywild plane and allowed players to create characters with connections to that world, and *Heroes of Shadow,* which did much the same thing but was themed to the Shadowfell realm.

Wizards announced that they were working on a new edition of the game in early 2012, and at the time it was referred to as *D&D Next*. It entered an open playtesting period that same year, with more than 175,000 people participating in testing the game throughout 2012 and 2013. *Dungeons & Dragons 5th Edition*, developed under lead designer Mike Mearls, released to the public on July 3, 2014, with the debut of a free digital PDF, *Basic Rules*, which contained complete rules for play. Its release coincided with the 40th anniversary of *Dungeons & Dragons* at large. That same month, the *Starter Set* debuted, which included the adventure module *Lost Mine of Phandelver* (intended for low-level characters), pre-generated characters to choose from, and basic instructions. The *5th Edition* returned to just the three core books from earlier editions – *Player's Handbook, Monster Manual* and *Dungeon Master's Guide*, all of which released by the end of 2014 – rather than having multiple volumes of each.

The *5th Edition* is largely a combination of several other past releases, while also simplifying many elements of gameplay that had proved difficult to manage. It also introduced the "advantage" mechanic, which removed a number of situational factors and replaced them by simply rolling two d20s in a given situation in which a character has an advantage or disadvantage, and taking the higher or lower score of the two, respectively. The game also returned to just using a single armor class rather than having to keep track of various defenses, and saving throws were also reworked.

Under *5th Edition, Dungeons & Dragons* continues to thrive and might be more popular now than ever before. Thanks to the continued popularity of the d20 system and OGL, there's plenty of new content that caters to a wide variety of players. And there's a more significant population of players than ever, largely thanks to the popularity of online streaming shows and podcasts, such as *Critical Role* and *The Adventure Zone*, that have normalized the game as just any other fun hobby.

ROLLING FOR INITIATIVE...
AND EVERYTHING ELSE

The basic idea of how *D&D* is played is pretty easy to explain – one person acts as a Dungeon Master (DM), while the rest of the players control individual characters. The DM's responsibility is to keep the story moving by describing scenes, controlling all non-player characters (NPCs) and enemies, and making sure rules are being followed correctly. The players each control and role-play their own characters, which they either create themselves by using the core rulebooks or simply by choosing a pre-made character available to them.

Each person participating generally needs to have their own set of polyhedral dice. While the most important of these tends to be the d20, other dice – 12-sided, 10-sided, 8-sided, 6-sided, and 4-sided – are used to determine damage dealt out in combat, among other things. It's also common for every player to at least have their own copy of the *Player's Handbook* for reference purposes throughout the course of play. Meanwhile, the DM uses the *Dungeon Master's Guide* and *Monster Manual* to keep things straight on their end; the DM will usually keep sheets and their own set of dice behind a "DM Screen," an opaque folio that allows them to hide the results of rolls and other game elements from the players.

When creating a character, players pick one of several races (Human, Elf, Half-Elf, Dwarf, Dragonborn, Gnome, Halfling, Half-Orc, Tiefling, among others) and then a basic class (Barbarian, Bard, Cleric, Druid, Fighter, Monk, Paladin, Ranger, Rogue, Sorcerer, Warlock, or Wizard, as of *5th Edition*). Some editions of *D&D* have added various paths for these different classes to go down, which have been referred to as "paragon" or "prestige" classes. The *5th Edition* instead uses subclasses of each base class which can be chosen to specialize the character in certain ways, and can usually be picked early on (usually at third level).

From here, players determine their statistics: Strength, Dexterity, Constitution, Intelligence, Wisdom, and Charisma. The values for these are usually determined by dice rolls during character creation, though many players opt for a "point-buy" system instead in order to keep things balanced.

Strength is used to determine a number of physical skills as well as most melee attack rolls. Dexterity affects other physical skills related to agility and reflexes, and is also used for ranged weapon attacks. Constitution determines a character's toughness and overall health, as well as certain resistances, and a higher score here usually means higher hit points. Intelligence determines learning and reasoning ability and can also influence the effectiveness of spells cast by certain classes (such as the Wizard); Wisdom, meanwhile, determines overall judgement skills and willpower, and influences divine spellcasters such as Clerics and Druids. Charisma determines a character's ability to persuade or otherwise influence others either by a sharp tongue or physical beauty, and bards and sorcerers draw on a high score here for spellcasting.

Once everyone involved is prepared, they generally get together and simply... have an adventure. Using pre-made adventure modules is common, especially for newcomers, as they outline a full experience. There's also the ability to improvise on a pre-made module in order to put a personal flair on things, and many people take to simply creating and writing out their own homebrew adventures as well. Depending on the amount of people and the personalities of those playing the game, a scenario can be finished in a few hours or over the course of several sessions (generally called a "campaign").

While not necessarily required, the use of miniatures and other set pieces is not uncommon, and accordingly there have been many official releases of minis and tile boards for *D&D*. Particularly with regards to combat or puzzle-solving, grid-based tiles are favored by many just to provide a visual aid of where things are happening. Outside of that, though, *D&D* is very much a "theatre of the mind" kind of game, with everyone interpreting the scenario presented on their own. The players explore towns, go on quests, delve into dungeons, and slay mighty beasts (including, of course, dragons).

WHAT'S WORTH COLLECTING?

Given that the game has been around for more than four and a half decades, there's a pretty significant breadth of material to collect. Books, miniatures, modules, mats – the list goes on for quite a ways. For those looking to get started on contemporary play today, it's best to start with current editions of the three core rulebooks. The *Player's Handbook, Dungeon Master's Guide* and *Monster Manual* all run about $50 a pop, brand-new. Popular supplemental material has included *Mordenkainen's Tome of Foes* and *Xanathar's Guide to Everything*, which expand upon the core books in huge ways – these also cost about $50 each. So to get started with a copy of the core books is $150, and another $100 to expand on that material – it's by no means a small investment.

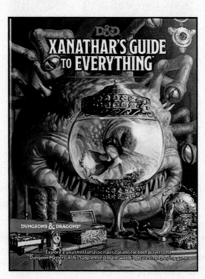

Adventures and campaigns can also run up to about $50 each, depending on how much material is being provided. However, in the digital age, many developers who are creating content for *D&D* under the d20 system and OGL have gotten into the habit of making them available as a digital download in PDF format, which often saves players a good bit of money.

One of the biggest upsides to purchasing the official material, though, is that almost everything is made available as a hardcover book. Not only do these look great when placed on a shelf with each other, but they hold up to the test of time (and wear-and-tear of usual play) much better than softcovers, pamphlets, or home-printed materials.

Dice, for the most part, are pretty inexpensive – maybe $10 or so for a full set of polyhedral dice. But there are some manufacturers out there that make what essentially boil down to "artisanal" dice sets, which are made out of fancier materials, such as wood, metal, or even animal bones. There's also folks out there who produce dice out of fancy minerals like malachite, jasper or quartz, which can carry a hefty price for a full set – usually several hundred dollars. There's even a company out there producing polyhedral dice out of meteorite, with each individual die costing at least $100.

When it comes to high-dollar collectibles within *Dungeons & Dragons*, though, you'll have to go back to the very beginning – the wood-grain box, hand-packed by the creators of the game, containing the original pamphlets for how to play. Given how few of them are out there (just 1,000 for that original first run), combined with the continued popularity and legacy of the game, it should come as no surprise that a complete original wood box set has sold for more than $5,500 on eBay.

A complete copy of the "white box" printing of the first edition can regularly generate prices of $300 to $600 or more online, especially if the box itself is still intact and in good condition. Even without the boxes, the manuals contained from the original release of *D&D*, when sold as a set, usually see prices of a few hundred dollars, depending on condition.

Convention exclusives can also draw high prices at auction, and GenCon has been host to many high-dollar items. The 2017 GenCon exclusive module, *Lost Tales of Myth Drannor*, has sold online for $200 or more in the time since its debut. There have also been convention exclusive dice sets and miniature figures, which tend to run about $50 online depending on the exact item.

There's also plenty of *D&D* related collectibles outside of the game itself. Vintage copies of *Dragon* and *Dungeon* magazines are collector's items, with some issues selling for $50 or more online. There's also been a number of successful video games based on *D&D*, with the most notable being *Baldur's Gate* and *Neverwinter Nights* – though these are hardly the only games that have used the *D&D* formula. There have been dozens of video games released based on various *D&D* campaign settings, and even focusing a collection on just those will be a huge investment. Some of these, particularly the computer games from the 1980s, can run for $75 or more online.

There's also board games, including 1975's *Dungeon!*, published by TSR. The game featured a six-level dungeon, and players were tasked with exploring it and defeating enemies. The game has been reprinted multiple times, though an original, complete-in-box copy of the '75 release can see prices of $150 or more in online auctions. Another popular choice is the *Dungeons & Dragons Computer Labyrinth Game*, published in 1980 by Mattel. This was actually one of the first computer/board game hybrids and accordingly is a collector's item for more than just *D&D* fans. A complete in-box copy of this can see prices of $75 or more online, particularly if the game itself still functions. Outside of games, *D&D* has expanded to a long-running series of novels, toys, and comic books. The comics have been produced by several different companies, including DC Comics, Devil's Due Publishing, and IDW Publishing.

Though it was the original fantasy RPG tabletop experience, *Dungeons & Dragons* nailed it on the first go and still in many ways has yet to be beat in terms of popularity and influence on the market. Today, it's more popular than ever, and seems destined to continue its growth in this industry renaissance.

MATT

MERCER

PHOTO BY PAMELA JOY

Matthew Mercer has become one of the top names when it comes to tabletop gaming thanks to the massive success of Critical Role, *the D&D-focused web series produced by Geek & Sundry, of which he is the host. Mercer has also made a name for himself in other forms of gaming, having lent his talents as a voice actor to smash-hit games such as* Resident Evil, Overwatch *and* Fallout 4. *His voice acting career has also extended to animation, in series such as* One Piece, JoJo's Bizarre Adventure *and* Attack on Titan.

Overstreet chatted with Mercer about his personal history with tabletop gaming, the impact that Critical Role *has had on gaming fandom, and more.*

[Editor's note: The following interview is compiled from questions and answers from two separate interviews conducted by Richard Ankney and Carrie Wood.]

Overstreet: What was your first exposure to tabletop gaming?
Matthew Mercer (MM): When I was in my freshman year of high school, a handful of older friends in our Popular Arts Club (our public-facing name for the Gaming & Anime Club) invited me to play in a campaign they were in. I had some of the books my mother had found at a garage sale before and got them for me, knowing I'd like them just for the art and ideas. I was excited to try it out, and while the story of that campaign wasn't exactly Shakespeare,

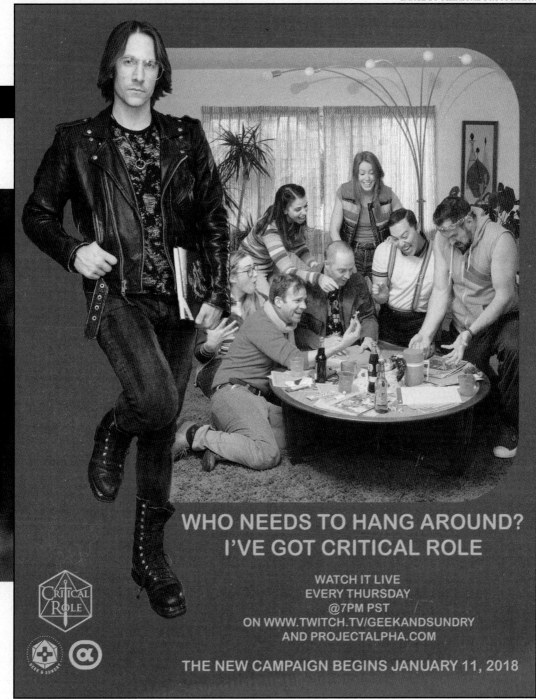

WHO NEEDS TO HANG AROUND?
I'VE GOT CRITICAL ROLE

WATCH IT LIVE
EVERY THURSDAY
@7PM PST
ON WWW.TWITCH.TV/GEEKANDSUNDRY
AND PROJECTALPHA.COM

THE NEW CAMPAIGN BEGINS JANUARY 11, 2018

it was enough to get me hooked on the idea of tabletop RPGs and gaming.

Overstreet: What is it about tabletop gaming – RPGs, board games or otherwise – that you think is able to draw people in the way that it does?

MM: I believe it provides a platform for verbal, communal storytelling and direct social interaction, an experience that was once such an important activity in human-ity's past history, but is now missing in much of modern media. It allows a group of friends an opportunity to meet with a purpose of enjoying a game together, challenging each other, and further develop their social skills and empathy in a safe space. At that table, you get to create memories that often aren't hindered by anything but the bounds of your imagination, and that is an invitation that anyone can take and enjoy.

Overstreet: There's been a clear resurgence in tabletop gaming of all types within the last few years. What do you think caused that?

MM: There are a lot of factors, I believe. After a generation of electronic gaming within a largely solitary experience, people are beginning to realize the joys of gaming socially, and in person. Seeing the faces of those you are playing with, and getting to know each other even better with each game night. The previous stigmas and misunderstandings about tabletop gaming have been dispelled in a very public way, with well-known personalities singing the praises of these experiences and showing the low bars of entry, making it easier for folks who were always curious to reach out and find gaming groups of their own. Older generations are rediscovering their love of tabletop gaming by watching so many new players enter the scene, providing them renewed pride in their older hobbies. There are so many factors here, but these are a few I believe have made a large difference.

Overstreet: As this book is inherently one focused on collecting, we have to ask – are you a collector of tabletop games at all? If so, what do you collect and why?

MM: I am a collector, though NOWHERE NEAR as some folks I know! I own roughly around 35 board/card games, and about 20+ RPG systems with a total of close to 100 books between them. They are all little windows into little worlds that have gotten me through tough times, or inspired me to create my own. Each has called to a part of me, and I enjoy knowing that they are never too far should I need to dive back in.

Overstreet: How did *Critical Role* first get going? What was the pitch?

MM: The pitch was to us, technically. One of the players, Liam [O'Brien], we were working on a video game together and I was talking about how I had played *D&D* with friends, and he missed playing *D&D* – he played it as a kid. So I told him, "Well, write me a one-shot sometime." So for his birthday he invited a bunch of mutual friends over who had never played before, and I ran the one-shot. They all had a great

time, so we turned it into a campaign. We played that privately for about two years.

Ashley Johnson, who's one of our players, mentioned to Felicia Day at Geek and Sundry about this *D&D* game that she loves and plays with a bunch of other voice actors. So Felicia reached out and said, "Hey, you guys should do this on our channel." Twitch was an emerging platform that allowed us to continue playing our game without having to change it for the media. That's a big thing for us – it's still a game that we're playing for ourselves, and we want to enjoy it as we have been. So that's kind of how it happened. It wasn't even really our idea originally, we were asked to do it.

Overstreet: When *Critical Role* first got started, did you ever think it would become what it is now – with well over 100 episodes, a comic book, and even campaign settings now available to the masses based on the show?

MM: Not by a long shot! We were pretty convinced it would flounder, and we were ready to just take it all back to the privacy of our own homes. Instead, it has become this incredible gift in a community of amazing people who inspire us. It's allowed us to make something we wholly created together as friends, and see that others connect with it as strongly as we do. It's unbelievable, and I'm ever preparing for it all to go away if I pinch myself too hard.

Overstreet: There's just a ton of people out there who watch you guys – you had around 100,000 people watch the second season startup.

MM: Yeah, that was crazy! I'm still kind of processing that. No one in their right mind should have ever believed that we would have, I believe, 125,000 there watching that first episode of the second season, to just watch me and my friends sit around a table, drink, roll dice, and make silly voices. It's crazy.

Overstreet: What do you think it is about *Critical Role* that keeps people continuing to tune in?

MM: It's hard to say. I'm sure it's different for many folks. Some grew up loving TTRPGs but are either too busy or have difficulty in finding their own groups, so they get to play vicariously through ours. Others are swept up in the story, with our campaign becoming their latest "show," only with the added thrill of random dice-rolls and improvised narrative that none of us know quite where it may go. Others still find a sense of acceptance and belonging among the positive voices of the community around it, taking the inspiration they draw from our show and pouring it into their own home games to forge new, lasting memories and friendships. I've heard stories like these, and many more, so the answers are as varied as there are people who watch.

Overstreet: You've clearly been going to a wide variety of conventions (anime, gaming, and otherwise) for a long time, as a fan, a cosplayer, and now as an industry guest. What's changed about the tabletop scene at conventions in the time you've been going?
MM: For one thing, I've seen the tabletop rooms and programming become FAR larger and more inclusive than it's ever been. What once may have been a few tables with perpetually open spots have become whole subsections of the convention, with sign-up sheets that often are full early in the day. I've seen small publishers begin to pop up

and thrive with new games in a space that was once withering away, and seeing the expansion of booths that represent that in convention halls makes me smile.

Overstreet: With regards to the gaming industry itself, you guys have had a huge influence on it – how do you feel about being a kind of ambassador to the general public when it comes to the gaming scene?
MM: It's a lot of pressure. I never anticipated or expected to be put in this position, but as an ambassador, I guess, to tabletop gaming, it's nice to be in a place where I feel I can represent a hobby that's so important to me that I feel has been misrepresented for so long by media and by social groups outside of it. I've heard so many misnomers about role-playing games and there are so many facets of the old gaming groups sometimes that can be very gate-keeper-y to what tabletop gaming used to be. It gives me an opportunity to kind of bridge that gap and break those assumptions. Hopefully, in my small way, it forms a better and healthier community.

Overstreet: How do you see the industry continuing to evolve from where it is today?

MM: In so many ways. I'm curious to see where tabletop games and technology can meet, allowing enhanced Alternate Reality Game experiences while not losing the personal, immediate, and improved nature that made these games so incredible to begin with. I can imagine more games catering to story and narrative flow over complicated rule sets, while the need for awesomely complicated rule sets will always be there. For me? I'm just excited to see kids like me in school being able to openly admit they love *Dungeons & Dragons*, and the response be, "Oh cool. Can I play too?"

Overstreet: How important are local game stores to the community, in your opinion?
MM: For me, the local game store is where I grew up. It's where I used to go for my comic books when I was a very young kid. It's where I got early sets of my Marvel cards when I was in elementary school. It's where I used to play *Magic: The Gathering* every day after school. It's where I bought all my role-playing game books. And today, I've been very particular to make sure we promote small stores around the country.

I remember there was a time in the 2000s when I got to watch two of my favorite gaming stores go away, and it broke my heart. In recent years, we've seen more and more stores start to show up, and that's been a heartening experience. So whenever we have the opportunity to shout out on Twitter or to go in and meet the people there and help foster awareness of these places – because it's not just a place for business, it's a place for community. It's a hub for people to come together with similar interests and meet friends and find gaming groups or find board gaming nights. I think it's super important. It's where gaming started. There were people who would play in a basement, but it all started from finding each other at game stores. That was where a lot of this whole culture began.

Overstreet: While *D&D* is clearly your go-to title, what other role-playing games are on your list of things to play?

MM: *D&D* is my favorite, partially because of the nostalgia, because it's where I started, but also as a person that grew up loving fantasy role-playing as a whole genre – it's my comfort food. But I really, really love the setting of *Deadlands*. The classic Old West genre is such a unique and interesting period of time, and to add to that these paranormal elements and faint bits of demonic magic and this kind of crawling essence of working towards an apocalypse if something isn't done – that's just *cool*! The original system was based around playing poker with the devil that you're borrowing magic from… it was just a really unique role-playing experience both narratively and mechanically. So *Deadlands* has a very special place in my heart.

If I had to pick another, I'd go with *Paranoia*. Very few games allow you to die in character creation or allow you to just play against your players in a way that's fun for everyone. A lot of games that have that competitive element can hit a territory where it's not fun and it gets too emotionally intense against each other. *Paranoia* has that sort of British satire vibe to it where you can't take it too seriously, and everyone's having a fun time just screwing each other over.

Overstreet: Besides tabletop RPGs, what other games to you like to play?

MM: I played a lot of *Warhammer Fantasy* back in the day, had my Skaven army for a while. And then I played *Warmachine* in recent years, with my Protectorate of Menoth and my wife, Marisha, had Cryx… we'd get very angry with each other. I enjoy wargaming, but I'm a little on the smaller scale there. *Warhammer 40K* is a little too big for my tastes, as far as army size. But I enjoy wargaming, and I enjoy board gaming too. We're heavy enthusiasts of *Mansions of Madness* and have been since the first edition. We love card games – *Red Dragon Inn* is a classic. If you've got a game, we'll play it!

Overstreet: What do you suggest a newcomer to tabletop gaming do if they want to get involved in the scene, with an RPG or otherwise?

MM: First, ask yourself what kinds of experiences and stories do you like – are you a fantasy buff who loves swords and sorcery? Do you prefer hard sci-fi and the challenges of the universes unknown dark? How much do you enjoy the nuances of strategy and competition? Have you a deep appreciation for historical events and conflicts? Whatever types of genre or story you love, there is most likely a game for you. Research around that, find some suggested products and read about them. If one seems to call to you, reach out to friends whom you think may enjoy it as well (and even some you'd like to introduce gaming to) and give it a shot! There is a plethora of resources and videos online now that can quickly show you how to play, what play looks like, and who these games might appeal to. Search, watch, learn, then enjoy!

Mercer can be seen on Critical Role *every Thursday evening on the Geek & Sundry Twitch and YouTube channels.*

PATHFINDER
ROLEPLAYING GAME

BY ALEX CARRA

Tabletop and board games are a uniquely polarizing beast, with a host of games inspiring a love-it-or-hate-it mentality in its players. Paizo's *Pathfinder* is no exception. Its long list of products, huge setting, and sometimes-complex rules don't help, and given its start as a derivation of the well known and well loved *Dungeons & Dragons*, it started with a stacked deck. But since the game's inception, Paizo has carved out a sizeable niche for itself, taking *Pathfinder* from a "*D&D* spinoff" to an industry heavyweight in its own right.

Like its predecessor, *Pathfinder* is a pen-and-paper roleplaying game. The success of a character's actions during the collaborative story is determined by rolling a 20-sided die and adding appropriate modifiers to meet or beat a target number, with other polyhedral dice used for secondary results, like damage or spell effects. Like other non-*D&D* games of the era, it adopted the term "gamemaster" for the player running the game from behind the screen, and a great deal of *Pathfinder*'s numerous books and supplements are designed with

the gamemaster in mind, building elaborate worlds and madness-inducing monsters for the players' characters to encounter.

Pathfinder builds on the typical character classes of classic *D&D* by retouching them, offering variant rulesets and bringing entirely new classes to the table. In later books, hybrid classes were added, such as the Skald (bard and barbarian) and the Warpriest (cleric and fighter), as well as completely original classes like the Oracle and Arcanist. Its only published game setting is a wizards-and-dragons high fantasy, though in August 2017 Paizo also released *Starfinder*, a space-faring revamp of the core game.

History

The *Pathfinder Roleplaying Game* began with its roots firmly entrenched in classic *Dungeons & Dragons*. The *Pathfinder* story and world setting first entered gaming circles as the spiritual successor to the *Dragon* and *Dungeon* magazines, which Paizo Publishing had been producing on contract for Wizards of the Coast. In 2007, when the contracts for *Dragon* and *Dungeon* were not renewed, Paizo continued the tradition of the two periodicals' adventure storylines, and began publishing *Pathfinder Adventure Paths*.

As the adventure paths were gaining traction, Wizards of the Coast was in development and playtesting for Dungeon & Dragons' rather polarizing *4th Edition*, creating a pocket in the market for those who wanted more content and more rules adjustments to 2003's *D&D Revised 3rd Edition*, or *Version 3.5*. As a result, when Paizo Publishing began writing and open-playtesting what would become the *Pathfinder Roleplaying Game*, it earned the nickname "*D&D 3.75*." To build the game,

Paizo used the Open Game License (OGL), which made available the vast majority of *D&D 3.5*'s bestiary and ruleset.

While Paizo was publishing the first handful of their adventure paths under the *D&D 3.5* rules, the Pathfinder game itself was in open playtest for a year. The *Pathfinder Roleplaying Game: Core Rulebook* was ultimately published in August 2009, closely followed by the *Pathfinder Roleplaying Game: Bestiary* in November of that year.

Core Products

In a departure from the *D&D* model, where core gameplay information is split across several books, *Pathfinder*'s *Core Rulebook* covers the gameplay rules for players and gamemasters, allowing a gamemaster to run a full and satisfying game with only the *Core Rulebook* and, optionally, the *Bestiary*. That being said, Paizo has yet to revise the game so substantially as to release a new edition of it, only new printings, so all the various *Pathfinder* books are compatible with each other, making the *Pathfinder* game and universe an ever-expanding beast.

The game's heart ultimately lies in a set of six books. The *Core Rulebook*, the *Bestiary*, the *Advanced Player's Guide* (2010), which introduced new rules and character class Archetypes, to provide new flavor to the core classes; the *Advanced Race Guide* (2013), which added new races to the game; the *Advanced Class Guide* (2015), which provided 10 new classes, including the Brawler and the Slayer; and *Pathfinder Unchained* (2015), which added variant rulesets for gamemasters looking to customize gameplay at their tables.

Paizo also published a total of seven books of monsters, five of which were direct sequels to the original *Bestiary*. The *Monster Codex* (2014) focused on specialized monsters, and the more general *Bestiary 2-Bestiary 6* were published between 2011 and 2017.

Beyond these core volumes, Paizo has also published a number of supplemental books, including *Mythic Adventures* (2013), which focused on epic-level play to take characters above 20th level; *Occult Adventures* (2015), which introduced several supernatural classes, like the medium and the psychic; and *Horror Adventures* (2016), which provided new character options and rulesets for games with a horror bent. Finally, a pair of books, the *NPC Codex* (2012) and the *Villain Codex* (2016), focused on supplementing the gamemaster's side of the screen, rather than that of the players.

Then, to collect the various options provided in the vast collection of *Pathfinder*'s supplement and setting sourcebooks, Paizo released a series of "Ultimate" books in the last several years: *Ultimate Combat* (2011), *Ultimate Magic* (2011), *Ultimate Campaign*

(2013), *Ultimate Equipment* (2016), *Ultimate Intrigue* (2016), and *Ultimate Wilderness* (2017).

To cap off the list, Paizo also released the *Pathfinder Beginner Box* (2011), designed for new players and presenting a simplified version of the *Pathfinder* ruleset, and in 2015 published a *Strategy Guide* to collate advice on building characters for both beginners and veterans of the game.

ADVENTURE PATHS

As of 2018, Paizo will have published 22 complete adventure paths, releasing two per year since 2008. To date, *Rise of the Runelords* and *Curse of the Crimson Throne*, the first adventure paths Paizo released, have been collected into hardcover anniversary editions, updated for use with *Pathfinder* rules, rather than the OGL rules. Those paths and the full gamut of Paizo's adventures, including *Council of Thieves*, the first adventure path to use the *Pathfinder* rules, *Kingmaker*, *Shattered Star*, and *Giantslayer*, are available as print sourcebooks and as PDFs.

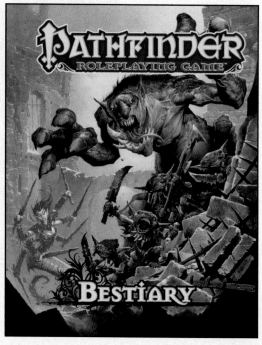

In addition to the more expansive, six-volume Adventure Paths, Paizo also published *Pathfinder Modules* (formerly *GameMastery Modules*) and *Pathfinder Companion*. *Modules* began as a monthly periodical in 2007, though it later switched to bimonthly releases in 2008 when *Companion* was announced. *Modules* focused on standalone adventures ranging from wilderness encounters to classic dungeons, game components that could be

easily dropped into the standard Pathfinder setting or even into homebrew games. *Companion*, which debuted in 2008 as a bimonthly periodical, explored themes from the Pathfinder campaign setting, with a focus on player options and the world as seen from the player's eyes. In 2012, *Modules* changed again, expanding from 32-page books to 64-page books, to be released quarterly, while *Companion*, having been renamed to *Pathfinder Player Companion* to clarify the series' intent, changed to a monthly release schedule.

CAMPAIGN SETTINGS

The *Pathfinder Campaign Setting* (hereafter PCS) products, originally called *Pathfinder Chronicles*, detail the various nations and lands of the staggeringly large planet of Golarion. Unlike the *D&D* model, which has an array of canonical settings, Golarion is *Pathfinder*'s melting pot, with a continent, region, and plane of existence for every type of game you could imagine. Particularly popular among Golarion's regions is the Inner Sea, which PCS has returned to several times in books like *The Inner Sea World Guide* (2011), *Inner Sea Gods* (2014), and *Inner Sea Races* (2015).

In contrast to the *Pathfinder Player Companion* series, the PCS sourcebooks delve deeper into the setting from the gamemaster's side.

A number of them were published as direct tie-ins to the Adventure Paths being published concurrently, such as *Guide to Korvosa* (2008; Curse of the Crimson Throne) and *Guide to the River Kingdoms* (2010; Kingmaker), but the PCS library also includes titles like *Cities of Golarion* (2009), *Faction Guide* (2010), *Lands of Conflict* (2017), and many more.

OTHER COLLECTIBLES

If Paizo's extensive library of supplemental sourcebooks and baseline rulebooks weren't enough to scratch the *Pathfinder* itch, Paizo has also licensed or directly published a number of other products to pair with or dovetail alongside their publications.

Where it concerns *Pathfinder* games at the table, Paizo partners with WizKids, best known for the Clix system, to produce *Pathfinder Battles*, a collectible miniatures battle game. Though *Pathfinder Battles* is a standalone game, the miniatures are just as likely, if not more likely, to see use as tabletop minis to represent in-game characters and monsters. For heroes and creatures not represented in *Battles*, Paizo has also partnered with miniature model creators like the companies Reaper and Bones, to offer greater customizability for players to see

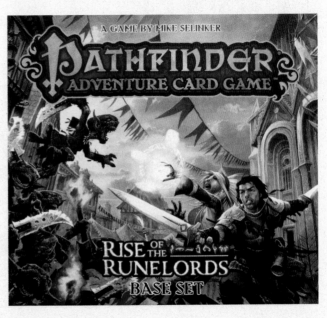

themselves on the grid. As Pathfinder gameplay rewards strategic combat thinking and pays homage to the original wellspring of both D&D and Pathfinder, wargames, a good map and minis can really help to put the battlefield in perspective when the dice come out in force. To that end, Paizo has also released a collection of map folios, many of which were direct tie-in products for adventure paths, to provide hex and square battle grid-enabled maps, as well as general regional maps.

Beyond the table, since 2010 Paizo has been publishing a series of novels expanding on the Golarion setting called *Pathfinder Tales*, including one by Dave Gross (*Prince of Wolves*), former editor of *Dragon Magazine*, and one by Ed Greenwood (*The Wizard's Mask*), who famously cre-

ated the Forgotten Realms setting licensed by D&D. In 2012, Paizo licensed Dynamite Entertainment to publish a series of comic books called *Pathfinder Comics*, some of which include maps and small-scale adventure pieces. Finally, Big Finish Productions, best known for its *Doctor Who* audio plays, has produced a series of audio dramas based on Golarion called *Pathfinder Legends*.

Not to be contained at just pen and paper play, Paizo also publishes the collaborative *Pathfinder Adventure Card Game*, designed by Mike Selinker of Loan Shark Games. The game began with a *Rise of the Runelords* set released in 2013, and has since added *Skull & Shackles*, *Wrath of the Righteous*, and *Mummy's Mask*, each based on the corresponding Adventure Path.

Finally, two *Pathfinder* video games have been announced. *Pathfinder Online*, a fantasy sandbox MMO, had a successful Kickstarter in 2013, while *Pathfinder: Kingmaker*, a computer-based roleplaying game, had a successful Kickstarter campaign in June 2017.

RARE PIECES

Between the core books, modules, adventure paths, player and gamemaster sourcebooks, maps, supplement card decks, and anything else that might strike your fancy, *Pathfinder*'s library of content spans literally thousands of titles. And all of them are available in PDF form on Paizo's website, with only a handful of exceptions. That being said, if you're planning to round out your bookshelf collection, you might be looking at ticket prices of hundreds, even thousands of dollars.

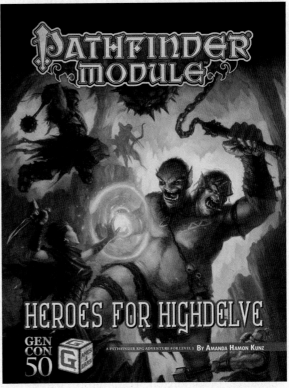

Nearly all of the map folios, adventure path single-volume books, modules, and other sourcebooks are, at this point, out of print if they're more than a couple years old. Some online offerings of these out-of-print books, especially for the earliest adventure paths dating back to 2007 and 2008, list at more than $800. The original map folio for *Rise of the Runelords* has even been listed, though with perhaps unrealistic optimism, for as much as $2,700. That being said, Paizo has injected its own

rarity in the past. *Pathfinder* has had a few exclusive promo offerings at GenCon events, including a module only available at GenCon 50 (August 2017): *Heroes for Highdelve*. Paizo also released, as online exclusives, a pair of limited edition leatherbound collections of the first two adventure paths, *Rise of the Runelords* and *Curse of the Crimson Throne*. These in particular originally retailed on the Paizo site for $200 and $75, respectively.

AN INTERVIEW WITH

Eric Menge is a game designer, writer and role-playing fan who has managed to spin his love of RPGs into part of his daily life. He's also contributed to D&D, having written for Wizards of the Coast (including the popular "Menzoberranzan: City of Intrigue") as well as on his own for the DM's Guild (with "Jungle Treks"). Overstreet chatted with Menge about the library of role-playing books he's amassed over the years and how he's turned that collection into a resource.

ERIC MENGE

Overstreet: First, can you tell us a little bit about yourself?

Eric Menge (EM): I'm Eric Menge. I'm a writer, game designer, and a small press publisher. I'm also an attorney, but I'm not actively practicing. I currently am the publisher of a digital community game called *Tattered Weave,* the writer for the webcomic *Snow by Night,* and a freelancer for Wizards of the Coast.

Overstreet: What first piqued your interest in tabletop RPGs to begin with?

EM: The stories. I love how you play out stories and the game becomes a form of cooperative storytelling.

Overstreet: At what point did collecting the books become a hobby on its own?

EM: Collecting for the sake of collecting still hasn't become a hobby on its own for me. My *D&D* collection is a resource for me so I treat it as a library. I freelance for Wizards of the Coast, and I am constantly making *D&D* adventures and supplements. Knowing what has come before is a huge boon in my work.

Overstreet: What kind of things have you included in your collection?

EM: For *D&D,* I have most of the second printing of 1e rulebooks, almost everything from 2e, most books from 3e (which took a lot because Wizards printed so much), and everything printed for 5e to date. I only have a few setting books for 4e.

Overstreet: Your collection is primarily focused on *D&D,* but what other tabletop games have you included?

EM: Outside of *D&D,* I collected my favorite RPGs. I have a great deal of books for *Deadlands, Ars Magica, Legend of the Five Rings, Middle Earth Roleplaying,* and a *Call of Cthulhu.* I have some other titles like *Numenera, Blue Rose, 7th Sea,* and *Tunnels & Trolls.*

Overstreet: What would you say is the single most valuable or otherwise rare piece in your collection?

EM: Probably my Issue #1 of *Dungeon Magazine,* but a true collector would scoff. I treat my RPG books as a library and a resource rather than collector piece.

Overstreet: Would you say you have a piece of your collection that maybe isn't monetarily valuable, but has a sentimental value to it?

EM: That would be the 1e Player's

Handbook. I still have all the names and phone numbers for my first *D&D* group from back in the '80s written on the inside cover. Because I've written notes all over it, it has no monetary value, but it brings back memories of fantastic times.

Overstreet: Is there a book or module out there for any tabletop RPG that you want but haven't been able to get your hands on?
EM: The first printing of the 1e *D&D* Deities & Demigods with the Cthulhu and Melnibonéan pantheons in it. TSR printed those without permission for the first (they thought Cthulhu as public domain) and Moorcock forgot he had already licensed it for the second. So both were removed from later print runs.

Overstreet: Tabletop games have seemingly seen a resurgence in popularity over the last few years. Why do you think that is?
EM: Tabletop RPGs are a great way to get together with friends and entertain yourselves by telling a story. And it's your story. There are no invisible walls, no right way to play the game, or restrictions on what you want to do. TSR billed *D&D* as "Products of Your Imagination" and it is. You make it up as the player, and every game is distinctly yours. I think people are craving that right now. They want to create something and be active participants.

Another reason is the broadcasting of games on the Internet. This has helped two ways. First, back in the '70s - '90s, no one learned how to play *D&D* by reading the rules. You learned by being taught by someone else. That is what is happening on these Twitch channels. You're watching other people play and learning the rules that way. Just with a much greater audience than before.

The other reason is the success of shows like *Critical Role* and success of *D&D* players like Anderson Cooper and Stephen Colbert. This showed fairly cool, well-adjusted people playing *D&D*. This removed a lot of the stigma and got people interested in the fun and the story.

Overstreet: For people who are new to tabletop gaming or collecting, what kind of resources would you suggest people use?
EM: For collecting, I use eBay a lot, but I'm picky about what I buy as it's often vastly overpriced. You can also pick up books from used book shops or conventions. Or check out yard sales. A lot of times you can find books there. The Internet is a great resource for figuring out which products have been printed and which ones you need.

For gaming, nothing beats the 5e Players Handbook and the 5e Starter Set. They are both quality products that can launch a lifetime of creative fun.

Overstreet: You're the writer for the online graphic novel *Snow by Night* – has your *D&D* experience played any kind of influence on how you create a story?
EM: Oh yes. Roleplaying has helped in almost every aspect of writing. All the improv acting in character helped me formulate characters better. What is my motivation? What are my goals? What are my mannerisms and speech patterns? Writing dialog draws on these skills.

Writing adventures to account for actions by hundreds if not thousands of players helps me identify plot holes and fill them. *D&D* players are always looking for solutions and solving complex problems with unexpected answers. So I'm constantly thinking, "what would happen if..." That has headed off a lot of plot problems.

Oh, and room descriptions in adventures! You want to tell the players a lot in a very short amount of time. All the descriptions of scenes that I've written over the years have trained me to boil my descriptions down to the most important details and remember my economy of words. This keeps the plot moving quickly when writing.

D&D adventures are just another medium of telling a story, and - like all writing – practice, practice, and more practice makes you a better storyteller.

WARHAMMER

BY ALEX CARRA

Images courtesy of Dave Taylor

For many, *Warhammer* is the biggest wargame that's maintained a foothold in popular culture, standing just on the edge between being a "nerd hobby" and something in the public eye. But in a more general sense, wargaming has existed for centuries. Toward the beginning of the 20th century, H.G. Wells kicked off the world of minis gaming with *Little Wars*. He established the first ruleset for players using small wooden or metal toys as stand-ins for units and tools of war, like soldiers and cannons. Since then, miniatures wargaming has grown and expanded in scope and focus. Large-scale mass-produced board games debuted in the 1950s, and the '60s and '70s saw a shift toward wargames set in fantasy and science-fiction worlds, rather than purely reflections of real historical battles.

Games Workshop (hereafter "GW"), a U.K.-based company founded in 1975, started out making boards for games like backgammon and Go. They became an importer for the U.S. RPG *Dungeons & Dragons*, established a newsletter called *White Dwarf*, and in 1979 partnered with Bryan Ansell to establish Citadel Miniatures, which remains a core part of GW's branding to this day. In the early 1980s, GW found a key gaming niche in the convergence of wargaming, Citadel Miniatures, and designers Richard Halliwell and Rick Priestley, who'd developed a miniatures wargame in 1979 called *Reaper* for the now-defunct company Tabletop Games. Halliwell and Priestley, along with Bryan Ansell, designed *Warhammer Fantasy Battle*, which GW published in 1983, ushering in a new era of minis wargaming.

How to Play

Like many other miniatures wargames of its era, *Warhammer Fantasy Battle* ("WFB") and its derivative *Warhammer 40,000* ("WH40K") simulate pitched battles between various forces of their respective fictional settings. Each player taking part in a battle selects regiments of soldiers from their army of choice: units of humans, elves, dwarves, orcs, or others, represented by models made of plastic or metal. These armies are often placed on tables strewn with model terrain, such as hills, trees, rivers, and buildings, to add interest and complexity to movement and unit line of sight.

Armies are built according to a point system, with each unit having a point value. Most games limit armies to values ranging from 750 to 3,000 points, to keep each side balanced. Players then place their troops and take turns moving units around the table, measuring units' movement in inches. Each unit has distance and combat ratings set out in the *Warhammer* rulebook and in supplemental texts, and players rely upon these books' guidelines to keep play balanced and fair. Like many wargames before *Warhammer*, the success of combat between units is determined by dice-rolling, with each player's turn covering several phases of action.

WARHAMMER FANTASY BATTLE

While *WFB* was not the first fantasy wargame, it *is* one of the biggest, and certainly one of the best known. Over its various editions and supplements, as well as additions in GW publications like the *White Dwarf* newsletter, *WFB* has filled out a rich fantasy setting loosely reminiscent of Tolkienian fantasy, with elves, orcs, goblins, dwarfs, and humans in large supply. The setting has grown to stand on its own merits, and has inspired many derivative works, including more than 150 novels, dozens of short stories and novellas, several board games, a dozen computer games, and a pen-and-paper roleplaying game.

After *WFB*'s first edition was published in 1983, GW published seven subsequent editions up until 2015, bringing in new mechanics, new armies, and adding variants to familiar ones. In 2006 *WFB* released Seventh Edition under the name *The Battle for Skull Pass*, marking the first time an edition had a scenario name. This trend continued with 2010's Eighth Edition, *Island of Blood*, as well as with its subsequent expansions. In 2011, two Eighth Edition expansions were released with *Storm of Magic* and *Blood in the Badlands*, and 2013 saw *Triumph and Treachery*, which included rules for multiplayer games of three to five people, and *Sigmar's Blood*, a five-scenario campaign. Another series of five books was released in 2014 and 2015 as a campaign titled *End Times*, with a final book *Archaon* covering the end of the *Warhammer* world as it had been. *Archaon* saw the forces of Chaos overcoming mortal defenders and very nearly destroying the world entirely.

In 2015 *WFB* was revitalized, relaunching as *Warhammer: Age of Sigmar* rather than publishing under the auspice of a ninth edition. *Age of Sigmar* picks up many years later after Chaos' victory, after the world rebuilds under the mortal-turned-god Sigmar's guidance. *Age of Sigmar* picks up with the return of Chaos as it invades the Mortal Realms yet again, and has continued releasing new product since.

WARHAMMER 40,000

With *WFB*'s popularity catching on like a wildfire in its first few years, GW returned to Rick Priestley to request a futuristic, science-fiction companion to the *WFB* franchise. Priestley drew upon a game he had been developing privately as well as upon the ruleset of *WFB*'s second edition to release a game that was similar to *WFB*, but with more of a focus on roleplaying, and which was best suited to small skirmishes, rather than full-scale battles. The game was released in 1987 under the title *Warhammer 40,000: Rogue Trader*, but supplemental materials in *White Dwarf* and other sourcebooks steered *WH40K: Rogue Trader* back to align more closely with *WFB* as a miniatures wargame. *WH40K*'s second edition, released in 1993, continued that trend, until now, where *WH40K* is, while distinct, ultimately very similar to *WFB* in its core premise and gameplay. The game continued streamlining play into 1998's third edition, and has continued launching new editions up to Eighth Edition, which was published in 2017.

The *WH40K* setting takes place predominantly in the 41st century of the *Warhammer* universe, some 38,000 years after the main timeline used in *WFB's* Warhammer Fantasy setting. *WH40K* presents a very dark, dystopian vision of *Warhammer's* future. The game's tagline, "In the grim darkness of the far future, there is only war," coined the term *grimdark* for hyper-dystopian, ultraviolent fiction – a term that has spread far beyond the reach of its inspiration.

Many of the key features of the *Warhammer* setting survive in some form, namely racial parallels (such as the Eldar, instead of Elves; Orks, instead of Orcs) and the persistence of Chaos as a primary foe. But *WH40K* also presented new themes, such as a subtle critique of organized religion in the reigning Imperium of Man and their fanatical devotion to the "Immortal God-Emperor."

A RICHER AND RICHER WORLD

Warhammer's success has prompted an absolute avalanche of derivative work, spinoffs, and supplements. Even setting aside the core, "canon" supplements like additional army writeups and codices and rulesets found in sourcebooks and *White Dwarf*, the two main settings have been explored in countless formats and media. Combined, *Warhammer Fantasy* novels and *Warhammer 40K* novels number in the hundreds, with dozens more novellas, short stories, and audio-dramas besides. Many of the novels, most of which were published by Black Library, a GW division founded in 1997, have also been collected into omnibus format.

Another of *Warhammer's* sub-categories is that of pen-and-paper tabletop roleplaying games, which introduced single-character focus and interaction and investigation to the general format of *Warhammer's* war-

games. In 1986, GW published *Warhammer Fantasy Roleplay*, intending for it to be a supplement for *WFB*. When this did not have the desired effect in boosting *WFB*'s miniatures sales, GW handed off the *Warhammer Fantasy Roleplay* materials to Flame Publications, a GW division. After Flame Publications failed financially and closed down in 1992, the game was in limbo and ultimately went through several other publishers, including an Italian company, Nexus Editrice, and a British company, Hogshead Publishing. In 2004 it was brought back under the GW umbrella into Black Industries, a part of Black Library, and finally found a home with Fantasy Flight Games in 2008.

Warhammer 40K took much longer to come to the RPG world. Only in 2008 did Black Industries release a tabletop RPG for the *Warhammer 40K* setting called *Dark Heresy*, which allowed players to pick up roles as Inquisitorial acolytes, with a balance between investigation and combat. Later, after Fantasy Flight Games picked up exclusive rights to GW's board, card, and role-playing games, they also took over support and expansion for *Dark Heresy*, and also released four more RPGs loosely based on *Dark Heresy*'s system: *Rogue Trader, Deathwatch, Black Crusade*, and *Only War*.

Warhammer's settings and wargames have also bridged into the general gaming sphere in a number of board games like *Warhammer Quest, Forbidden Stars*, and *Horus Heresy*, card games like *Warhammer 40K: Conquest* and *Dark Millennium*, and other minis spinoff games, like *Inquisitor, Space Hulk, Gorkamorka*, and *Warhammer Ancient Battles*, a real-world spin on WFB and WH40K.

Warhammer has also made a mark in the digital world with dozens of video games. Several were developed and released under license by companies famous for their tactics and wargames, like Strategic Simulations, of *Panzer General* fame, which in the 1990s developed *Warhammer 40,000: Chaos Gate, Warhammer 40,000: Rites of War*, and *Space Crusade*. THQ and Relic Entertainment, known for several games including *Homeworld*, also published a number of *Warhammer* video games under license in the early 2000s, including *Dawn of War* and several expansions, *Fire Warrior*, a first-person shooter, and *Warhammer 40,000: Space Marines*. *Warhammer Fantasy*, too, saw a number of video games, including Mindscape's 1995 *Warhammer: Shadow of the Horned Rat* and EA's 1998 sequel, *Warhammer: Dark Omen*. In 2008, EA, by way

of Mythic Entertainment, released *Warhammer Online: Age of Reckoning* as *Warhammer*'s first, and so far only, massively multi-player online RPG.

Let's Talk Collection

Warhammer has always been known – even mocked – as a pricey habit. The models themselves aren't cheap, but add to that the cost of the paints, brushes, glue, terrain, and model bases, plus the time investment of assembly and painting, and it's not exactly a wallet-friendly hobby. Many basic army components cost several dollars per unit, with some starter kits of 30-plus miniatures running upwards of $160.

And if you're looking to set up a particularly expansive collection, you'll really watch the numbers climb. *Warhammer: Age of Sigmar* presents four main factions comprising dozens of races and organizations, and over its many editions *WFB* and *WH40K* have each offered more than 20 armies, some with several notable sub-divisions. That said, like with reprinted cards in collectible card games, the value of some early or particularly powerful units can be deflated by recasts in later editions and by to-order models offered by sources like Forge World, a GW subsidiary that specializes in resin recasts of rare and hard-to-obtain models like the Chaos Dwarf Juggernaut/War Machine.

Some of the rarer units though – in particular metal-cast models from early in the games' histories – can still fetch a good price on resale sites due to their relative rarity. If you're looking specifically for rare models, you'll probably want to focus on early models, like those cast for the first-edition eras of *WFB* and in particular *WH40K: Rogue Trader*. Early Citadels Miniatures products also top the resale-value lists, like the so-called "Chicken Dragon," an extremely ambitiously cast Imperial Dragon model nicknamed for its size. The model clocked in at around two feet long, or roughly the size of a small chicken, and has sold for more than $1,000.

Due to the nature of the game, wherein any player can bring most any unit to the table that they can afford, build, paint, and finance within the army-construction constraints, and due to the fact that Games Workshop doesn't really run tournament support to the degree that many card game companies do, *Warhammer* doesn't see as much prevalence for rare, promotional units. Not that there aren't any. The late '90s in particular saw some limited run models like the Racing Nob, a Gamesday prize in '97 that today fetches usually around $50-$75, as well as a Rogue Daemon model that was a prize for a U.S. painting competition that goes for about the same price.

But aside from the occasional really big-ticket model like Forge World's Warlord Titan, a staggeringly tall multi-piece resin-cast model that can, all together, run well over $1,500, *Warhammer* doesn't see as many limited edition models as card companies printing limited-run cards. Whether that's due to GW's prerogative or greater difficulty in ensuring product legitimacy is anyone's guess. Even GW's anniversary edition models, like the *White Dwarf* 30th anniversary White Dwarf XXX model and the *WH40K* 25th anniversary Crimson Fist Space Marine Captain may see recasts, both legitimate and otherwise.

For all its quirks, oddities, and cost, *Warhammer* stands as the spiritual successor to a long and proud tradition of historical wargaming and tactical simulations. With it, Games Workshop brought together the inventiveness of fantasy and science-fiction, the precision and artistry of miniature models, and the brutal strategy of historical combat reenactment, leading the traditional miniatures wargame into a new era, both on tables and in digital landscapes. And despite its financial stumbles along the way, Games Workshop has brought their community into the internet age with web forums and countless online resources, creating spaces for their players to come together and foster a love of the game that will keep Games Workshop busy for many years to come.

THE FANTASY MINIATURES GAME

MINIATURES

MINIATURES

AN INTERVIEW WITH
DAVE TAYLOR

Miniatures have long been a part of tabletop gaming, from role-playing adventures to war games. Many gamers end up with a collection of minis simply by amassing them over many years' worth of play, while others specifically seek them out in order to have certain lines. Dave Taylor has been painting miniatures for nearly three decades, and we spoke with him about the ups and downs of the hobby and how far it's come.

Overstreet: First, tell us a little bit about yourself.

Dave Taylor (DT): My name is Dave Taylor, and I've been painting miniatures as a hobby since 1991. I've also worked in the "toy soldier industry" since 1994. I started out painting miniatures for Games Workshop's *Warhammer*, *Warhammer 40,000*, and *Blood Bowl*, and it really snowballed from there. I started working for Games Workshop in a retail store in 1994 in my hometown of Newcastle, Australia, and after a few years working in and opening up GW retail stores, I moved into the Promotions Studio. There I was editor/publisher of the Australian edition of *White Dwarf* magazine, and organized the first Games Days and Grand Tournaments in Australia.

In 2002 I moved to Baltimore, USA, to work for the U.S. arm of Games Workshop, also in the Promotions Studio. In 2008 I left Games Workshop and joined the team at *Wargames Illustrated*, the world's premier tabletop wargaming magazine. There I had the opportunity to work with many different miniatures manufacturers and paint a lot of great minis. In 2014 I launched my own business - Dave Taylor Miniatures - which is all about helping miniatures companies bring new products to market, and sell more of their existing products. Over that time, my love of painting minis has not dulled at all. In fact, I've probably painted over 10,000 miniatures in that time.

Overstreet: When did you first get into the miniature side of the hobby?

DT: In the early to mid-'80s I painted a few minis for use in my *AD&D* games, but it wasn't until 1991 that I really started painting armies of miniatures for wargaming purposes.

Overstreet: At what point did miniatures turn from just another part of tabletop gaming into a full-blown collection/hobby for you?

DT: It was always cool to be able to have a miniature that represented a character (or a party of characters) on the tabletop, but the idea of being able to field armies of painted miniatures that I could command was really cool. In 1991 I saw some lovely looking minis in a local hobby store (amongst the RC cars and train sets) and I was sold.

Overstreet: What is it about miniatures that make them so appealing to collect?

DT: Well-sculpted miniatures have a real character to them, something that harkens back to the toys of my youth (*Star Wars* and *He-Man* action figures in particular). I'm sure there's a connection there, but I really enjoy gaming with miniatures in a

setting that fits with the story of the world/ universe the minis are from: war-ravaged gothic cities for *Warhammer 40,000*, the dusty plains of the Iberian Peninsula for my Napoleonic gaming. Imagining the models coming to life to march into conflict. There's something about that I find really appealing.

Overstreet: Are there any specific miniature figures (or lines) that you know of to be "holy grail" type situations for collectors? What makes those specifically so valuable?

DT: For most miniatures gamers/collectors, the "holy grail" is typically a very personal thing and depends, I think, on the childhood of the collector. In recent years there has been a great surge of nostalgia for the early days of modern gaming and most "holy grails" come from that era (late '70s to early '80s). The value of models from this time is, of course, really quite arbitrary, but much of the pricing is driven by scarcity and condition, and also by the intent of the buyer. Some collectors are willing to pay considerably more for something they can display, making packaging surprisingly valuable too.

Overstreet: Is there any part of your own collection of miniatures that is particularly valuable or collectible?

DT: I must admit I'm not usually into collecting the older miniatures. Although they certainly have their charms, I prefer the latest and greatest sculpts. Sculpting skill and casting technologies have advanced considerably over the last few decades, and many modern miniatures are works of art in their own right.

Overstreet: Is there any part of your collection that stands out as a sentimental favorite?

DT: I really like a lot of my collection of minis, but I think the *Warhammer 40,000* Imperial Guard army I painted in 2003 will remain a sentimental favorite. The army has a very "World War I" feel to it, and is an extensive kit bash of Games Workshop's Bretonnian and Cadian miniatures. There are over 150 models in the army, and all of them are converted in some way to make them unique.

Overstreet: In your time collecting and painting miniatures, what about that part of the industry has changed for the better?

DT: Advances in skills and technologies has improved the sculpting and casting of miniatures, and crowdfunding has really opened things up and brought many more great games and miniatures to the market. Wonderful ideas that would otherwise have never seen the light of day are now a reality.

Overstreet: What has changed for the worse?

DT: In recent years this "golden age" of miniatures games has given gamers a lot of options, but has also aided in the fragmentation of the gaming community. Wargamers are typically fiercely loyal to their favorite game and with so many games available, the community isn't as cohesive as perhaps it once was.

Overstreet: What advice would you have for someone looking to start including miniatures into their tabletop RPG play for the first time?

DT: There are quite a few great manufacturers that make minis perfect for a variety of RPGs - Reaper Miniatures make a range called Bones that is vast and covers all manner of RPG archetypes for a very reasonable price. I'd recommend picking up some of those, a "starter paint set" from any of the major paint manufacturers (GW, Vallejo, Army Painter, etc.). Check out YouTube for a lot of great painting tutorials and just have a go, and ask questions. It may be tough at first, but stick with it. Painting minis is an incredibly rewarding hobby.

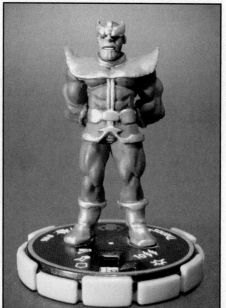

BY ALEX CARRA

Wargaming, especially miniatures wargaming, maintains a massive presence in the tabletop gaming industry. Many of the genre's heavyweights include unpainted, user-assembled miniatures, and rulesets meant to imitate real life rules of engagement and war, allowing players to simulate real or close-to-real battles. But the more lifelike the combat, the more complex it is, necessitating complex rulebooks and lists of unit statistics, which can bog down the speed of the game and complicate play.

Enter WizKids' Clix system, designed in the early 2000s. Pre-painted miniatures stand on top of bases, similar to other miniatures games, but with an added feature: the base can be twisted like a dial, with a small window revealing a unit's current statistics and power values. The Clix system introduced a much simpler way to track the evolution of play, with a unit's statistics and powers changing as the game continues. Units could sustain damage that weakened them, or even empowered them, and all without a pen and paper or stacks of rulebooks.

WizKids first used this system for its game *Mage Knight*, and would also make use of it in *MechWarrior: Dark Age* and similar games. But the game that truly put WizKids on the gaming industry map was its 2002 release *HeroClix*, which applied the Clix system to licenses for Marvel Comics superheroes. As the game progressed, HeroClix introduced

sets of DC Comics characters, and even additional heroes from Image Comics and Dark Horse Comics.

In 2003, though, The Topps Company bought WizKids, and five years later, Topps shuttered the HeroClix line to focus on other products. For half a year HeroClix was inactive. Early in 2009 several companies were in talks to buy the rights to the line, including a new company called Piñata Games that was specifically formed by fans and former WizKids employees to buy the game's rights, but these talks fell through. In 2009 National Entertainment Collectibles Association (NECA) released a promotional mini that was never released by WizKids: a large Thor's Mighty Chariot piece. The mini launched in July 2009 at Comic-Con International: San Diego, and in doing so, NECA tipped its hand. In September NECA announced it had bought the rights to HeroClix, and to this day the company markets and produces the game, and provides event and tournament support, as WizKids did before its sale.

LET'S GET CLICKING

Like other wargames, HeroClix is meant to simulate combat scenarios. Unlike classical wargames and minis wargames, HeroClix is focused not on wartime strategy, ships and infantry, but on teams of superheroes and villains duking it out for the good of the world. HeroClix simplifies the wargame core concept, making for a game that's more accessible to younger players, and keeps the high-flying, bad-guy-punching feel of the comics that fans know and love.

As with many modern minis wargames, HeroClix characters each have a unit point value, which each player uses to build teams of characters up to an agreed-upon team value (usually 300). However, *unlike* most minis wargames that use terrain and a map meant to reflect a real (or imagined) place, with troop movement measured in inches, HeroClix uses a grid map printed on top of scene imagery, reflecting buildings, town squares, alleyways, and more. These maps, and the game's lack of micro-level movement rules, help to simplify play and let the game move more quickly, with units' speed scores listed on their respective dials, along with health and power levels.

HeroClix doesn't really impose player restrictions, but generally the game works best with two to four players. All players take turns moving their characters and attacking enemy units or using individual powers, which are denoted on the dial. Over time, the game began releasing units with a corresponding reference card to explain each character's powers more completely. Since HeroClix has been in production for some time and occasionally some

bizarre power combinations and conflicts come up, HeroClix has rule booklets and reference guides online to demystify the play-to-play questions.

The core Clix system, in which the miniature bases are built on dials with hidden counters to track unit damage and strength, matters more as gameplay progresses. As characters are hit by enemies, a character's respective player will "click" the dial clockwise to reflect that damage. Generally this weakens units, but some (for example, as one might imagine, the Incredible Hulk) get more powerful the more damage they've sustained, which is reflected on the unit's strength dial as its health drops.

Generally speaking a game ends when only one player has units that haven't been knocked out (dropped to 0 health), but some also play with time limits. If more than one player is standing at the end of the match, each player counts up the point values of all the units they removed from play. Whoever knocked the most (or most valuable) units off the board wins.

MARVEL VERSUS DC

While WizKids' products started with Marvel in May 2002 with the *Infinity Challenge* set, DC licensing was close behind, entering the game in September of that year with *Hypertime*. Under WizKids and then Topps, HeroClix would release a total of 35 sets. Mostly these portrayed

Marvel storylines, including *Ultimates*, two different *Galactus* sets, *Days of Future Past*, *Avengers*, and the last Topps-led release, the July 2008 *Secret Invasion*. DC sets included *Cosmic Justice*, *Origin*, *Green Lantern Corps*, with a final Topps-led *Arkham Asylum* in October 2008. In October 2003 HeroClix also added the *Indy* set, which introduced independent comic characters to the game. In that vein, the game also gained a set of figures linked to *Watchmen*.

Since NECA took over production in 2009, HeroClix has added more than 40 more sets. Many of these sets have coincided with Marvel Cinematic Universe and DC Extended Universe movie releases, like Marvel's *Guardians of the Galaxy Vol. 1* and *Vol. 2*, *The Avengers Movie Set*, and *Captain America*, as well as DC's *The Dark Knight Rises*, *Joker's Wild* (released just a few months after *Suicide Squad*), and *Wonder Woman*.

Under NECA, HeroClix has also expanded the game's offering with tie-in sets for Middle Earth, to align with the release of *The Hobbit: An Unexpected Journey*, and a *Pacific Rim* set that launched in 2013. NECA also released a spinoff game to align with some of the newer *Star Trek* movies, though the game is mostly incompatible with other HeroClix sets, and generally stands alone as its own game. In partnership with Disney's *The Lone Ranger* movie, NECA also released a *Lone Ranger* set.

NECA also produced a few more unconventional tie-in sets, including a number that partnered with video game franchises, such as one tied to *Assassin's Creed* that launched in October 2012 and a *BioShock* set tied to the release of *BioShock Infinite*. NECA also added sets in September 2011 for *Halo* and in August 2011 for *Gears of War* and *Street Fighter*. Perhaps most odd of all, though, was the May 2013 release of an *Iron Maiden* set, featuring mascots and iconography from the band.

COLLECTORS' CORNER

Over the years the HeroClix unit hierarchy of rarity hasn't changed too substantially, though as with any game, some kinks have been worked out along the way. Originally there were six tiers of rarity, identified by numbers and categorized only loosely according to manufacturing numbers, but WizKids didn't track the statistics as closely as is common in modern games, so exact percentage odds of pulling particular figures out of a booster pack was almost impossible to calculate.

A year or so before the game's brief period of inactivity while Topps found a buyer, HeroClix recast its hierarchy to present only five official tiers, with each tier color-coded for ease of identification. Commons have a white ring, Uncommons green, Rare silver, and Super Rare uses gold. The fifth tier uses a copper ring and are called "Chase" miniatures, and are significantly

HANDYMAN
Armor, Brute, Founders, Monster, Robot

☆ **Thrown into Action** Handyman can use Super Strength. When he has no action tokens, he can use Telekinesis as a free action, but may only place on an adjacent friendly character.

Clearing the Decks Handyman can use Charge and Leap/ Climb. When he uses Charge, after actions resolve, he may use Force Blast as a free action.

RELENTLESS (Charge)

CAUGHT IN CERAMIC FISTS (Plasticity)

ANGRY (Quake)

ARMORED SHELL (Invulnerability)

POINT VALUE: 150

BIOSHOCK INFINITE

rarer than any of the other four. According to most collectors' math, only one Chase exists in every case of booster packs. Super Rares are generally valued on the resale market between $5 to $20. The value of a Chase is generally higher, but they also have a wider range of values, based on the respective power of the unit. Some Chases with low power values, and thus low impact on a team, might be worth only about $10 or $11, with more powerful Chase figures coming in as high as $65.

In addition to the Chase figures, though, HeroClix has released a number of limited edition figures over the years. Of particular value are Masterpiece figures, some of which were given out as tournament prizes and some distributed in booster packs as Chases. Each of the Masterpiece figures have only 50 copies in existence, with the most valuable and rare being the *Mutant Mayhem* Spider-Man figure: due to its visual similarity to other, standard Spider-Man figures and the ease with which some buyers overlooked the figure's certificate of authenticity, not all 50 have been accounted for. As a result, certified-authentic Masterpiece Spider-Man figures have an estimated resale value of over $200.

Another of the most valuable figures, with a somewhat similar story, is the Black Costume Infinity Challenge Wolverine promotional figure made in 2002 to help promote HeroClix at the game's initial launch. Fifty were made, but as the game had not yet gained much traction, most were discarded or outright junked. While this makes the original figure a particularly pricey entry for collectors, purchasing one can be a gamble. Like the man Logan himself, there have been so many derivations and remakes that verifying a figure's authenticity can be difficult.

But we can't talk rare HeroClix figures without mentioning a fabled Clix figure of the esteemed Stan Lee, armed with a giant pencil. The figure was not made by WizKids, but was a promo and a tournament prize, and so retains a sort of "unofficial official" classification. Only a few exist, with one given to a tournament winner at Emerald City

Comic Con, a second awarded by charity raffle, and a third, allegedly, printed for Stan Lee himself.

SPEAKING OF TOURNAMENTS
Being "wargame lite," HeroClix lends itself very well to traditional tournaments, but in addition to classic tournaments, WizKids also developed an "Organized Play" event format to capitalize on HeroClix's primary content: superheroes. These Organized Play events reflect big comics storylines, and often span several months at a time.

The Organized Play storyline events often combine standard tournament styles with additional mechanics or new twists on classic gameplay, such as a storyline in 2016 that emulated the story of Marvel's *Civil War*. HeroClix's Civil War event chain used a Battle Royale draft tournament for-

mat to simulate the harsh team lines drawn during the events of the comic storyline, with groups of four players drafting teams and engaging in a grand melee. Winners drafted units out of a prize pool at the end, and proceeded to the final tournament in a four-month event.

Keeping the spirit of WizKids' intention, NECA continued running these Organized Play events after it took over production of HeroClix. NECA also continued WizKids' event support, providing and producing limited edition figures as event prizes for tournaments and Organized Play events alike.

A GAME THAT JUST... CLICKS
In addition to the wealth of Marvel, DC, and miscellaneous figures that have been released as official, tournament-compatible HeroClix, the Clix system and HeroClix's popularity have spawned a number of derivative games and sets. These spinoffs, while not always fully compatible with HeroClix, operate on the Clix system and use similar rules.

HorrorClix, which launched while WizKids still held possession of HeroClix's product lines, was designed in a similar way but had only limited compatibility at official tournaments, as were the *Star Trek* HeroClix launched by NECA in 2012. The *Star Trek* HeroClix sets originally

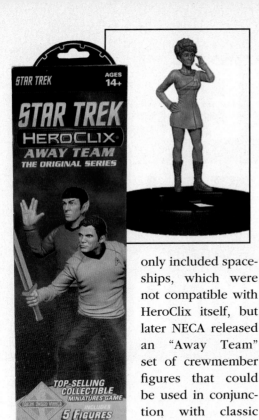

line and HorrorClix, such as four Chase figures dubbed "Marvel Zombie" figures, which had both a HeroClix character card and a HorrorClix monster card. Later in 2007 more zombie HeroClix figures were added, but these did not have a monster card. Hellboy and six Bureau for Paranormal Research and Defense figures were also released with compatibility in both games, but aside from these, there's been very little cross-game support.

only included spaceships, which were not compatible with HeroClix itself, but later NECA released an "Away Team" set of crewmember figures that could be used in conjunction with classic HeroClix. In 2013 NECA also produced a line of *Yu-Gi-Oh!* HeroClix inspired by the trading card game of the same name, and made use of a new "SwitchClix" mechanic. This allowed a player to flip over a figure's

Despite its commercial woes and corporate shuffling, HeroClix has sustained a relatively steady tenure in the games industry, bolstered in part by its simplicity and the overall quality of their figures. Given the comically disastrous painting errors that can sometimes occur in pre-painted figures, HeroClix's general caliber is noteworthy, and has definitely had a significant role in the game's continued success. Given the financial success of the Marvel Cinematic Universe and the DC Extended Universe and the way both have become cultural touchstones breaking new ground with box office smash hits like *Black Panther* and *Wonder Woman*, it's safe to say that by maintaining its position on the coattails of the superhero industry in general, HeroClix too can look forward to many more years of success.

dial, such that a feature could be set and then hidden, which let HeroClix adopt a "trap/spell" mechanic based on the *Yu-Gi-Oh!* card game.

Over the years HeroClix has added a few figures that were compatible with both that

OTHER TABLETOP ROLE PLAYING GAMES

The most popular and best-known role-playing games, such as *Dungeons & Dragons* and *Pathfinder*, have generally been set in a high fantasy, medieval-inspired world. And while that sort of setting has a massive fanbase, it's certainly not for everyone, and it's important to keep in mind that role-playing is hardly restrained to that kind of atmosphere. Regardless of your personal tastes, there's likely a tabletop RPG out there to suit your exact style.

For those who prefer a more gothic or horror-inspired world, there's a whole lot to choose from, but *Call of Cthulhu* will likely be the first to come to mind. The game, first published in 1981 by Chaosium, uses the Basic Role-Playing (BRP) system that had been originally created for *RuneQuest*. *Call of Cthulhu* is set in a world inspired by the stories of H.P. Lovecraft – a darker, more mysterious version of Earth in which players control ordinary folks who are interested in the mysterious happenings

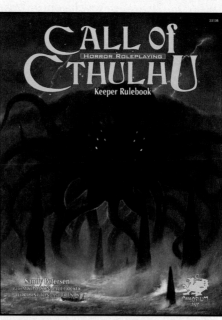

taking place. The game relies on percentile dice to determine whether or not a skill is successfully used, and while player characters will get better at using skills by rolling successfully, a leveling system is not present in the game.

Call of Cthulhu has, so far, seen seven different main editions since its debut in 1981, as well as one in-between release, "Edition 5.5." There was also a version of the game that made use of the d20 system, released by Wizards of the Coast in 2001; this enabled the *Call of Cthulhu* lore to be adapted for *Dungeons & Dragons*. Chaosium has worked with a number of other companies over the years to produce other *Cthulhu*-licensed products and games, most of which act as stand-alone adventures separate from the core series. A pair of card games, *Mythos* and *Call of Cthulhu: The Card Game*, have also been produced, as well as multiple video games.

Most books for *Call of Cthulhu* are fairly easy

to find and fit well within most budgets, though, as with many long-running games, there's a few stand-outs worth making note of. "Anniversary Editions" of the main rulebook have been released, and these typically draw high prices in online auctions. The *20th Anniversary Edition*, a green leather hardcover release, can go from about $100-$300 in online auctions, depending on the exact condition of the example; the *30th Anniversary Edition* draws about $100-$200 in similar venues, and is a red leather hardcover release. "Masks of Nyarlathotep" is one of the most highly-acclaimed and easily the most popular of the *Cthulhu* campaigns, and the hardcover anniversary release of this supplement sees prices of about $100 or so (compared to about $30 for a contemporary standard release).

A decade after the arrival of *Call of Cthulhu*, another horror-inspired role-playing game came onto the scene – *Vampire: The Masquerade*. Rather than being a pure horror experience, *Vampire* was a brood-

ing, moody, urban gothic story setting that favored a more narrative experience rather than one based on combat. By focusing more on story than on battle, *Vampire* was quickly recognized as a game that was far easier for newbies to pick up and play than many other RPG systems.

Vampire: The Masquerade uses White Wolf, Inc.'s Storytelling System (previously known as the Storyteller System). A number of other games published in the years since have used these systems, including *Werewolf: The Apocalypse, Mage: The Ascension, Trinity, Exalted*, and *Orpheus*, among many others.

After its debut in 1991, *Vampire* was almost immediately recognized as an interesting new choice for gamers, and picked up the Origins Award for *Best Roleplaying Rules of 1991*. A number of different editions of *Vampire: The Masquerade* have released, and a sequel game, *Vampire: The Requiem*, first released in 2004, which also has seen a second edition release. In addition to the

main tabletop experience, there have been successful card games, video games, novels, and even a live-action role-playing system.

Most books within the *Vampire* line are going to be in the same budget range of most other mass-produced RPG systems, with a core rulebook running about $40-$50 and supplementary materials going for about $20 or so. But there are some highlights for collectors, notably including the 20th Anniversary Core Rulebook *Grand Masquerade* limited edition, released in 2011 – and only available in New Orleans. Bound in black leather with "New Orleans 2011" stamped on the cover, this book has commanded prices of $400 or more in online auctions. White Wolf has also produced some limited accessories as tie-ins to the game, including cigarette cases and lighters, both of which tend to draw prices of $50 or more.

While horror-flavored adventures have long been popular stories to explore, science-fiction has also been dominant as a genre. Few games have breathed new life into what sci-fi can be quite like *Shadowrun*, which was first published in 1989. The game combines traditional sci-fi with elements of fantasy, horror and noir to create a truly unique world, and one that has not often been matched in terms of popularity.

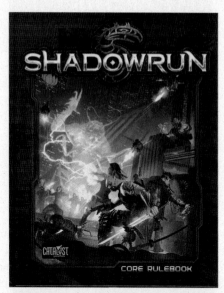

Shadowrun's setting is in the near-future of 2050 (as of the first edition; later editions take place in later decades), where, after the Mesoamerican Long Count Calendar ended, magical creatures and powers emerged. Alongside magical developments were technological and scientific ones, allowing for people to augment their bodies and abilities. Players control shadowrunners, specialists who exact missions for various sponsors.

By balancing a unique story setting and interesting gameplay mechanics, *Shadowrun* has enjoyed significant popularity over the last three decades. The series has also expanded to include a card game, numerous novels, and several different video games. In fact, some of the *Shadowrun* video games are more valuable and collectible than the tabletop books themselves – the Super Nintendo game regularly sees prices of $50 or more for just the cartridge, while a complete-in-box game can draw upwards of four times as much in online auctions. The 1996 Sega Mega-CD *Shadowrun* game, which was a Japan-only release, often sees prices of $200 or more as well. But when it comes to the tabletop materials themselves, Catalyst Game Labs has done some limited edition releases of the core rulebooks and other materials since 2005, all of which tend to fall in the range of $75-$150 or so, depending on the condition of the book in question.

There's also been plenty of licensed tabletop role-playing games, for those interested in dipping their toe in an RPG system but want to do so in a setting already familiar to them.

For gamers who enjoy a good spy adventure, there's a number of espionage games out there – and at one point that included *James Bond 007: Role-Playing in Her Majesty's Secret Service*. The game was published from 1983 to 1987 by Victory Games, and only ended up discontinued due to the licensing lapsing. Thanks to an easy-to-learn system and the overall popularity of the *Bond* films, the game was pretty popular. Today, materials related to the game usually go for $50 or more in online auctions.

Fans of stories from a galaxy far, far away have a pretty significant variety when it comes to *Star Wars* RPGs, with systems having been published by West End Games in 1987 (*Star Wars: The Roleplaying Game*), Wizards of the Coast in 2000 (*Star Wars Roleplaying Game*), and Fantasy Flight in 2013 (*Star Wars: Edge of the Empire; Star Wars: Age of Rebellion;* and *Star Wars: Force and Destiny*). Each has their own style of play, some of which are more

suited to newcomers than others. The Wizards of the Coast version of the game made use of the d20 system, and therefore bears the closest resemblance to *D&D*. When it comes to collecting these games, books and minis from the West End Games production tend to have higher prices than pieces from the newer games, simply due to their vintage. However, materials from all three publishers are generally easy to find.

Other RPGs based on licensed properties of note have included multiple *Star Trek* games (*Star Trek: The Role Playing Game; Star Trek: The Next Generation Role-Playing Game*, among others), DC Comics games (*DC Heroes, DC Universe Roleplaying Game*), Marvel Comics games (*Marvel Heroic Roleplaying, Marvel Universe Roleplaying Game, Marvel Super Heroes Adventure Game*, and others), Tolkien-inspired settings (*Lord of the Rings Roleplaying Game, Middle Earth Role Play*), and many more.

Thanks to contemporary technology allowing for instantaneous publication and distribution of new materials, there's more role-playing games and systems being developed than ever before. Regardless of what your personal taste may be, there's sure to be an RPG out there to suit your needs.

A HISTORY OF

WIZARDS OF THE COAST

Few companies have been quite as synonymous with tabletop game publishing over the years as Wizards of the Coast (WotC). The company was founded in May 1990 by Peter Adkison and Ken McGlothlen; Adkison had previously self-published a wargame called *Castles and Conquest* and had written the *Chaldea* campaign for *Dungeons and Dragons* in the 1980s. The name "Wizards of the Coast" was actually based on an in-game guild from one of Adkison's role-playing experiences.

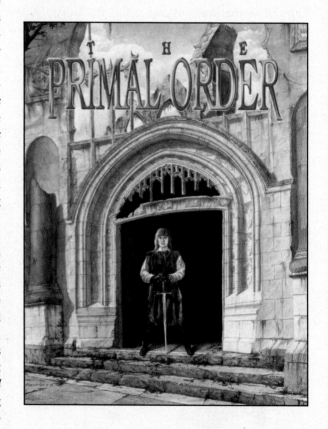

One of the first titles WotC began working on was a role-playing game called *The Primal Order*, which was designed by Adkison. The game didn't release until 1992, but it did introduce the "Capsystem" concept, which allowed for game runners to integrate various other titles that used the same system into *The Primal Order*. WotC also began publishing the third edition of the already-established *Talislanta* around the same time.

The company struck gold early in its history with *Magic: The Gathering*. The card game's creator, Richard Garfield, had approached WotC in '91 with an idea for a board game, *RoboRally*; however, the game was shot down because of how expensive it would have been to produce. Instead, Garfield was asked to create a portable game that was easy to learn and could be finished quickly – the result was *Magic*, though it was originally called *Manaclash*. The game debuted in the summer of 1993, where it was exhibited at both Origins Game Fair and Gen Con. The company had produced about 2.5 million cards, anticipating that it would be enough to last them through the end of that year, but *Magic* proved to be so exceptionally popular that they sold out of the entire supply by the time Gen Con was over.

Magic has since won dozens of industry awards in the two and a half decades since its original launch and is still a seemingly unbeatable juggernaut when it comes to collectible card games. Plus, thanks to the success of the game, WotC was able to expand from a small operation essentially running out of Adkison's basement into a massive publishing company that employed several hundred people. Garfield's original board game *RoboRally* was also eventu-

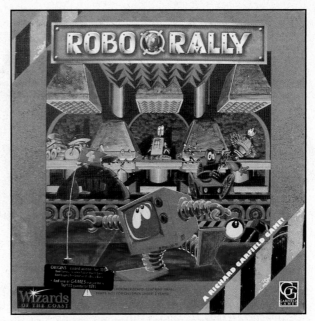

ally published in '94, and that too picked up several industry awards. Other games published by WotC around this time included *SLA Industries, Ars Magica, The Great Dalmuti*, and *Everway*.

In April 1997, WotC acquired TSR, the publisher of *Dungeons and Dragons*. TSR had been struggling financially for years at that point, and the company had been sitting on years' worth of unsold stock; TSR actually entered 1997 more than $30 million in debt. That summer, the Third Edition of *D&D* entered development, allowing for Adkison and WotC as a whole to essentially put their own spin on the classic role-playing

game. *D&D*'s Third Edition would release in 2000, alongside the d20 System and the Open Game License, which allowed other publishers to use the systems most closely associated with *D&D*.

While WotC had already established themselves as the go-to company for card games thanks to the wild success of *Magic*, another game came along that essentially allowed lightning to strike twice – *Pokémon*. The *Pokémon Trading Card Game* was first published by Media Factory in Japan in 1996, and WotC was able to secure the rights to publish it in America. The colorful card game had already seen massive success in Japan (unsurprising, given the enormous popularity of the franchise at large at the time), and in January 1999, WotC began publishing the game in English. The game proved to be hugely popular in the U.S. and around the world, and exceeded

WotC's sales projections by about 10 times what they had expected. Several millions of *Pokémon* cards had been sold within just the first year once the game was made available in English.

In September 1999, WotC was acquired by Hasbro for $325 million, and Avalon Hill (which had been acquired by Hasbro the previous year) was made a subsidiary of WotC. That same year, WotC purchased the gaming retailer The Game Keeper, and turned those stores into Wizards of the Coast stores. They could be found in malls across the country and played host to various events, such as *Dungeons and Dragons* nights, *Magic* tournaments, and the *Pokémon* Trading Card League.

In January 2001, Peter Adkison resigned from Wizards; he would go on to take over Gen Con the following year and is still the

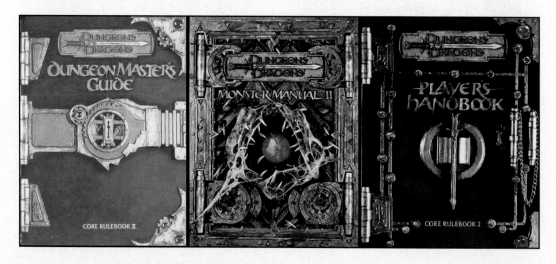

owner of the convention today. Around the same time, WotC began outsourcing its various magazines (*Dungeon, Dragon, Polyhedron*) to Paizo Publishing – Paizo has since become perhaps better-known as the publisher of the *Pathfinder* role-playing game, which uses the d20 system that WotC had released years before.

All Wizards of the Coast retail locations were closed by the spring of 2004, as the company opted to focus entirely on game design and publication. WotC has continued to publish various card games, board games, and tabletop games in the years since (the company no longer publishes *Pokémon*, as that game was taken over by The Pokémon Company in 2003). In 2008, the Fourth Edition of *Dungeons and*

Dragons released, aiming to be more accessible to new players by offering a more streamlined set of rules. This was followed up in 2014 with the Fifth Edition, which features further rebalancing of gameplay that draws from various previous editions of the game.

Meanwhile, *Magic: The Gathering* continues to be the driving force when it comes to collectible card games, with new sets and expansions releasing multiple times per year. In 2016, Hasbro announced Chris Cocks as the new President of Wizards of the Coast, who joined the company after spending several years working for Microsoft.

Though there have certainly been ups and downs for the company throughout the years, Wizards of the Coast remains one of the most recognizable names in tabletop gaming. Having continued to play host to some of the biggest games out there, Wizards remains a titan in the industry and is sure to remain one for years to come.

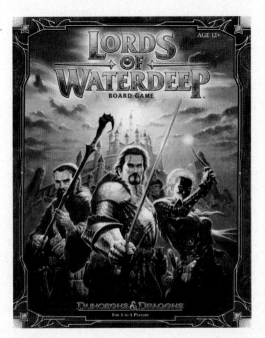

AN INTERVIEW WITH
PETER ADKISON

Peter Adkison is the founders of Wizards of the Coast, the company that's been home to such games as Magic: The Gathering, Dungeons & Dragons *and many more over the course of its long history. After leaving the company in 2001, he purchased Gen Con, and has been running it ever since. Overstreet caught up with Adkison at Gen Con 50 to discuss his legacy in the industry and the state of tabletop gaming today.*

Overstreet: Tell us a little bit about the Gen Con museum – who did you reach out to in order to cultivate and put it together?

Peter Adkison (PA): The idea for the museum came from [John Peterson] who came to me with it. I said, "well, I don't know where to get all this stuff to put into a museum." Even though I've run collectibles businesses, I've never personally been a collector. And John kind of smiled the way that he does and said "I've got you

covered." So really, most of the museum content came from really three collectors. John knows them because he bids against them at auctions on special items.

So [Bill Minehart], who focuses on role-playing games and might have the biggest collection in the world of role-playing first prints and so forth, and [Paul Stormberg], who overlaps a lot with role-playing games and the board gaming and runs a lot of events [joined John.] So it was really

between the three of them. But they said – "really, we only collect the older stuff. We don't really collect much of the newer stuff like *Magic: The Gathering*." Well, I had them covered there! My dad actually is a huge *Magic* collector, and I also know the guy who runs the Pokémon Company. And then there was Mike Carr, who's the only person who's been at every single Gen Con since it started, and he's got a bunch of great items.

After that it tailed off into the onesies and twosies – very important onesies and twosies. It just went on after that. At some point it was throwing out the net to the friends and family network – old industry veterans – and asking people what they had.

Overstreet: When you, as either a collector or as a hobbyist, are looking at a game that you want to add to your collection, what specifically are you looking for? What catches your attention personally?

PA: I don't actually collect anything as a collector! [laughs] I know, I know. I was the founder of Wizards of the Coast and Wizards of the Coast was known for *Magic: The Gathering* and *Pokémon*. I pursued *Magic* and making it and us publishing it because I like playing the game! I do like to collect them – my dad's a big collector, he's really into it – but if I'm buying a game, it's because I think it's going to be fun to play.

Overstreet: So speaking of Wizards of the Coast and *Magic: The Gathering*, did you know or even have a feeling that *Magic* would become the juggernaut of a game that it is?

PA: We knew at some level that it was possible, right? It was always possible. But when you're a publisher, you generally don't let yourself dream that way. You gotta keep your head down out of the clouds and be practical about your forecasting. The deeper we got into it, the more confident we became that *Magic* was going to be some level of successful – it was going to be a hit of some degree. But, you know, on a totally different scale than what it turned out to be, which was hundreds of magnitudes more. But then there's also the sustainability – how long would it last? We lived through the '90s thinking, "When's the bubble going to break? What's

Magic took off there and was a huge success. At one time, Japan was 30 percent of our sales – not Asia, but just Japan was 30 percent of our sales – which was incredible. One day, I remember we went and visited HobbyJapan and Mr. Sato informed us that *Magic* was no longer the number-one trading card game in Japan. And we were like "What? How is that possible?"

By then we had seen several other trading card games come into the market and then leave. And he said "Well, there's this company called Pokémon." So we learned about it from that angle.

At first it was a little bitter – it's hard not to when someone's beating you competitively. But when we looked closer at the game, we realized it was a totally different thing. It's targeted younger, it's got TV support; this is not a game that competes with *Magic* but was a game that would train *Magic* players. It was the gateway drug.

The creator of *Pokémon* came to our offices – that kind of surprised us, that he asked to visit with us, and he met Richard Garfield. And he asked if we would consider being their partner for bringing *Pokémon* to the United States. All of a sudden we went from these feelings of bitterness to "Oh, we *love* Pokémon!" [laughs] We saw it in a whole new light! It was absolutely wonderful that we had that opportunity. I

going to happen on the other side, at the end of this tale?" We knew this thing had to have some sort of bubble, so how badly was it going to crash on the other side?

Overstreet: Guess we'll learn that someday!
PA: Yeah, we're still waiting! [laughs]

Overstreet: When you saw the success of *Magic: The Gathering* as it was, which was ramping up pretty consistently over the expansions, along came *Pokémon*.
PA: Talk about lightning striking twice!

Overstreet: No kidding! What was it about *Pokémon* that was attractive to you to bring it over to the States?
PA: It was based on what we were seeing in Japan. We were partners with a company called HobbyJapan, which is our distributor into the Japanese market. They were selling lots of *Magic*; just like everywhere else,

like to think if I was still at Wizards, maybe Wizards would still be making *Pokémon* – I don't know.

Overstreet: You're a huge supporter of indie games on sites like Kickstarter. What is it about these games that draws you to them?

PA: I love indie RPGs especially. Small press role-playing games is a place in the industry that's a personal hobby of mine. First of all, a lot of times, if you don't catch these games on Kickstarter you're not going to get them anywhere else! Kickstarter is, in many cases, the only distribution model for those games. But it's what I love!

Overstreet: As far as Kickstarter goes, do you see that – even though you may not be a collector – things like exclusives or stretch goals affect the collectability or desirability of something?

PA: I don't know, maybe I'm overly simplistic, but I think collectability just depends on future popularity. All this old stuff in the museum that relates to, say, *Dungeons & Dragons* – the only reason it's interesting is because it's *Dungeons & Dragons!* Now, there are other games in there – we've got a first printing, first-edition copy of *Warhammer Fantasy Roleplay* and so on – these games were all important. But there's also a lot of games, thousands of role-playing games that weren't in there, because nobody cares. I think that you can have all

these different types of collectability, but if the total print run of a game is just 500 copies, then who cares if the game isn't good?

Overstreet: Despite not being a collector, if there was a "holy grail" for you to have, what would that item be?

PA: In the museum, I found this *Avalon Hill General*, which was a magazine dedicated to war gaming from way back in the '60s. I read the *General* when I was a teenager. I read every issue of the *General* cover to cover. This was before I discovered role-playing games, so I was a board gamer at the time. And I found that there were three different issues from three different years where the *General* covered Gen Con as "the nation's premier war gaming convention." So that's very surreal for me, to think that I now own a convention which was on the front cover of a magazine that I read as a boy. I was given a blown-up poster-sized version of the cover, but now I'm aiming for the real thing.

A History of Collectible Card Games

Like board games and role-playing activities, card games have a long and storied history that dates back several hundred years. Some of the earliest known records of playing cards date to the 9th century, during the Tang dynasty in China – woodblock printing started to arise around this time, making the manufacturing of game cards possible. A text that dates to this period, the *Collection of Miscellanea at Duyang*, contains one of the first references to card games, in which it describes the daughter of the Emperor playing a "leaf game" with her husband's family.

The exact game that the princess was playing is unknown, though other texts that came later continued to describe the activity of playing the "leaf game." Other card games – usually played while drinking alcohol in a social setting – began play around this time, though the rules to most of these have been lost to history. One of the earliest Chinese games that can still be played today thanks to the preservation of the rules is *Madiao*, which dates to the 14th century. *Madiao* is played with 40 cards, with three people playing against a fourth, who acts as the banker.

But card games were hardly limited to Asia, with evidence pointing to card games being played in regions of Africa – Egypt, in particular – around the same time. Some of the oldest surviving playing cards have dated to 12th-century Egypt. Many of the cards from this era depict clear suits, and would often feature intricate and abstract artwork.

The traditional four-suited playing cards known today first showed up in Europe in the 14th century, and were seemingly inspired by the Egyptian cards of the same era. Playing cards became quite common by the end of the 1300s, and by the 1400s, many began to enter card-making and printing as a profession. The four suits most commonly seen at the time were Cups, Coins, Clubs, and Swords; the contemporary Anglo-American suits of Hearts, Diamonds, Clubs and Spades were derived from these. The tarot deck was also introduced to Europe around this time, with the earliest documented references to tarot cards dating to the 1400s (and the oldest surviving tarot cards being from this period). Most tarot decks used between 50 and 60 cards, though an expanded deck would contain more than 90. A number of different games could be played using a tarot deck, with rules varying depending on the region it was being played in. Today, tarot cards are more closely associated with divination and the occult, with a 78-card deck being used to conduct cartomancy and fortune-telling.

In the 1600s, *Hanafuda* became popular in Japan. *Hanafuda* literally translates to "flower cards," and accordingly the cards typically feature full-color artwork of different plants. The game features 12 dif-

ferent suits, each representing a different month of the year and being designated by a different kind of flower. The game actually came into existence after Japan banned gambling and, along with it, banned foreign playing cards. *Hanafuda*, alongside other games like *Unsun Karuta*, were created as a workaround.

As cultures around the world rebelled against gambling, items closely associated with the activity – mainly cards and dice – were accordingly shunned, or at the very least considered unsavory to have out in public. However, the traditional deck of playing cards eventually came back into favor, and the 52-card, four-suit deck is used today for a wide number of games.

When it comes to collectible card games, though, those didn't arrive in true form until the 20th century. Most CCGs are based around a system of two different products – pre-built decks of cards, and booster packs. In order to get the most powerful cards available, or collect every card in a series, a person has to buy blind boosters and hope for the best.

One of the early predecessors to today's CCGs was *Batter-Up Baseball*, which was

published in the 1950s and 1960s by the Ed-u-Cards Corp; this was followed up by Topps' *Baseball Card Game*. Topps' game was similar to CCGs in that cards were bought in blind packs and there was a focus put on collecting a whole set in addition to actually playing with the cards. *Strat-O-Matic Baseball*, first released in the early 1960s, also introduced some concepts that are used in contemporary CCGs, insomuch that each card had a specific set of stats that had to be taken into account in order to form appropriate

strategies to win. Strat-O-Matic as a company went on to produce similar games for hockey, football, and basketball; their main competitor has long been APBA, which produced a line of similar games.

Magic: The Gathering's arrival in 1993 heralded in a new age for card games and for tabletop gaming at large. It set the standard for how a CCG is played and produced, and its instant popularity led to dozens of other CCGs entering production in an attempt to capitalize. By 1995, one-third of the total games announced at that year's GAMA Trade Show was a CCG.

The CCG market has been largely up and down since the 1990s, but many aspects (and series) have remained remarkably stable in that time. CCGs have come and gone, and many other types of card games, such as deck-builders (such as *Dominion*) have come into popularity as well. Card games have enjoyed – and will likely continue to see – huge popularity due to generally easy learning curves and accessible entry price points. Whether for the love of the game or the joy of collecting, people worldwide have confirmed that CCGs continue to be worth paying close attention to.

Magic: The Gathering

BY ALEX CARRA

Magic: the Gathering is and has been, since its launch in 1993, the genesis and undisputed king of the collectible card game. And it stands to maintain that position for a long time to come. Building on the backs of classic card games and collectible games like Ed-u-Cards Corp's 1947 *Batter Up* and Topps' 1951 *Baseball Card Game*, Richard Garfield developed *Magic: the Gathering* first under the name *Mana Clash*, after Wizards of the Coast suggested he design a game that would be low-cost to produce and quick to play, with the intention of using its sales to fund another game that Garfield had pitched to them, *RoboRally*.

Wizards of the Coast *would* ultimately publish *RoboRally*, but it would be hard to compete with the success of *Magic: the Gathering* (hereafter "*Magic*"). *Magic*'s first printing in August 1993, dubbed Limited Edition Alpha, sold out within just a couple months, and Wizards of the Coast scrambled to print a second run (Limited Edition Beta) in October, and a third (Unlimited Edition) in December. Wizards of the Coast struggled to stay ahead of demand, and barely a year after *Magic*'s release, new games hoping to capitalize on *Magic*'s rampant success flooded the market.

HOW TO PLAY

Magic established several key gameplay features that would become mainstays of the collectible card game genre for decades to come. It's a competitive dueling game, in which two (or more) players are pitted against each other, taking on the roles of rival Planeswalkers: magicians who can move between the planes of the Magic multiverse and draw upon mana, the power of the land, to cast spells and summon creatures to do their bidding. Players build a deck averaging about 60 cards, which forms the player's "Library," and while turn by turn a game of *Magic* is determined somewhat by luck of the draw, much of the strategy and skill of the game is decided in initial deck-construction. Of particular importance is the balance of Land to other spells; a deck with too few Land cards may fail to support spells with a higher casting cost, as a player must pay for every spell they cast with Land cards already in play.

Magic nominally divides its cards into five colors. Red cards favor impulsivity and often feature quick bursts of power or direct attacks on an opponent's health, while Green cards favor slow, sustainable resources, usually building up more slowly to bring out big, hard-hitting creatures. Black cards focus on weakening those cards already on the field, and favor riskier play, with some cards even gambling the player's health to fuel spells, while White focuses on healing and shoring up defenses, creating nigh impenetrable walls of creatures to keep opponents at bay. Blue often presents itself as the wild card category, favoring powers that control or amplify the random aspects of the game, often focusing on getting desired cards from the player's deck into play, while trashing cards from an opponent's hand to keep needed cards out of their grasp.

Cards that transcended color appeared as early as the 1994 expansion Legends, but have gained more prominence in modern expansions to the game, most often appearing as cards with a gold background instead of one of the five colors. Hybrid cards, which can be paid for with one of two listed colors, were introduced in the 2005 Ravnica Block of expansions. Conversely, some cards have no color association at all, and have grey backgrounds. These colorless cards can be played effectively from any deck, and featured prominently in the 2003-04 Mirrodin Block of expansions.

To play a game of *Magic*, two or more players prepare their respective decks and begin with 20 life points each. The ultimate goal of the game is to be the last Planeswalker standing, usually by bringing any and all opponents' life counters to 0 through creature combat or other magical abilities.

Land cards are the more straightforward category of *Magic* cards, representing locations associated with a particular color: Mountains for Red, Forests for Green, Plains for White, Swamps for Black, and Islands for Blue. Some Lands, especially in later expansions, have multiple colors, or have extra abilities, but in general, each Land is fairly simple. A player can play one Land per turn, and to make use of that Land once it is on the field, the card is tapped (turned 90 degrees from its usual face-up position) to add a mana point of the corresponding color to the player's pool. Tapping, a facet of *Magic* that was famously patented by Wizards of the Coast, is a core mechanic of the game, and signifies that a card has been used, and cannot be used again until the next turn, when all of that player's cards "untap."

The mana gained by tapping Land cards is then used to cast spells, the meat and potatoes of a player's Library. Spells fall into several categories: Creature, Sorcery, Instant, Artifact, Enchantment, and Planeswalker.

Creatures represent everything from elves to magical beasts to humans to ghosts, and come with a core pair of statistics for strength and defense ("Power" and "Toughness," respectively). Once summoned, creatures remain on the field until they are destroyed by another card effect or by combat with creatures controlled by an opponent. Creatures can possess a wide range of abilities, indicated by "Keywords" like *Flying*, a quality that renders a creature impossible to block or attack except by another flying creature or one that is specifically allowed to interact with a flying creature, and *First Strike*, which indicates that a creature hits its defender first and resolves its damage, potentially killing the defender before it can counter-attack. Some Creatures even have abilities that require the Creature to be tapped, forcing the player to choose between activating that ability, or keeping the Creature in play to be used in combat.

Some sets also include Creature Token cards, which are not shuffled into a player's deck as usual. Only some spells or occasionally Creature abilities can create Tokens, so the stand-in card is only used when a Token is brought into play.

Sorceries and Instants are both cast-and-done spells that cause their listed effect and then are discarded to the Graveyard, *Magic*'s in-world term for the discard pile. They can range in power from minor effects that are relatively cheap to cast to big, expensive cards that can really change the tide of a game. In most ways, Sorceries and Instants are exactly the same, except that Instants can be cast during an opponent's turn to interrupt something that's happening, where Sorceries may only be played on the turn of the player using them.

Artifacts and Enchantments, like Creatures, are "permanent" spells that remain in play until removed. Artifacts sit on the field of play for the player who controls it, and usually can be tapped, like Mana or Creatures, to activate abilities. Enchantments generally are not tapped, but are placed on a Creature, to weaken or strengthen it, or on other cards in play, to interfere with their use and abilities. Some enchantments, for example, might block a card from being un-tapped at the start of a player's turn, such that for as long as the enchantment is in play, the enchanted card cannot be reactivated.

Planeswalkers were introduced as a new card type in 2007. Though some Planeswalkers are represented on several different cards, to date there are only a couple dozen named Planeswalkers within the *Magic* lore that appear in the game. In keeping with the fact that within the

world's lore players are Planeswalkers in and of themselves, these cards function as allies alongside the player who plays them, with powerful abilities that can be activated to boost the player or interfere with an opponent. Planeswalker cards look similar to traditional creatures, but are ultimately very different, and do not have Power and Toughness stats quite the way Creatures do. Each Planeswalker card instead has a personal store of health, and like a player, a Planeswalker card can be targeted by an opponent's cards and creatures in attempts to remove a Planeswalker from play.

Players take turns drawing cards, activating spells and powers, and besieging opponents with their summoned creatures. The most common ending conditions stipulate that a player loses when they are reduced to 0 life, or when they are required to draw more cards than are remaining in the player's Library, but some expansions have introduced other loss conditions, such as accruing 10 "poison counters." Some cards even specifically state that under a particular condition, such as accruing counters, a coin-flip, or having specific cards in play, a player loses or wins, while others might indicate that the controlling player cannot lose, but the other player(s) also cannot win, forcing the game to continue until that card is removed from play or the controlling player wins.

WHAT'S ON ORDER

Since its first year, *Magic* has followed a fairly simple release format, with an annual or biannual core set of cards that form the skeleton of gameplay, and are, with only rare exceptions, reprints of cards released in either prior core sets or expansions. Expansions are released usually on a seasonal basis, averaging two to four expansions per year since the game's inception. Expansions introduce new card mechanics and explore new parts of the *Magic* multiverse, exploring new storylines and conflicts that feature into the lore and flavor text of cards, as well as spinoff novels.

The initial core sets, released between 1993 and 2007, mostly followed a numbered edition format, starting with the 1993 Limited Editions Alpha and Beta and Unlimited Edition, then the 1994 Revised Edition, and then the Fourth to Tenth

Editions, which were published every other year from 1995 to 2007. In 2009 Wizards of the Coast began holding prerelease events and switched naming conventions, releasing *Magic 2010*, and switching to an annual release schedule until *Magic Origins* in July 2015, which Wizards of the Coast designated the last core set. In honor of the game's 25th anniversary, however, a revamped printing of the *Magic Origins* set is slated for release in 2018. Core sets and expansions alike are generally sold in 60-card preconstructed decks and randomized booster packs of, for modern sets, 15 cards. Throughout the game's history the size of a booster pack has varied, ranging from 8 in some expansions like *Arabian Nights* and *Fallen Empires*, to 12 in *Alliances* and *Chronicles*.

All *Magic* sets include cards of different rarities. Common cards form the backbone of any set, with Uncommon next, then Rare. The Mythic Rare, denoted by a red-gold expansion icon, was introduced in the 2008-09 Alara Block, just before *Magic 2010*'s release. According to Wizards of the Coast, a Mythic Rare replaces a Rare card in one out of every eight booster packs.

The first expansion, *Arabian Nights*, was released in December 1993, just months after the Limited Editions were printed and sold out. Only during its development did Garfield codify the idea that *Magic* expansions would introduce new mechanics and elements of gameplay, and briefly Garfield intended for the card backs of *Arabian Nights* cards to in fact be a different color, to distinguish them from the core sets. Players objected to the plan and pushed for the expansion to have the same backing, thus maintaining the possibility of integrating *Arabian Nights* cards into games using the core set of cards. Wizards of the Coast agreed, and to distinguish it from the core set, a scimitar icon (keeping with the set's *Thousand and One Arabian Nights* inspiration) was added to the layout of the card. Every expansion since *Arabian Nights* has used a unique icon, ranging from weapon icons in keeping with a particular expansion's lore to setting-specific icons, like a trio of icicles for the 2006 *Coldsnap* expansion.

In October 1996, after the release of seven more expansions (*Antiquities, Legends, The Dark, Fallen Empires, Ice Age, Homelands,* and *Alliances*), Magic began releasing con-

tent in blocks, sets of expansions that all focused on a particular setting, and usually a particular new mechanic or group of mechanics, such as the 2011-12 *Innistrad Block* introducing double-sided cards that could flip and "transform" in the middle of play. Between the 1996-97 *Mirage Block* and the 2014-15 *Khans of Tarkir Block*, all but two blocks have comprised three sets. *Khans of Tarkir* marked another shift in Wizards' release format, and is to date the last block to contain three sets. The 2007-08 *Lorwyn* and its 2008 companion block *Shadowmoor* both had only two sets, as have the 2016-17 *Kaladesh Block*, the 2017 *Amonkhet Block*, and the 2017 *Ixalan Block*.

Blocks focus on particular planes, or parts of the *Magic* multiverse, and a number of them feature a departure and later return, such as the 2005-06 *Ravnica Block* and the 2012-13 *Return to Ravnica Block*. These paired blocks, like *Ravnica*, the 2003-04 *Mirrodin*/2010-11 *Scars of Mirrodin Blocks*, the 2009-10 *Zendikar*/2015-16 *Battle for Zendikar Blocks*, and the *Innistrad*/2016 *Shadows over Innistrad Blocks*, reflect storylines wherein the players, as Planeswalkers, return to a region to discover that things have gone very wrong while they've been busy resolving conflicts elsewhere.

Elements of the stories of these various planes frequently impact other expansions, with the best example possibly being the *Phyrexian Invasion*, which impacted dozens, perhaps hundreds of planes, and made appearances in a number of the game's early expansions, including the *Mirage Block*, the 1998-99 *Urza Block*, the 1999-2000 *Masques Block*, the 2000-01 *Invasion Block*, and the *Scars of Mirrodin Block*. The 2001-02 *Odyssey Block* deliberately picked up more than a hundred years after those events, in another part of the multiverse, and the Phyrexian storyline has not been substantially revisited since.

It's hard to predict what the future has in store for Magic, but the expansion released in April 2018 is *Dominaria*, referring to the multiverse nexus that has featured in numerous prior expansions. Blocks after *Dominaria* are slated for September 2018, January 2019, Spring 2019, September 2019, January 2020, and Spring 2020. These have code names "Spaghetti," "Meatballs," "Milk," "Archery," "Baseball," and "Cricket," respectively, according to Mark Rosewater, head designer for Magic.

In addition to these baseline expansions, Wizards of the Coast published several introductory sets that were intended for novices: *Portal* (June 1997), *Portal Second Age* (June 1998) and *Portal Three Kingdoms* (May 1999), as well as *Starter 1999* (July 1999) and *Starter 2000* (July 2000). All these sets were initially illegal in sanctioned tournaments until 2005, when they became viable in Legacy and Vintage tournaments.

Wizards has also, over the decades, printed several compilation or reprint sets, many of which were printed to commemorate events like big matches or anniversary sets. The Multiverse Gift Box, for example, was released in 1996 and contained booster packs from various sets, all printed in different languages. A long roster of Duel Decks was also released, each of which contain two preconstructed decks presenting often mythic dueling pairs. These often pit well-known, named Planeswalkers against each other, like in the *Garruk vs. Liliana* Deck set, or reflect major in-world conflicts, such as *Phyrexia vs. the Coalition*. Starting in 2008 Wizards also released limited bursts of reprinted foil cards in their From the Vault series and Premium Deck series, and in 2013 they began releasing reprint sets of older cards from *Magic*'s history in sets like *Modern Masters* (catering to Modern-rules tournaments) and *Eternal Masters* (which broadened scope, to also serve Vintage and Legacy tournaments).

Other smaller, more unique sets include the Masterpiece Series, which began with the *Kaladesh* block. Masterpiece Series cards have a unique expansion symbol, but are often special reprints of cards from the set in which they appear. Starting in 2009, Magic also began releasing special sets that focused on multiplayer play, like *Planechase*, *Archenemy*, *Conspiracy*, and *Commander*, the last of which was a special variant on classic *Magic* where decks include no repeated cards, and add a special, oversized "Commander" card that grants special abilities to its controlling player.

Perhaps most odd of all *Magic*'s sets are three satirical sets. Unlike most of *Magic*'s other sets, the "Un-sets" are all English-language-only (attributed to its heavy use of English wordplay), and began with *Unglued*, in 1998. The idea for a set of nominally unplayable cards came from all the cards that had ended up on the cutting-room floor from prior expansions. The set's themes, including chicken and dice-rolling, made it inappropriate for anything like serious gameplay, but that was the point. It wasn't exactly commercially successful, but it sparked a cult following, and two more similar sets were released: *Unhinged*, in 2004, and *Unstable*, in 2017. In part due to the oddity and unconventional, full-card artwork, the basic land cards in the Un-sets have seen surprisingly high valuation among collectors, with some *Unstable* basic lands selling for $2-$4 per card.

COMPETITIVE PLAY

It's hard to talk *Magic* collecting without focusing on the impact that tournament play has had on the game's collecting culture. While for some, card collecting is about completing sets or mining for the rarest, earliest printings, most collectors are focused on playability and deck construction, tracking down the rarest and

most powerful cards for use in casual play and in particular in *Magic* tournaments.

Owing largely to the sheer scope of the game and its long, prolific history, *Magic* tournaments have been divided into several formats. All formats fall into two categories, Limited and Constructed, which refer to the state of a player's deck before the tournament starts. Limited games include Sealed Deck games, common at prerelease events where players are given an equal number of packs or a preconstructed deck and make the most of what they have in play, and Draft games, where players are offered a set of booster packs, pulling cards from a shared pool to build the best deck they can.

Constructed tournaments refer to all other formats, in which players arrive with a deck they've constructed from their own collection. Constructed formats, therefore, focus on the legal pool of playable cards, rather than the source of those cards. Standard tournament format, the most common, allows cards from the current core set and the most recent two blocks (even if that block has not yet been fully released). The Block Constructed format has the smallest card pool of all tournament styles, using only the cards from a particular block and no others, while Vintage tournaments have the largest pool. In Vintage format, just about every white- or black-bordered card ever printed are fair game, though the format does have a list of banned cards (mostly cards from the Un-sets) and a list of restricted cards, cards that may only appear once in a deck instead of the standard four-copy maximum. The Legacy format is the next-largest pool, as it bans the cards on Vintage's restricted list, but deems playable most everything else since the Limited Edition Alpha printing.

One of the most popular formats, and especially common in *Magic*'s Pro Leagues, is the Modern format, which allows most cards after Eighth Edition, save for a ban list and some exclusions, like cards from multiplayer sets like Commander and Conspiracy.

The Vintage and Legacy formats in particular have kept the earlier printings alive, granting importance and new life to cards that would otherwise have eventually become obsolete and only the purview of the most expansive collectors. This works both ways, though, as the Modern tournaments led to reprintings, like the aforementioned *Modern Masters* set, essentially

making old cards new again. This satisfies some of the demand for the players' market, and simultaneously adds even more value to the rarest, earliest printings, while weakening the value of middle editions, a move that some collectors who are focused on value dislike.

Since 2000, Wizards of the Coast has been promoting numerous types of tournaments. Friday Night Magic (FNM), the game's most simple, novice-friendly tournament style, is meant to cater to the casual player, and usually uses the Standard Format. Friday Night Magic can be found hosted at local game shops every week the world over, and especially with Wizards of the Coast's promotional support, including special promo cards granted to winners, FNM has been one of the company's most popular game events they've ever run.

DOWN TO BRASS TACKS

With *Magic* being so expansive, starting a collection is an exercise in picking a niche. For most collectors joining the arena in modern *Magic* gaming, the draw of collecting is to focus on deck construction, but some who are looking for the completionist joy of a more classic collection will focus on collecting a copy of each card in a particular expansion or block. But with a game as large as *Magic*, it's important to pick a theme. Some collect by artist, or focus on collecting all versions of a specific card; some focus on a favorite mythical creature, like angels, dragons, or griffins, while others go for a particular in-world creature type, like *Mirrodin*'s Myrs, or civilizations, like Merfolk or Vampires.

But most often, collectors are focused on sheer playing power, and that can mean cards racking up into the hundreds of dollars.

Tarmagoyf, a famously valuable powerhouse of a card that, due to a minor fluke of card-development where it was rewritten from memory by a designer, is a potentially *very* powerful Creature card that's almost comically inexpensive to summon to the field. Foil *Tarmagoyf*s especially can run for over $100, but the market has also seen one particularly infamous copy in 2015, a foil card that was opened in a Modern Masters pro tournament draft, and thus also bore the tournament's special stamp. After the tournament, that card sold at auction for $15,000, with half the proceeds being donated to charity by the player who drafted it.

Another big contender, a Land card from the 1994 *Legends* expansion called *The Tabernacle at Pendrell Vale*, stands to cripple opponents by charging an added cost to keep their creatures on the board. Due in part to its singular printing and its power, it regularly sees listing prices over $1,400.

Promo cards also top some of the cards valuation lists, with cards like a special print of *Force of Will*. The card originally appeared in the 1996 Alliances expansion, which sees listings ranging from $50 to $75, but in 2014 it also saw a reprint with new art that was exclusively granted to judges for *Magic* tournaments. This judge-only promo version can run over $300.

Due to the prevalence of Wizards of the Coast's tournament-friendly reprints, the real money is in early-release cards, with cards from the Limited Edition Alpha and Beta printings often selling for thousands of dollars, especially those of the "Power Nine." These extremely valuable and extremely powerful Alpha-print cards include five cards colloquially referred to as "The Moxen," five artifact cards that, when tapped, even in the middle of an opponent's turn, grant mana of the corresponding color (*Mox Emerald* for Green, *Mox Pearl* for White, *Mox Ruby* for Red, *Mox Jet* for Black, and *Mox Sapphire* for Blue). The Moxen regularly run $2,300 to $3,600, depending on the color, with *Mox Sapphire* as the most valuable, clocking in at $6,300.

The remaining four of the Power Nine include *Timetwister*, which causes both players to shuffle all their cards together and basically reset the game, running about $1,600; *Time Walk*, which grants an extra turn and can run the average collector $3,000; and *Ancestral Recall*, which lets the player draw three extra cards, about $6,500.

But if your goal is to round out a collection of the Power Nine, your wallet may not thank you. The last entry in the list is the infamous *Black Lotus* card, which can be played for free and then tapped and discarded, even on another player's turn, to gain three mana of any one color. It was printed only in the first three sets, and is generally considered the rarest non-promotional card ever printed, aside from misprints. The average listing even for an Unlimited Edition version is over $6,000, with the Beta printing breaking $8,000. As recently as 2017, it's almost impossible to find a listing for an original Alpha copy for less than a whopping $13,500.

MAGIC'S STAYING POWER

Magic's rampant commercial success has made it the cornerstone of the collectible card game sphere, and Wizards of the Coast has, perhaps wisely, sought to leverage that success into other sectors. Chief among these are licensed novels and comic books exploring the game's lore, delving into the worlds detailed in various expansions and exploring the stories of named characters, especially Planeswalkers like

Jace Beleren and Chandra Nalaar. Most of the comics have been published by IDW Publishing and ARMADA, an imprint of Acclaim Comics, with additional entries published by Dark Horse and Gotta Comics. In addition to these, more than 60 novels have been published exploring the storylines featured in various expansion blocks. Some of these novels were published by Harper Prism, while most were published directly by Wizards of the Coast, alongside art guides, player guides, and even a couple graphic novels.

In 2015, Wizards of the Coast partnered with Hasbro to produce *Magic the Gathering: Arena of the Planeswalkers*, a tactical board game evoking aspects of the card game as it pits Planeswalkers against each other on a customizable board. As of 2016 the game has had two expansions: one themed from content in the *Battle for Zendikar* block, and one for *Shadows over Innistrad*.

Wizards of the Coast has also made or licensed a number of video games for *Magic*, including their own *Magic: the Gathering Online*, the digital version of the game that most closely mirrors paper-card tabletop play. Other licensed products include MicroProse's *Magic: the Gathering*, Acclaim's unsuccessful *Magic: the Gathering: Battlemage*, and Stainless Games' *Magic: the Gathering – Duels of the Planeswalkers*, which started out on Xbox 360 and was later ported to PC and PS3, and which had yearly updates until 2015. Hiberium and D3 Publisher licensed *Magic* for the mobile game *Magic: the Gathering – Puzzle Quest*, and Cryptic Studios and Perfect World Entertainment have announced plans to create a *Magic* MMORPG for PC and consoles.

And then in the cinematic sphere, after Universal Studios dropped it from their schedule, in 2014 20th Century Fox acquired rights to produce a Magic film. A documentary about life on the *Magic* Pro Tour called *Enter the Battlefield* was released in 2016.

No matter how you look at it, *Magic* is an absolute titan of the gaming world. It's dominated the collectible card game industry since 1993, it changed the face of card gaming in general, and it doesn't hurt that the game has about as much pull in foreign markets as domestic, with cards printed in 10 languages besides English. Even occasional dissent among fans and players over Wizards of the Coast's tournament banned card lists and subsequent reprints devaluing particular cards can't stop it. And with new and exciting things ahead in 2018, the year of *Magic*'s 25th anniversary, the game is a juggernaut, and not looking like it'll slow down any time soon.

KEY TO THE CARDS

The name of the card.

The card's Mana Cost. This is how much Mana needs to be generated in order to summon this card into battle. In this case it's one red Mana, plus two generic Mana - generic Mana can be Mana of any color.

The Type Line, which tells what kind of card you have. There are six basic types - creatures, lands, artifacts, instants, enchantments, and sorceries. As this is a creature card, it further describes the creature itself. Many decks are built around specific kinds of creatures, so it's important to keep that in mind.

The card's Expansion Symbol. Each set has its own corresponding symbol to denote cards as being from a specific release. This card came from 2013's Theros set.

The main text in the box below the image is the card's effect. In this case, 'Haste' grants this card a boost when it's first played. Cards (usually creatures) that do not have an effect are usually called 'vanilla' cards.

The italicized text on a card is simply its flavor text, which tells the player a little bit about the lore of the card itself.

Power/Toughness. This is the card's main stats. The left number is Power, which is how much damage this card can deal in combat, while the right is Toughness, or how much damage it can sustain before being knocked out of the battlefield.

The artist information. This lets you know who created the artwork for the card itself.

The collector's number. This denotes what number card this is in its respective set.

Minotaur Skullcleaver

2 🔴

Creature — Minotaur Berserker

Haste
When Minotaur Skullcleaver enters the battlefield, it gets +2/+0 until end of turn.

"Their only dreams are of full stomachs."
—Kleon the Iron-Booted

Phill Simmer

2/2

Pharika's Cure

🔴🔴

Instant

Pharika's Cure deals 2 damage to target creature and you gain 2 life.

"The venom cleanses the sickness from your body, but it will not be pleasant, and you may not survive. Pharika's blessings are fickle."
—Solon, acolyte of Pharika

—Igor Kieryluk

Trained Armodon

1 🟢🟢

Creature — Elephant

Armodons are trained to step on things. Enemy things.

—Gary Leach

3/3

Spearpoint Oread

2 🔴

Enchantment Creature — Nymph

Bestow 5 🔴 *(If you cast this card for its bestow cost, it's an Aura spell with enchant creature. It becomes a creature again if it's not attached to a creature.)*

First strike
Enchanted creature gets +2/+2 and has first strike.

—Todd Lockwood

2/2

MAGIC The Gallery

Magic: The Gathering has been the go-to collectible card game for more than two and a half decades now. Accordingly, there are a number of cards that are highly valuable and significantly collectible, due to their rarity or simply their power in the game itself. Here, you can find a number of highlights from *MTG* along with pricing info on various printings of the card. Prices shown reflect a range representative of online auction sales as of this book's publication and are meant to represent an aggregated average. Your final buying or selling price will vary.

ANCESTRAL RECALL
ALPHA: $4,000-$6,000
BETA: $2,000-$3,000
UNLIMITED: $1,200-$3,000

BLACK LOTUS
ALPHA: $10,000-$20,000
BETA: $10,000-$15,000
UNLIMITED: $4,000-$9,000

BIRDS OF PARADISE
ALPHA: $900-$1,200
BETA: $600-$800
UNLIMITED: $60-$150

CHAOS ORB
ALPHA: $1,000-$2,000
BETA: $1000-$2,500
UNLIMITED: $300-$600

DEMONIC TUTOR
ALPHA: $300-$400
BETA: $250-$350
JUDGE GIFT: $300-$350

FORCEFIELD
ALPHA: $2,000-$4,000
BETA: $500-$1,500
UNLIMITED: $150-$300

GAUNTLET OF MIGHT
ALPHA: $700-$1,000
BETA: $400-$650
UNLIMITED: $250-$350

GOBLIN KING
ALPHA: $250-$800
BETA: $125-$300
UNLIMITED: $15-$30

HOWLING MINE
ALPHA: $300-600
BETA: $150-$250
7TH EDITION FOIL: $150-$300

ILLUSIONARY MASK
ALPHA: $200-$400
BETA: $200-$350
UNLIMITED: $75-$150

ISLAND SANCTUARY
ALPHA: $75-$200
BETA: $50-$100
UNLIMITED: $15-$30

LICH
ALPHA: $300-$500
BETA: $150-$350
UNLIMITED: $50-$100

LIGHTNING BOLT
ALPHA: $150-$300
BETA: $75-$100
JUDGE GIFT: $200-$300

LORD OF ATLANTIS
ALPHA: $300-$500
BETA: $250-$450
7TH EDITION FOIL: $50-$100

LORD OF THE PIT
ALPHA: $250-$500
BETA: $125-$225
UNLIMITED: $10-$15

MAHAMOTI DJINN
ALPHA: $400-$700
BETA: $100-$200
UNLIMITED: $10-$15

MIND TWIST
ALPHA: $400-$600
BETA: $500-$750
UNLIMITED: $35-$50

MOX EMERALD
ALPHA: $2,000-$4,000
BETA: $2,000-$3,500
UNLIMITED: $1,000-$2,000

MOX JET
ALPHA: $3,000-$5,000
BETA: $2,000-$4,000
UNLIMITED: $1,000-$2,000

MOX PEARL
ALPHA: $2,000-$5,000
BETA: $1,000-$3,000
UNLIMITED: $1,000-$2,000

MOX RUBY
ALPHA: $2,500-$5,000
BETA: $1,500-$4,000
UNLIMITED: $1,000-$2,000

MOX SAPPHIRE
ALPHA: $3,500-$7,000
BETA: $3,000-$6,000
UNLIMITED: $1,500-$3,000

NIGHTMARE
ALPHA: $200-$400
BETA: $150-$250
UNLIMITED: $10-$20

PERSONAL INCARNATION
ALPHA: $150-$400
BETA: $50-$100
UNLIMITED: $5-$15

ROYAL ASSASSIN
ALPHA: $350-$500
BETA: $100-$200
UNLIMITED: $25-$75

SAVANNAH
ALPHA: $1,000-$2,000
BETA: $800-$1,500
REVISED: $80-$125

SCRUBLAND
ALPHA: $1,200-$2,000
BETA: $700-$1,200
UNLIMITED: $150-$250

TIME VAULT
ALPHA: $1,500-$3,500
BETA: $850-$1,300
UNLIMITED: $500-$750

TIME WALK
ALPHA: $2,500-$4,000
BETA: $1,500-$3,000
UNLIMITED: $1,000-$1,800

TIMETWISTER
ALPHA: $1,500-$3,000
BETA: $1,300-$2,500
UNLIMITED: $1,000-$2,000

TROPICAL ISLAND
ALPHA: $1,500-$3,500
BETA: $1,300-$2,800
UNLIMITED: $300-$500

TUNDRA
ALPHA: $2,000-$3,000
BETA: $1,500-$2,500
UNLIMITED: $200-$500

WHEEL OF FORTUNE
ALPHA: $2,000-$3,000
BETA: $800-$1,200
UNLIMITED: $100-$200

FAN TO PRO

GAVIN VERHEY

While Magic: The Gathering *has established itself as the go-to card game around the world, few of its many millions of players have ever made the leap from player to professional. Gavin Verhey is one of those lucky few, who went from a childhood fan to a well-known professional player and is now working full-time in product design for Wizards of the Coast. We spoke with Gavin about his history with* Magic, *the impact the game has had on the industry in the last 25 years, and what's next for this legendary card game.*

Overstreet: First, tell us a little bit about yourself!

Gavin Verhey (GV): My name is Gavin Verhey and I'm a Senior Game Design and Product Architect in *Magic* Research and Development at Wizards of the Coast. What all those long words and proper nouns basically boils down to is this: I design the abilities of new *Magic* cards, and help decide what kind of sets we make and

release each year! It's absolutely fantastic getting to work on a game with such history behind it and such a passionate group of players. *Magic* has been such a huge part of my life in every way possible – and now it's a pleasure helping to create those memories for a whole new generation.

If you're not familiar with *Magic*, it's a strategy game where each player brings a deck of cards to the table – but you get to choose what cards go into the deck. You both start at 20 life points, and use your cards to try and get the other player to 0 before they do the same to you. We release new sets of cards all the time, so strategies and decks are always evolving. You really never have the same game twice!

In addition to *Magic* and games, in my personal life I really enjoy writing, sampling new kinds of food, and traveling the world. A major life goal is to visit every single country – I'm at nearly 80 countries so far, which for age 27, I'd say isn't too shabby!

Overstreet: *Magic* has obviously been around for quite some time now – 25 years! What was it about the game that drew your attention in the first place?

GV: I first picked up *Magic* when I was just 10 years old, back in January 2001! I was interested in other games at the time, and the woman behind the store counter recommended *Magic* to my mom. I brought it home, read through the rules, began playing with my brother… And instantly fell in love.

One of *Magic*'s greatest strengths – and one of the things we constantly have to juggle working on the game now – is that it's not really just one game: it's a hundred. You can play casually on your kitchen table. You can play in big tournaments with thousands upon thousands of dollars on the line. You can play in ways with decks you bring, of all sorts. You can play a form of *Magic* called "booster draft," where you open the cards you're going to use right there. You can simply collect cards. You can be an admirer of the art of the game. You can follow the storyline shown on the cards. This is a huge part of *Magic*'s success. It is the game you want it to be.

And when you're brand new – let alone 10 years old – and playing your first few games, a lot of this potential hits you right away, and in a ton of different ways. It was this potential which completely enraptured me with the game and quickly caused me to have *Magic* cards strewn all over my bedroom carpet (sorry about that, mom): there was just so much to learn about and discover, and so many ways to do it in. The game truly felt like an endless expanse to uncover.

Overstreet: At what point did you make the decision to go from a casual player to something more serious?

GV: I know this moment exactly. I will never forget it.

When I was 10 years old, I started playing *Magic*. So, naturally, by the time I was 11, I had made up my mind: I was going to get a job making *Magic* cards.

Trying to design *Magic* cards became my focus. I would invite friends over to my house, and we would make *Magic* sets together and play with them. I had my mom buy me books on game design so I

could devour them. At 11!

Fortunately for me, I lived in Seattle at the time, and, since Wizards was based in Renton, Washington, just outside of Seattle, occasionally Wizards employees would come and visit our events. It was the special early prerelease event for the Fall 2001 set Odyssey, and Randy Buehler, the Vice President of *Magic* R&D at the time, was there playing *Magic* against all-comers. So, I went up to him, introduced myself, and said one very simple, but life changing question: "I want to come work for you making *Magic* cards. How can I do it?"

Randy looked at me very seriously, despite me maybe measuring up to the height of his chest at best. He nodded.

"Alright. If you want to come work for us, you're going to need two things," he began. "The first thing you'll need is a college degree."

And my heart just sunk.

I was 11! College? That was forever away! How long was it going to take to get one of those?

"The second thing, though, is you need to be someone we recognize from *Magic*. We hire mostly from people we know are good at *Magic*, like Pro Players."

Well, I didn't know about this whole "college degree" thing… But professional *Magic*? How hard could that possibly be, anyway?

And that was the moment I decided: I was going to need to go Pro. I dedicated a ton of effort toward doing just that.

I'll also note, as a fun aside, that I started college at 16 through an early entrance program in part so that I could graduate early, still following Randy's exact advice. I started playing on the Pro Tour around the same time. Four years later, I graduated college just as I turned 20 – and then I started at Wizards a year later, at 21. I guess his words of wisdom really were quite accurate!

Overstreet: Can you describe the lifestyle of a professional *Magic: The Gathering* player?

GV: There really is nothing else like it – in every way possible.

You get to travel the country and world. *Magic* is really played all over (we had 73 countries represented at our last World *Magic* Cup in 2017, for example), and you get to meet and make friends… Everywhere. And despite going to all of these places, you begin to see similar faces. You know, "Oh hey, there's that guy from Brazil I met in Berlin, and there's that lady from London who I've seen at the past few events, and hmm, I wonder what new deck the Japanese friends I have brought into the tournament…"

It really is this crazy universal language. I can't speak much Japanese, or Portuguese, or Swedish, but we all understand the language of a *Magic* game. We all fly under the flag of *Magic*.

On top of the amazing friends you make along the way and places you get to see, a *Magic* tournament is a pulse-pounding competition for the competitors. In an event like a Pro Tour, one of our largest events which happens several times a year, you'll play 16 best-of-three matches against individual opponents over the course of two days, all competing for a total prize pool of $250,000. (As of this writing.) And in addition to the prize money, there are invitations to future events and status in a "Pro Players Club" – a club which awards you everything from free airfare at events to automatic appearance fees just for showing up – on the line. How you do in a single match could make or break your entire tournament, so it really can be intense as a player. Focus and careful play are paramount.

And yet, it's some of the most alive I've ever felt.

Of course, it is hard and draining, too. There is a lot of preparatory work. You will spend long hours playtesting with somebody else to try and figure out which deck is most strong, playing the same decks over and over again with tiny changes. You might fly across the country or world for an event and not do well and end up with little to show for it. And on top of all of this, you have to manage everything else going on in your life as well – even when some weeks you feel compelled to dedicate 80+ hours to working on *Magic*.

For most of my professional *Magic* career, I was a student. And so I would go to class Monday through Thursday, fly off to a tournament somewhere in the world on Thursday night, play all weekend, fly back early Monday morning and do my homework on the plane, then get into class. While it felt like being some kind of superhero, *Magic* did end up taking up most of my weekends. And that was something I had to be okay with to be a professional player.

I will note that it's becoming easier and easier to break into the professional scene in other ways too. With the addition of streaming matches online, writing and making videos about the game, mentoring, and simply better ways to share information online, there are tons of ways to showcase yourself and learn quickly.

Overstreet: How were you able to go from a fan, a player of the game, to working for Wizards?

GV: As Randy told me all those years ago, it really is important you can catch Wizards' eye to come work on designing the cards. And really, I did just that.

Playing professionally was a great start. But in addition to that, I also was a weekly columnist on StarCityGames.com, one of the most-read *Magic* websites, and that was very important: it gave me a platform to talk about the game and show that I could think and discuss both the strategy and design on a weekly basis. And finally, I created a new format – a new way to play *Magic* around the world – before I was hired there. This format garnered a lot of attention – and with me at the center, it definitely helped catch the eye of the department. Between all of those things, I was contacted, interviewed, took a test, and, ultimately, hired on.

I will note that if you want to work for Wizards, it's a lot easier than it may sound. Sure, this was my route into R&D – but there are almost always jobs up on our website. I encourage you to go and take a look at what's there. Everybody inside Wizards can have a chance to come down, playtest *Magic*, and give feedback, so really, getting your foot in the door is a great step toward getting to do design work.

Overstreet: What has your experience at Wizards been like so far?

GV: Absolutely phenomenal. And I'm sure there are a number of people who may be thinking, "Well, of course he's going to say that, he works for them" – but I truly, truly mean it.

The people who work at Wizards are some of the most intelligent, passionate, and fun to talk with people I know. They're more than coworkers: they're friends. We spend time with each other outside of work. We collaborate in ways that I don't think many workplaces can. And we have such a wild diversity of talent.

For example: I studied Creative Writing – poetry and fiction, and all that. Working right next to me is someone who studied Communications and used to work in Hollywood, on the other side is someone with a Masters in Marine Biology, and on the other side of him is someone with three Ph.D.'s in Computer Science, Math, and Philosophy. Across us, we span a very wide range of ages. It's a really amazing conflux of viewpoints, experience, and background – who have all united to bring our unique experiences to making this game. And that's incredible.

There's always a story to tell or something to think about. I really do love it.

Also, oh yeah – we get to play and talk about games all day. Not much to complain about there, either!

Overstreet: What are some of the biggest challenges when it comes to developing new sets and expansions?

GV: *Magic* is in its 25th year now, which is truly astounding. However, that also makes it that much harder: how do you design new content for a game that's 25 years old? To make matters more difficult, remember how earlier I said one of *Magic*'s strengths is that it's 100 different games in one? Well, you also have to make sure you design content for everybody – even when they have different interests and they all started the game at entirely different points. How can you create a set for both the 25-year veteran and the brand new player?

We've done a lot of work on this. And ultimately, we've pulled a few different tricks.

For one, in our largest sets each year we really do try and make sure sets have something for everybody – or at least

many people. When we were working on *Dominaria*, the expansion releasing in April 2018, for example, we made sure to include cards that appeal to several different kinds of players and playstyles; cards that could appeal to both individual play formats and history.

Additionally, we've made sure to create several different products for different players. Sure, you can buy booster packs of *Dominaria* if you want an assortment of brand new cards – or if you're brand new you could buy a *Dominaria* Planeswalker Deck, a product aimed at teaching new players the ropes, instead. The experienced player is probably going to gloss over that product, but it's crucial for the new player. Creating different products for different people is part of the recent secret to *Magic*'s success.

Before I came to Wizards, something I was worried about – and something I think many players have been worried about at various points – is: "Will *Magic* run out of ideas soon?" And after being here for nearly seven years, I have an answer: and it's a resounding no. The amount of ideas and ingenuity I've seen in this building – solely the ones I have seen – could fill decades. My job is to make sure *Magic* lasts forever. And I am confident that when I someday get married and have kids, when I retire, even when I die and am long buried, *Magic* will have plenty of ammo to keep existing. It's truly amazing!

Overstreet: What would you describe as the most rewarding aspect of working on a game like *Magic*?
GV: When I started at Wizards years ago, I was overjoyed. I had a job working on something I really cared about, with people that were wonderful to work with. It was instantly wonderful.

But, I'm an ambitious person. I care a lot about the state of the world. And in the back of my mind, a thought lingered: I was working on a game. I was spending my time and energy, day to day, working on a card game. Shouldn't I be out there causing the world to be a better place?

And then, maybe a year in, the first Make-A-Wish kid came by. His final wish was to spend time with us.

Us. *Magic* R&D. The makers of a game.

And then, as my designs started getting out there in the world, I started receiving letters every now and again. About how *Magic* pulled someone through a dark time in their life. About how soldiers stationed thousands of miles away from home bonded over *Magic*. About how entire communities, lifetime friendships, and even marriages have been created through *Magic*.

And I slowly began to realize: entertainment is important. *Magic* isn't "just a game" – it's a vehicle for happiness and friendship and inspiration for millions of people around the world.

I keep that in mind as I work. It, above the many, many wonderful perks of working at Wizards, is what gets me most excited about working on our game. We really do change lives – and I don't know what could possibly be more rewarding than that.

Overstreet: Do you happen to collect *Magic* cards or any other trading cards (or even other tabletop games)?
GV: My *Magic* collection now spans two entire closets, most of a spare bedroom, an entire garage, and… many boxes in storage that I left at my mom's house. (Once again: sorry, Mom.) I am pretty sure I will continue to find *Magic* cards in random crevices in my house for the rest of my life.

Because you get to play with your cards, *Magic* for me is really a collection of memories. I'll go back through and find old decks, or even individual cards, I haven't touched in years and be reminded of a time, or a place, or an event where I got them. Different sets occupy different times in my life. A trip through any given storage box of cards can lead to hours of nostalgia.

On top of *Magic* cards, the one other thing I really intentionally collect is magnets. I try to get a magnet from each country, or at least region, I go to, as a reminder of where I've been whenever I go to the fridge. Not quite cards, but a collectable nonetheless!

Overstreet: What is it about *Magic* and similar games that you think drives the collector's market?
GV: Consider this: With just the *Magic* cards that exist today, there are many, many, many more possible *Magic* decks than atoms in the known universe. And yet, as *Magic* players, we want to try as many of them as possible!

And so for *Magic*, it really is all about those different kinds of play; how *Magic* is really so many different games in one. Different people want different cards – but they all have somebody who wants them. Players trade for cards for all kinds of reasons, from because a card shows off a key moment in the story, to because it's a card they need for their tournament deck. It's that personal need and excitement to try a card out that really tends to get

people excited. And that's really the, well… "*Magic*" of it.

Overstreet: What kind of resources are out there for newbies to Magic?
GV: If you're brand new to *Magic* and want to check it out, I really recommend heading into your local game or hobby store. We currently send stores these decks that teach you the basics called Welcome Decks, which are totally free and a great place to get started. They can also help direct you to whatever the best learning decks are at the moment. If you're reading this shortly after the guide releases, I'd recommend checking out Core 2019 which is a set designed in part to help people get into *Magic*. If you're reading this later on, look for another Core Set of the appropriate year – or ask your local game store.

Additionally, there's a wealth of information online too. You can check out Magicthegathering.com, which should point you in the right direction as well.

Overstreet: Where can people go to keep up with what you (or WotC in general) are working on?
GV: Dailymtg.com, a part of Magicthegathering.com, is where you can find daily updates on what is new and coming to the world of *Magic*! Aside from that, if you have any questions, feel free to reach out to me! You can find me on Twitter @ GavinVerhey, or send me an e-mail at BeyondBasicsMagic@Gmail.com.

Thank you very much! It's been a pleasure talking with you. And I invite anybody reading to come check *Magic* out – it's a great time to start!

The *Pokémon* series began in February 1996, when the original Game Boy titles, *Pokémon Red* and *Pokémon Green*, released in Japan. In these games, players take on the role of a Pokémon trainer, collecting the creatures and battling them en route to becoming the Champion of the Pokémon League. In October of that year, the basic concept was translated to tabletops for the first time through the Pokémon Trading Card Game.

The PTCG first arrived in October 1996 in Japan, where it was originally published by Media Factory; it arrived in the U.S. at the start of 1999, where the publishing was at first handled by Wizards of the Coast. By 2013, worldwide publication of the game was being taken care of in-house by The Pokémon Company.

PLAYING THE GAME

Much like the video games, the PTCG put its players in the role of Pokémon Trainers, who face off against each other in one-on-one matches. Each player has a deck consisting of 60 cards; the cards in the deck are divided between Pokémon, Trainer and Energy cards. Pokémon themselves are the creatures that each Trainer controls, Trainer cards can be played to have a variety of different effects during each player's turn (such as drawing additional cards, discarding them, healing Pokémon, or influencing the opponent), and Energy cards are to be attached to Pokémon cards in order to meet the requirements for attacks. Pokémon cards are further divided into Basic Pokémon (which can be put as an active or benched creature with no restrictions), and Stage 1 or 2 evolutions. Stage 1 cards evolve from Basic cards, and Stage 2 from Stage 1 cards; accordingly, the appropriate prerequisite must already be on the playing field to place a Stage 1 or 2 evolution.

To begin a game, each player first sets six cards face down as Prizes. Each player then draws seven cards, and places one basic Pokémon face-down as their active creature. If a player does not have any basic Pokémon in their starting hand, they must show their opponent their hand, reshuffle their deck, and redraw. After placing their active Pokémon, players may place up to five more basic Pokémon on their bench, also face down. A coin toss determines who goes first.

Each Pokémon has a set amount of hit point (HP). Players take turns, which end with one active Pokémon attacking the other or by the player ending their turn voluntarily without attacking. On each turn, players draw one card from the top of their deck. They are permitted to attach one Energy card to either their active Pokémon or one on the Bench, play Trainer cards and execute those effects, and then attack.

Each attack does a set amount of damage, which is tracked by Damage Counters. Once a Pokémon has taken damage equal to its HP, it is knocked out and placed in the discard pile (alongside any Energy or other cards that were attached to it), and the Trainer who knocked out their opponent's Pokémon takes one of their Prizes and adds that card to their hand. The person who's Pokémon was knocked out must choose a new active Pokémon from

the bench. Certain attacks can inflict status ailments, such as paralysis, poison, sleep, or confusion.

Besides attaching energy and attacking, other actions that can be taken during a turn include: evolving Pokémon (so long as the evolution is not taking place on the same turn that the prerequisite Pokémon was placed), using Trainer cards, using any abilities or Pokémon Powers that Pokémon on the field may have, and retreating an active Pokémon to the bench to swap for a new active Pokémon. Besides beginning the turn with a card draw and ending it with an attack or voluntarily without an attack, actions may be taken in any desired order.

There are three ways to win a match. The first and generally most common way to win is when one player has knocked out enough of their opponent's Pokémon in order for them to draw all six of their prizes. The second win condition is when one person knocks out their opponent's active Pokémon, and the trainer is unable to place a new active Pokémon from the bench; this ends the match immediately regardless of how many prizes are left. The third win condition occurs when one player runs out of deck cards and cannot draw from their deck at the start of their turn, leading their opponent to immediately be declared the winner – this is commonly called simply "decking" and is the least-common occurrence of the three.

The PTCG is a popular form of competitive card gaming, and the Pokémon Company International runs Play! Pokémon (formerly known as Pokémon Organized Play). There are tournaments and regulated League play held throughout the year, culminating with the Pokémon World Championships, typically held in August. Players are divided between Junior, Senior and Masters divisions.

COLLECTING BY SETS

The slogan for the *Pokémon* franchise at large has long been "Gotta Catch 'Em All" – so the idea that the PTCG itself would be huge for collectors was ingrained from the start. There are as many ways to collect as there are Pokémon out there, but perhaps the most straightforward way is simply collecting by set.

As of this book's publication, there have been 75 different card sets released in English, and 69 in Japanese. This, of course, means that there are that many different sets available to collect. Complete sets of *Pokémon* cards – like any other type of cards – are generally pretty desirable, with older sets of particular interest to most old-school fans.

The original English set, simply called *Base Set*, arrived on January 9, 1999 and contained 102 different cards. As the first set, it was fairly well-rounded, not focusing at all on a particular type of Pokémon like later sets would tend to do. Four different "theme decks" were produced, as well as a two-player starter set. Notably, the first and second printings of this set had some subtly differences from the "unlimited" third issuing, such as somewhat brighter colors, a lack of shadow around the Pokémon images, and the year 1999

printed twice in the copyright notice at the bottom of the card. "Shadowless" Pokémon cards are generally considered more desirable, as there were far less of them printed.

The first expansion set was the *Jungle* set in June 1999, followed quickly by the *Fossil* set that October. Both of these sets were fairly small – introducing 64 and 62 cards, respectively – but have some notable attributes. *Jungle* was the first set to have both holographic and non-holo editions of rare cards (which, in effect, made those holographic editions that much more desirable). Of those holo cards, some were mistakenly printed without the correct symbol denoting it as a Jungle set card; these error cards demand a higher price than their correctly-printed counterparts.

These original three sets were then compiled into *Base Set 2,* which contained 130 reprinted cards; Wizards of the Coast would continue the trend of these rereleases/compilation sets throughout the time they held the license to publish the PTCG.

Expansions from *Base Set 2* included *Team Rocket* (which focused on the villainous team from the franchise and introduced the "Dark Pokémon" that had been corrupted), *Gym Heroes* (focusing on the first four Generation One gym leaders and introducing "Owner's Pokémon" for the first time), and *Gym Challenge* (focusing on the latter four gym leaders from the first generation).

As the video game franchise would continue to add new regions and new Pokémon with each new generation of the games, so accordingly would the card game.

Second generation sets arrived starting with *Neo Genesis*, in October of 2000. This was the set to introduce the two new types,

Dark and Steel, as well as Baby Pokémon. It was followed by *Neo Discovery* in June 2001, *Neo Revelation* in October 2001 (which introduced Shining Pokémon), and *Neo Destiny* in February 2002. Additionally, a small promotional set, the *Southern Islands* collection, was also released; containing only 18 cards, the set came in a special box and the cards would form a larger illustration when put together correctly.

The second compilation set, the *Legendary Collection*, released in May 2002. It consisted exclusively of reprints from the *Base, Jungle, Fossil*, and *Team Rocket* sets.

Additionally, three sets were produced that made use of the Game Boy Advance peripheral, the e-Reader. Players could scan their cards with the e-Reader to produce various effects on the Game Boy Advance. These sets included the *Expedition Base Set* in September 2002 (the largest set ever produced at 165 cards), *Aquapolis* in January 2003, and *Skyridge* in May 2003. *Skyridge* would be the last set published by Wizards of the Coast, as the Pokémon Company took over publication in July of that year.

The third generation kicked off in July 2003 with the first of the EX Sets (derived from the presence of Pokémon-ex in each set): *EX Ruby and Sapphire* in July 2003, *EX Sandstorm* in September 2003, *EX Dragon* in November 2003, *EX Team Magma V.S. Team Aqua* in March 2004, *EX Hidden Legends* in June 2004, *EX Fire Red and Leaf Green* in September 2004, *EX Team Rocket Returns* in November 2004, *EX Deoxys* in February 2005, *EX*

Emerald in May 2005, *EX Unseen Forces* in August 2005, *EX Delta Species* in October 2005, *EX Legend Maker* in February 2006, *EX Holon Phantoms* in May 2006, *EX Crystal Guardians* in July 2006, *EX Dragon Frontiers* in November 2006, and *EX Power Keepers* in February 2007.

Fourth generation sets began in 2007. The first was the *Diamond and Pearl Base Set* in May 2007, followed by *Mysterious Treasures* in August 2007, *Secret Wonders* in November 2007, *Great Encounters* in February 2008, *Majestic Dawn* in May 2008, *Legends Awakened* in August 2008, *Platinum Base Set* in February 2009, *Rising Rivals* in May 2009, *Supreme Victors* in August 2009, *Arceus* in November 2009, *HeartGold/SoulSilver Base Set* in February 2010, *Unleashed* in May 2010, *Undaunted* in August 2010, and *Triumphant* in November 2010. A compilation set, *Call of Legends*, released in February 2011, essentially as a filler set as the time between the releases of the fourth and fifth generations of games was longer than normal.

The fifth generation began with *Black and White – Base Set* in April 2011, followed by *Emerging Powers* in August 2011, *Noble Victories* in November 2011, *Next Destinies* in February 2012, *Dark Explorers* in May 2012, *Dragons Exalted* in August 2012, *Boundaries Crossed* in November 2012, *Plasma Storm* in February 2013, *Plasma Freeze* in May 2013, *Plasma Burst* in August 2013, and *Legendary Treasures* in November 2013.

The *XY* generation was the sixth generation of PTCG sets, and began in February

2014 with the *XY Base Set*. It was followed by *Flashfire* in May 2014, *Furious Fists* in August 2014, *Phantom Forces* in November 2014, *Primal Clash* in February 2015, *Roaring Skies* in May 2015, *Ancient Origins* in August 2015, *BREAKthrough* in November 2015, *BREAKpoint* in February 2016, *Fates Collide* in May 2016, and *Steam Siege* in August 2016.

Generations released in February 2016 to commemorate the 20th anniversary of the *Pokémon* franchise at large, and was not considered part of the *XY* family, instead being considered as a special/extra expansion. It focused on reprints from early sets, such as *Base Set, Jungle,* and *Fossil.* Of note was that *Generations* booster packs couldn't be purchased individually and were only included as pack-ins with other 20th Anniversary merchandise.

The sixth generation came to a close with *Evolutions* in November 2016, which notably featured updated reprints of original *Base Set* cards, keeping the original artwork and style of those cards while rebalancing them to current gameplay standards. *Evolutions*, due to its reprinting of original cards, accordingly focused on Generation One Pokémon; the set was also made to commemorate the 20th anniversary of the franchise.

The *Sun and Moon* set started the seventh generation when it arrived in February 2017. Its expansions have included *Guardians Rising* in May 2017, *Burning Shadows* in August 2017, *Shining Legends* in October 2017, and *Crimson Invasion* in November 2017.

Outside of the main, mass-produced sets, there have also been a number of smaller promotional sets released over the years. These have included promotional cards released in conjunction with one of the *Pokémon* films, as well as a number of promotional sets released as part of League play events. Promotional cards typically have a black star with the word "PROMO" on it in lieu of the traditional expansion symbol to differentiate them.

One last "set" of note worth discussing is the Pokémon Demo Game Pack, which was a limited production run distributed in December 1998. It contained 24 *Base Set* cards (all of which were shadowless) and an instruction manual for the game. These were distributed to select retailers around the country, at card shows, and at the 1999 Electronic Entertainment Expo. As the very first introduction of the game to the U.S. market, it's accordingly desirable – especially in its original packaging. As of 2018 there's just 11 of these sets in the PSA Population, and it's estimated that there's just about 100 or so of them left still in the packaging. Accordingly, these sets regularly fetch at least a few hundred dollars in online auctions.

INDIVIDUAL CARDS

In terms of individual card rarity, there are symbols printed in the bottom right-hand corner of each card that denotes how common or uncommon they are within each set. Cards with a circle are common cards, while ones with a diamond symbol are uncommon, and ones with a star symbol are denoted as rare cards. Most common and uncommon cards aren't going to be worth more than a few cents each, and even most rare cards may only fetch a couple of bucks. But there's definitely a few standouts over the two decades' worth of history with this game.

As with many other types of card collecting, there's a clear "Holy Grail" card for the PTCG – "Pokémon Illustrator." The card is more commonly colloquially known as "Pikachu Illustrator" in reference to the image of the series mascot in the illustration on the card. Pokémon Illustrator was exclusive to Japan and was only ever distributed as an award for illustration contests held by *CoroCoro Comic* magazine between 1997 and 1998.

The contest invited fans to draw their favorite Pokémon and submit the artwork, with the best drawings being awarded various prizes. These included 20 copies of a card featuring their illustration, as well as one copy of Pokémon Illustrator. With only three of these contests ever being held, it means that only a handful of the Illustrator cards were ever produced, making it the rarest Pokémon card in existence.

The card featured an image drawn by Atsuko Nishida (the character designer responsible for Pikachu's creation) of Pikachu holding a pen and a brush, and text that translates to: "We certify that your illustration is an excellent entry in the Pokémon Card Game Illustration Contest. Therefore, we state that you are an Officially Authorized Pokémon Card Illustrator, and admire your skill."

A PSA 9 Mint copy of Pokémon Illustrator sold at Heritage Auctions in November 2016 for $54,970, making it easily the single most valuable Pokémon card ever.

There were two other card-related contests held in Japan, one by *CoroCoro Comic* and the other by the TV show *64 Mario Stadium*. Both of them were held in 1999, and both had fans submitting their best photos from the Nintendo 64 title *Pokémon Snap*; winners would have their photo printed on a real Pokémon card. These are not to be confused with the Pikachu promotional card featuring an image of the character from *Pokemon Snap* – that card saw a fairly high print run and features the black PROMO star symbol, while these feature a camera symbol instead. The winners of the *CoroCoro* contest each received 20 copies of their winning card, though it's unknown how many cards the *64 Mario Stadium* winners received. On the rare occasion that these cards hit the auction block, they have been known to realize prices well into four figures.

Some cards have only ever been given out at special events, making them valuable just due to their scarcity. These have included the "Master's Key" card, which was given out in 2010 at a championship event in Japan. Only about 30 copies or so were ever made, making it one of the rarest cards out there. When these have hit auctions, they can realize several thousands of dollars. Other championship-related card releases have included the "No.1 Trainer," "No.2 Trainer" and "No.3 Trainer" cards, given out to the players who place accordingly at these events. These cards have been released at Japanese championship events since the game's earliest days, though the ones released in the 1990s are the most desired.

The individual cards discussed so far have all been only available in Japanese. In terms of English-language releases, there's no card more desired than the *Base Set* Charizard. Since the *Base Set* saw multiple print runs, it's important to distinguish the variants of the Charizard accordingly. Shadowless, first-edition prints of the card in a high grade (Mint or as close to it as possible) regularly see prices well into four figures, and even without a proper grade can go for $1,500 or more.

To compare to that remarkable price, a *Base Set* Charizard from a later printing (a shadowed image and no first-edition denotation), graded highly only sees prices of about $100 or so in online auctions. Ungraded examples of these cards see prices ranging from $20-$50 depending on the condition.

Most holo cards from the early sets see pretty significant prices, especially if they receive a high grade or are first editions, but standouts include the *Base Set* Blastoise ($25-$50) and Venusaur ($25-$75), the *Jungle* Jolteon ($15-$20), and the *Fossil* Dragonite ($10-$25).

A type of rare card introduced in the second generation was "Shining Pokémon," reflecting the fact that, on rare occasions, players of the video games will find a Pokémon of an unusual color for that species. Shining Pokémon all fall into the "Secret Rare" category – a card that's numbered outside of the set number (for example, the Shining Magikarp card is numbered 66 out of 64). The value of the Shining cards varies wildly with regards to what exact Pokémon it is; Shining Charizard is the most desirable (like-ly due to the popularity of Charizard as a character) and regularly sees prices of $125 or more, while the weak Shining Magikarp only demands about $30 or so.

EX cards are also fairly in-demand. These cards are generally super powerful in gameplay, feature a shining silver border, and all show "ex" after the Pokémon name. Valuable examples of EX cards include the *FireRed/LeafGreen* Charizard ($50-$100), the *Team Rocket Returns* Rocket's Mewtwo ($50-$150), and the *Unseen Forces* Lugia ($30-$50). Many EX cards can be found for $10 or less, though – it all depends on the popularity of the Pokémon depicted. In general, though, the EX cards from *Team Rocket Returns* are the most in-demand.

A more recent rare card type has been the "Full Art" card, introduced in the fifth generation. There are both trainer cards and Pokémon cards that are of this type, which feature artwork of the character taking over the entirety of the card itself, with text printed on top. Besides being aesthetically pleasing, many of these cards are super useful in gameplay. Standouts among the Full Art lineup include the *Noble Victories* N ($80-$120), the *Plasma Freeze* Professor Juniper ($30-$50), the *Boundaries Crossed* Bianca ($25-$35), and the *Steam Siege* Professor Sycamore ($15-$25).

Other types of cards that tend to demand higher prices than normal are LEGEND cards, Prime cards, Gold Star cards, Crystal Type cards, Lv. X cards, Ace Spec Trainer cards, Mega EX cards, BREAK cards, and GX cards.

Ultimately, as with many other types of card collecting, the final price realized on any given card will come down to factors that include scarcity, demand and condition.

OTHER COLLECTING

Besides seeking out the most valuable cards or simply trying to complete a set, there's plenty of other ways to collect Pokémon cards. One popular subset of collecting is to get every available card of a given character, which can be more difficult depending entirely on the character chosen. Certain Pokémon, like Pikachu, Eevee, Mewtwo and Charizard, have enjoyed long-lasting popularity across all forms of the franchise due to cool or cute designs or because of their powers. More popular Pokémon generally see more cards made of them accordingly.

It should come as no surprise that series mascot Pikachu has seen more than 120 different cards featuring its likeness. Meanwhile, fellow Generation One Pokémon Pinsir has only been featured on 14 different cards. Pikachu is a cute electric mouse while Pinsir is an angry-looking bug – no shock that Pikachu is inherently more popular.

With the artwork depicted on the cards, many people elect to collect by artist. There's plenty to choose from, though Ken Sugimori would be the first to discuss. Sugimori has been involved with the *Pokémon* franchise from the beginning, acting as the character designer for the original games. He is easily the best-known artist to be associated with *Pokémon* at large. To date, Sugimori has illustrated more than 850 different PTCG cards, making him the most prolific of the artists featured in the game.

Other notable artists have included Hironobu Yoshida, who has been involved with *Pokémon* since the release of *Pokémon Yellow*, Tomoaki Imakuni, a comedian and musician whose cards are usually gags and not meant to be used in serious matches, and Atsuko Nishida, Pikachu's original designer

who has illustrated more than 400 cards on her own. With more than 100 artists having contributed to PTCG artwork, there's been a lot of different styles featured over the years – and a lot of different ways to collect.

The card game can actually be incorporated into a video game collection, and not simply because it's based on a video game, but because a video game based on the card game was made for the Game Boy Color. Simply called *Pokémon Trading Card Game*, the video game first released in Japan in 1998 before making its way elsewhere in 2000. It featured a plot revolving around the player's desire to inherit the powerful Legendary Cards. Similar to how the mainline video games worked, the player would travel to eight different Clubs, defeat the Club Masters, and eventually face off against the four Grand Masters before becoming the champion. The game featured cards from *Base Set, Jungle,* and *Fossil* as well as a handful of promotional cards and was a faithful digital recreation of the tabletop game.

A sequel, *Pokémon Card GB2: Here Comes Team Great Rocket!,* released in Japan in 2001, and accordingly was focused on the *Team Rocket* expansion of the card game. It was similar to the first GBC title in many ways and was received fairly well. However, for reasons unknown, the game was never released outside of Japan.

Though dismissed by many as simply a game for children, the *Pokémon* Trading Card Game has proven to be a viable collectible in the 20-plus years since its inception. With many prices well into the thousands of dollars, the appreciation in value for some of the earliest cards printed is obvious. Both as a tabletop game and as a collectible, *Pokémon* continues to shine.

KEY TO THE CARDS

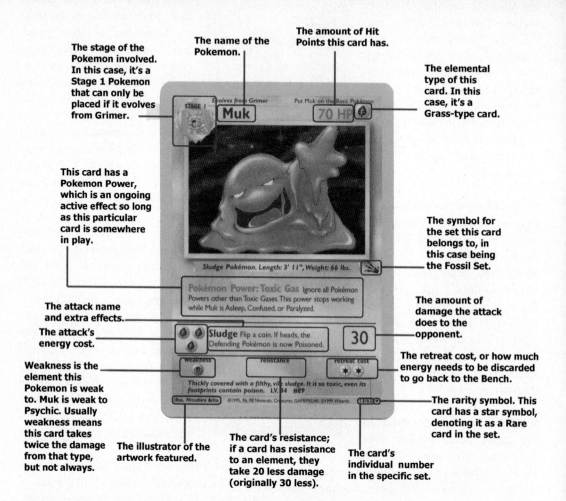

The stage of the Pokemon involved. In this case, it's a Stage 1 Pokemon that can only be placed if it evolves from Grimer.

The name of the Pokemon.

The amount of Hit Points this card has.

The elemental type of this card. In this case, it's a Grass-type card.

This card has a Pokemon Power, which is an ongoing active effect so long as this particular card is somewhere in play.

The symbol for the set this card belongs to, in this case being the Fossil Set.

The attack name and extra effects.

The attack's energy cost.

The amount of damage the attack does to the opponent.

The retreat cost, or how much energy needs to be discarded to go back to the Bench.

Weakness is the element this Pokemon is weak to. Muk is weak to Psychic. Usually weakness means this card takes twice the damage from that type, but not always.

The illustrator of the artwork featured.

The card's resistance; if a card has resistance to an element, they take 20 less damage (originally 30 less).

The card's individual number in the specific set.

The rarity symbol. This card has a star symbol, denoting it as a Rare card in the set.

The highest sale price for any *Pokémon* card at auction, as of this book's publication, went to the "Pokémon Illustrator" card when it was sold through Heritage Auctions on November 18, 2016. Graded at a PSA 9 Mint, the card brought in $54,970 – a world record for the card individually as well as for any *Pokémon* card overall.

Due to the illustration on the card, it's also colloquially known as "Pikachu Illustrator." The image on the card features the franchise mascot, Pikachu, holding illustration tools.

an Officially Authorized *Pokémon* Card Illustrator and admire your skill." Accordingly, it has no use in the context of the TCG itself, and is purely a collectible rather than a playable card.

The illustration of Pikachu depicted on the card was done by Atsuko Nishida, an artist who has been involved with the *Pokémon* franchise at large since its earliest days. Nishida was actually the artist who designed Pikachu; she also designed Pikachu's evolution, Raichu, as well as the Alolan variant of Raichu that was first seen in the *Sun* and *Moon* games. Other Pokémon Nishida designed have included numerous Eevee evolutions (Vaporeon, Espeon, Umbreon, Leafeon, Glaceon, and Sylveon), as well as the Munna, Cottonee, Minccino, and Petilil evolutionary lines. Nishida has also worked as a character designer on several of the *Pokémon* films and on multiple seasons of the anime series.

"The Pikachu Illustrator Card was given in January of 1998 to winners of the *CoroCoro Comic* Illustration Contest," said Barry Sandoval, Director of Operations for Comics at Heritage Auctions, in a press release. "Only 20-39 copies of this card were released, 10 of which are graded in top condition and it is unknown how many still remain with the public."

CoroCoro Comic is a Japanese magazine that regularly highlights *Pokémon* products, including the card game; in Japan, the *Blue* edition of the *Pokémon* Game Boy games was offered exclusively through the magazine. *CoroCoro Comic* held a handful of contests between 1997 and 1998 for the readers to submit illustrations of their favorite Pokémon. Winners each received 20 cards that featured their illustration as well as a copy of Pokémon Illustrator.

The card is in the same layout as a typical Trainer card in the game, though it reads "Illustrator" where "Trainer" usually is at the top. The card's flavor text reads: "We certify that your illustration is an excellent entry in the *Pokémon* Card Game Illustration Contest. Therefore, we state that you are

With only three of these contests ever being held, it means that only a handful of the Pokémon Illustrator cards were ever produced – 39 at most. And with the nature of *Pokémon* cards being aimed primarily at young children who played the game, rather than at collectors, there's really no way to tell how many of the 39 cards produced are still out there.

Pokémon Illustrator previously sold for about $23,000 in the early 2000s; Heritage credited the new world record price partially to the resurgence in *Pokémon*'s popularity due to the arrival of the *Pokémon Go* mobile game around the same time. With such a limited amount of these cards out there – and with so few of them with known whereabouts – it's entirely possible that this world record could be surpassed in the future.

The Gallery

While the *Pokémon Trading Card Game* may have experienced its greatest heydey in the late 1990s and early 2000s, it never totally went away. Thanks to the success of some of the more recent video games as well as *Pokémon Go*, the card game has managed to enjoy success for more than 20 years. The following pages contain highlights from throughout the history of the game. Pricing information is an average range as of the publication of this book and should be considered a starting point for those looking to collect - your final buying or selling price will vary.

CHARIZARD
BASE SET
1ST EDITION: $800-$2,000
SHADOWLESS: $500-$1,000

BLASTOISE
BASE SET
1ST EDITION: $200-$600
UNLIMITED: $50-$100

VENUSAUR
BASE SET
1ST EDITION: $200-$500
UNLIMITED:

PIKACHU
BASE SET
RED CHEEKS MISPRINT: $25-$75
YELLOW CHEEKS: $2-$10

JOLTEON
JUNGLE
HOLO: $15-$30
NON-HOLO: $5-$10

SNORLAX
JUNGLE
1ST EDITION HOLO: $20-$50
UNLIMITED HOLO: $10-$25

DRAGONITE
FOSSIL
1ST EDITION HOLO: $40-$100
UNLIMITED HOLO: $10-$30

DARK CHARIZARD
TEAM ROCKET
1ST EDITION HOLO: $50-$100
1ST EDITION NON-HOLO: $10-$25

BLAINE'S MOLTRES
GYM HEROES
1ST EDITION HOLO: $50-$100
UNLIMITED HOLO: $10-$30

BLAINE'S CHARIZARD
GYM CHALLENGE
1ST EDITION HOLO: $100-$200
UNLIMITED HOLO: $25-$75

LUGIA
NEO GENESIS
1ST EDITION HOLO: $50-$100
UNLIMITED HOLO: $25-$45

UMBREON
NEO DISCOVERY
1ST EDITION HOLO: $50-$100
UNLIMITED HOLO: $25-$50

HO-OH
NEO REVELATION
1ST EDITION HOLO: $150-$300
UNLIMITED HOLO: $40-$100

SHINING GYARADOS
NEO REVELATION
1ST EDITION HOLO: $100-$250
UNLIMITED HOLO: $30-$80

SHINING MEWTWO
NEO DESTINY
1ST EDITION HOLO: $200-$400
UNLIMITED HOLO: $100-$200

NIDOKING (CRYSTAL TYPE)
AQUAPOLIS
$150-$250

CELEBI (CRYSTAL TYPE)
SKYRIDGE
$200-$500

DRAGONITE EX
EX DRAGON
$20-$50

REGIROCK EX
EX HIDDEN LEGENDS
$25-$75

MUDKIP (GOLD STAR)
EX TEAM ROCKET RETURNS
$200-$500

RAYQUAZA (GOLD STAR)
EX DEOXYS
$500-$750

PIKACHU (GOLD STAR)
EX HOLON PHANTOMS
$150-$350

TIME-SPACE DISTORTION
MYSTERIOUS TREASURES
$20-$50

LEAFEON (LV X)
MAJESTIC DAWN
$20-$40

SNORLAX (LV X)
RISING RIVALS
$20-$50

N
NOBLE VICTORIES
$50-$100

MEWTWO EX
NEXT DESTINIES
$15-$40

DARKRAI EX
DARK EXPLORERS
$25-$75

COMPUTER SEARCH
(ACE SPEC)
BOUNDARIES CROSSED
$25-$75

ULTRA BALL
PLASMA FREEZE
$75-$150

LYSANDRE
FLASHFIRE
$15-$50

MEGA GENGAR EX
(SECRET RARE)
PHANTOM FORCES
$20-$40

SOLGALEO GX
(RAINBOW SECRET RARE)
SUN & MOON
$25-$40

Yu-Gi-Oh!

BY ALEX CARRA

A few years after *Magic: the Gathering* hit shelves, manga artist Kazuki Takahashi started publishing a series through *Shonen Jump* magazine called *Yu-Gi-Oh!*. The story focused on a teenage boy and his friends as they navigated high school, encountered zany villains both large and small, played a fantastically popular card game called Duel Monsters, and – oh yeah – dealt with the possessing spirit of a millennia-old pharaoh. (And you thought your high school was bad.) The story was later adapted into two anime series, one by Toei Animation that aired in 1998, and another by NAS and Studio Gallop (*Yu-Gi-Oh! Duel Monsters*) that aired from 2000 to 2004. The series was wildly well-received, and sparked numerous spin-off shows that air to this day.

In 1999, Konami launched a collectible card game based on the rules, characters, and even specific cards of Duel Monsters. It was marketed in Asia as the *Yu-Gi-Oh! Official Card Game* and, later, as the *Yu-Gi-Oh! Trading Card Game* internationally. The game was extremely successful even from the outset, building on the success of *Magic: the Gathering* and

other entries in the collectible card game gold rush of the middle and late 1990s. The game faced some legal trouble concerning counterfeit cards distributed by The Upper Deck Company, *Yu-Gi-Oh!*'s international distributor from 2002 to 2008. Despite this, the game was recognized with a Guinness World Record for best-selling trading card game in 2009. As of 2011, it had sold more than 25 *billion* cards worldwide.

IT'S TIME TO D-D-DUEL

Like many of the classic collectible card games, *Yu-Gi-Oh!* and its fictional inspiration, Duel Monsters, feature duels between rival players called duelists. Each duelist has a deck of 40-60 cards, comprising three types of cards: monsters, spells, and traps. Each player begins the duel with a number of life points, usually 8,000, though in the manga and the anime series it sometimes ranges from 2 to 4,000, and casual players may choose to use other numbers. The game ends when one player is reduced to zero life points, a player cannot draw a card when they are supposed to do so, or when a special card's win condition is met.

Somewhat unique to *Yu-Gi-Oh!,* and key to its strategy, is the ability to play cards face-down, rather than face-up. Traps must be played face-down, while spells may be played either face-up or face-down. Similarly, nearly all monsters *can* be played face down, though any face-down monster is played in "defense mode," where it is turned 90 degrees to the left and serves as a barrier to the owner's life points. A monster in "attack mode," face-up and pointed toward the player's opponent, can attack and potentially destroy a combatant, but the winner deals damage to the loser's player equal to the difference in attack values. A monster in defense mode cannot counter-attack, but blocks any damage from being dealt to its owner, even if the aggressor has more attack strength than the defender has in defense.

Each player's side of the game board includes a space or "zone" for the deck and graveyard (discard pile), a zone for the Extra Deck, five zones for Monsters, five zones for spells/traps, and one zone for a special Field spell, if one is in play. Later expansions also added additional zones, such as Pendulum zones, that tie into particular card effects.

Monsters, the bread and butter of *Yu-Gi-Oh!,* are creatures that duelists can summon for battle against the opposing player's monsters. Each one has an attack and defense score that determines the winner in combat between monsters. Deck them-ing comes into play largely with regard to monsters' attribute (such as Light, Dark, Wind, and Fire) and type (such as Spellcaster, Fiend, Dragon, and Machine). Monsters are also ranked by level, where bigger, more powerful monsters require a "tribute" to summon: one or more monsters already on the field that must be destroyed as sacrifice for the new one.

Monsters are also grouped by type, with early card sets including just Normal, Effect, Fusion, and Ritual. Normal monsters and most Effect monsters can be played directly out of hand, while Ritual monsters require that the duelist play a special spell card to summon it. Fusion monsters, on the other hand, are not included in the main deck at all, but are kept to the side in a special Extra Deck. When the duelist has the relevant fusion material monsters in hand or on the field, they can play the spell card Polymerization to discard the material monsters and summon the Fusion monster to the field.

Later expansions to the game built upon these special summoning conditions and added other monster types based on new mechanics that were introduced in subsequent anime spinoff series. These include Xyz monsters, where component monsters are overlaid on top of each other beneath a special, extra monster, and Synchro monsters, which can be summoned from the Extra Deck by offering a special Tuner monster as tribute.

Spells come in multiple sub-categories, and can cause a wide range of effects, from direct damage to the duelist's opponent to healing lost life points to summoning cards from the duelist's graveyard. Most "normal" spells are played only on the duelist's turn, while Quick-Play spells can be used even to interrupt the other player's turn. Equip spells use a spell card zone but attach to a monster in play, usually to boost its attack or defense. Continuous spell cards are cards that are not immediately discarded upon use, and Field spells, a special kind of continuous spell, have their own zone, and usually affect play in a way that is beneficial to the duelist who played it—but can also help the opponent. Any spell card (other than a Field spell) can be played face-down, in which case it is merely kept on the board, inactive but available for activation at the player's discretion. One reason to do so is to keep a manageable number of cards in hand, but another common reason is to provide a smokescreen or a sort of impromptu shell game, with which to hide trap cards.

Trap cards are both strategically vital and something of an in-joke in the *Yu-Gi-Oh!* fanbase, largely due to the prevalence of a key phrase in the anime: *"You've activated my trap card!"* Traps must be played face-down on the owner's turn, but after that, they can be activated at any time, even on the opponent's turn. Like spells, trap cards have several categories. Normal traps are discarded after they've been flipped, but Continuous traps remain active on the field, face-up, until and unless another card is used to destroy it. Counter traps are special traps that can even be activated in response to another trap. Traps can (and have, in the story) turned the tide of countless duels, and are a key part of all great duelists' strategy.

TWO DECADES OF CARDS

From 1999 to 2002, *Yu-Gi-Oh!* was published exclusively in Japan, releasing a total of 22 sets across Series 1 through 3. The 22 sets were then combined two at a time into larger sets that were released internationally from 2002 to 2004, starting with *Legend of Blue-Eyes White Dragon*, which was a combination of a Japanese reprint set of the same name and a second reprint set called *Phantom God*. The last international-catchup set was *Ancient Sanctuary*, a combination of the Japanese Series 3 sets *The Sanctuary in the Sky* and *Pharaoh's Inheritance*.

After *Ancient Sanctuary*, the two games (the Asian *Yu-Gi-Oh! Official Card Game* and the international *Yu-Gi-Oh! Trading Card Game*) converged, and began following the same release schedule. This constituted the games' Series 4, starting with the *Soul of the Duelist* set, which launched in Japan in May 2004 and internationally in October. Since then the game has expanded to Series 10, with 54 more sets released globally. The most recent sets to launch as of this book's publication were *Flames of Destruction*, which was released in Japan in January 2018, and *Cybernetic Horizon* in April 2018.

Each set contains cards of numerous rarities, including Common, Rare, Super Rare, Ultra Rare, and Ultimate Rare. Japanese Series 1-3 sets also included Secret Rare cards, but these were not used in international releases, and due to problems with the prevalence of online sales, they were dropped in Series 4 when the games converged. They were later brought back in 2006 internationally, and in 2014 in Asia. Other special rarities have also been used, such as the Prismatic Secret Rare, which appeared on international video game promotions, and a special rare introduced in 2007 that appears only once in each set: the Holographic Rare (in the Asian game) or Ghost Rare (in the international version).

The sets are mostly sold in nine-card booster packs, but each set is also marketed in pre-built Starter Decks and Structure Decks, and in special collectible metal tins featuring particular monsters or characters from the manga and anime series. Unlike some other golden age collectible card games, *Yu-Gi-Oh!* favors small sets of only about 100 cards that introduce new cards and mechanics, and are predominantly brought into play via booster packs. The pre-built decks, on the other hand, are not limited to particular sets, and instead focus on a deck or character theme. This makes collecting a single set comparatively easier, as there's fewer cards to track down if your goal is to complete by sets. On the flipside, though, the game's printing schedule causes some problems for those trying to collect rarer cards, as this prevalence for reprinting devalues all but the first print runs of new sets, which are all marked "1st Edition" at the bottom of the card.

Other special booster packs have also been marketed in the game's history. Special booster packs were granted to those who

attended tournaments, most of which had fewer cards than a standard booster. In 2009 *Yu-Gi-Oh!* also started marketing "Duelist Packs," which focused on collectability for new players, with a large block of classic cards sold as a unit. The last big way to get *Yu-Gi-Oh!* cards is in Battle Packs, a pack type Konami premiered in May 2012 with an eye at a particular type of tournament play that *Yu-Gi-Oh!* had not yet courted.

Tournament play is one of the best ways to keep a collectible card game alive, and *Yu-Gi-Oh!* is no exception. Up until 2012, *Yu-Gi-Oh!* had two main formats: Advanced and Traditional. Advanced Format has both a restricted list (where only one or two copies of a card can be used in a given deck) and a banned list, a list of cards that cannot be used under any circumstances. The Traditional Format is less restrictive, so it does not have a ban list, but any card that is banned in Advanced is restricted to a single copy. In 2012, though, with the launch of "Battle Pack: Epic Dawn," Konami sought to expand into sealed-pack tournament play, better known as drafting.

Secondary Market

Like most collectible card games, *Yu-Gi-Oh!* has a robust secondary market, complete with numerous sales and price-tracker sites and a thriving community of resellers on social media. Of most value are promotional cards, which can number in mere tens or hundreds due to release rarity, and 1st Edition printings. Due to the game's propensity for reprints, most sets see an initial burst of value during the 1st Edition print, and then see a precipitous drop once the first print rolls over into the Unlimited Edition printing, satisfying tournament duelists' need for the new cards.

While many card games see a focus in collections based on art, or set, or card types, *Yu-Gi-Oh!* also sees a prevalence among collectors for aping a particular character's style or constructing decks that match a deck used in the show. Building Light/Dragon-themed decks, after Seto Kaiba's deck, for example, or a Spellcaster/Fiend deck based on Yugi's deck, or an Xyz deck based on Yuma's deck from the *Yu-Gi-Oh! Zexal* series, add a new layer of collectability to the game.

Of particular note, but low financial pull, are some of the promotional cards based on cards that are rare in-world, such as the five pieces of "Exodia, the Forbidden

One," and the three "Egyptian God" cards. The Egyptian Gods, in particular, saw significant fluctuation in value. Initially, the three cards were given solely promotional printings, and were released with various video game releases and an "ani-manga" paired to the *Yu-Gi-Oh! The Movie: Pyramid of Light*. These were not legal in tournament play, and after release they saw incredible values in the secondary market. They were also subject to heavy counterfeiting, mostly in East Asia. Later, though, the Egyptian Cards were also given tournament-legal printings with heavy caveats and weaknesses not present in the "canon-compliant" promotional cards.

However, due to their prevalence for reprinting and promotional draw, these cards have actually attained a certain level of market saturation, and particular Limited Edition runs might hit upwards of $200. But despite their in-story value, these aren't the bank-breaker cards.

For those, instead you'll want to look to tournament prize cards and special printings. Foreign-language promo cards in particular tend to run high, like a special Chinese printing of the *Blue-Eyes White Dragon* that can go for between $1,300

and $3,900, or an early Japanese promotional copy of the *Dark Magician Girl*, which was given to tournament winners and players in 1999. That card in particular can sell anywhere between $1,100 and $6,600, depending on its condition.

Other such rare prize cards include *Gold Sarcophagus* ($1,370) and *Des Volstgalph* ($1,530), each of which have only 20 copies in existence. *Minerva, the Exalted Lightsworn*, despite being printed as only a Super Rare card, was a tournament prize and is also very valuable for its playability, and can sell for around $1,900. *Cyber Stein*, awarded to winners of the Shonen Jump Championship, can list for as much as $4,500.

Crush Card Virus, another Shonen Jump Championship prize, tends to sell around $2,475, but its fame underlines the deep impact of the *Yu-Gi-Oh!* story on the game. In the show, the nominal villain and sometimes-deuteragonist Seto Kaiba claimed that the card is a crucial component of his deck, cementing its value among fans. But even that isn't scratching the surface of some of the most valuable cards in the *Yu-Gi-Oh!* roster. A prize from the 2006 World Championship Series, *Armament of the Lethal Lords*, was

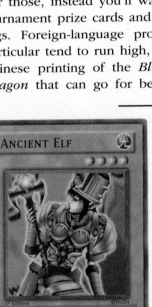

once reported as selling for $1.2 million on eBay in 2007. While that story wasn't actually true, it *has* sold for about $9,000, and regularly sees listings for $8,000.

But top of the list is a one-of-a-kind copy of the *Black Luster Soldier* that was in fact printed on stainless steel, and granted as a prize during the 1999 *Yu-Gi-Oh!* Championship in Japan. It was allegedly later sold for $2 million.

DIGITAL DUELS AND THE *REAL* RAREST CARD

Yu-Gi-Oh! knows its demographic, and even early on, it deployed an ingenious marketing move to tap into another gaming sector rising in popularity in the late '90s and early 2000s: video games. Konami spread *Yu-Gi-Oh!*'s story and gameplay to more than 50 video games between every console, from the Nintendo GameBoy to Xbox to mobile apps. Many of these came with special promotional cards, but Konami wisely made sure the game's physical-to-digital integration went both ways. Nearly every physical card bears a special eight-digit code, and some of the games, including *Yu-Gi-Oh! Forbidden Memories* (marketed as *Yu-Gi-Oh! True Duel Monsters: Sealed Memories* in Asia) and *Yu-Gi-Oh! The Duelists of the Roses* (or *Yu-Gi-Oh! True Duel Monsters II: Inherited Memories*), allowed players to enter physical card codes in order to receive digital copies of the cards in-game.

Yu-Gi-Oh! is ultimately, like so many shonen stories, a tale of friendship, trust, and good overcoming evil. The story touched hearts and brought a fun twist to the collectible card game genre as it was entering the social consciousness, thanks to the "gold rush" games of the middle to late '90s. The *Yu-Gi-Oh!* card games then brought that into readers and viewers' homes in a very real way. And then in 2005, Konami (with some help from the Make-A-Wish Foundation) made good on that theme in a big way, turning a fan-drawn card into *Tyler, the Great Warrior*, in honor of the artist: a young boy diagnosed with liver cancer. The card was printed as part of a special Make-A-Wish Foundation set, and only one copy exists. Since Tyler survived and came out the other side of his cancer in good health, the card is still in his possession. It's safe to say it's hard to put a price tag on that.

While it never had quite the same universal pull that other late '90s card games had, *Yu-Gi-Oh!* carved out a niche in the gaming community and hasn't budged since. It hasn't been knocked out of its Guinness World Record slot for best-selling trading card game since it took the record in 2009, and with yet more sets slated for release in 2018 and beyond, it doesn't look like it's planning on giving up that title for a long time to come.

Our thanks to Billy Saccardi for providing many of the card images shown.

The name of the card.

The card's elemental attribute.

The card's level. Cards that are levels 1-4 do not require a Tribute to be sacrificed and can be played immediately. Level 5-6 cards require one monster on the field to be sacrificed as a Tribute in order to be played, while cards that are level 7 or higher require two Tributes.

The card's Type. Many pre-built theme decks will focus on a specific Type of monster and there are many cards that can be used in game to benefit specific Types as well.

The description of the card. If this card has any sort of specific effects or requirements in the game, this is where that information will be described.

CELTIC GUARDIAN

EARTH

[WARRIOR]
An elf who learned to wield a sword, he baffles enemies with lightning-swift attacks.

ATK/1400 DEF/1200

SDY-009

91152256   ©1996 KAZUKI TAKAHASHI

The Card Number. This denotes the set this card is from and its respective position in that set.

The attack and defense statistics for this card.

The Passcode for this card. This serves no purpose in the card game but can be used in various video games in order to render this card digitally in those games.

Yu-Gi-Oh! The Gallery

"It's time to duel!" Arriving at the tail end of the 1990s in Japan before making its way to the rest of the world in the early 2000s, the *Yu-Gi-Oh!* Trading Card Game instantly took hold as a popular TCG choice thanks to its easy learning curve and accessiblity. The anime and manga that featured the game prominently also helped! Here, we take a look into some of the most popular and most valuable cards from throughout the game's history. Prices shown are aggregated from online auction results and are meant to show an average range - your final price will vary.

ASH BLOSSOM & JOYOUS SPRING
MAXIMUM CRISIS: $50-$100

BLUE-EYES SHINING DRAGON
RETRO PACK 2: $400-$500
MOVIE PACK: $10-$20

BOOK OF MOON
CHAMPION PACK- GAME ONE: $100-$300
DUEL TERMINAL 3: $10-$30

BORRELOAD DRAGON
CIRCUIT BREAK: $50-$100

CRUSH CARD VIRUS
SHONEN JUMP 2007 PRIZE: $2,000-$3,000
DUELIST PACK- KAIBA: $15-$20

CYBER-STEIN
SHONEN JUMP 2004 PRIZE: $2,500-$4,000
DARK BEGINNING 2: $15-$30

DARK MAGICIAN
DARK DUEL STORIES PROMO: $100-
$200
SHONEN JUMP VOL. 9 PROMO:
$20-$50

DES VOLSTGALPH
SHONEN JUMP 2005 PRIZE:
$1,500-$2,000
GOLD SERIES 2009: $15-$25

ELEMENTAL HERO
SPARKMAN
MATTEL PROMO: $400-$500
DEMO DECK 2015: $5-$10

EVENLY MATCHED
CIRCUIT BREAK: $50-$100

EXODIA THE
FORBIDDEN ONE
DARK DUEL STORIES PROMO:
$30-$100
RETRO PACK: $25-$75

FORTRESS WHALE
TOURNAMENT PACK 7:
$150-$250

GATLING DRAGON
DARK REVELATION VOL. 3:
$30-$75
FLAMING ETERNITY: $15-$30

GOLD SARCOPHAGUS
SHONEN JUMP 2007 PRIZE: $800-
$1,100
GOLD SERIES 2009: $15-$40

HEAVYMETALFOES
ELECTRUMITE
EXTREME FORCE: $30-$100

JUDGMENT DRAGON
TURBO PACK BOOSTER ONE:
$50-$100
LIGHT OF DESTRUCTION:
$25-$50

MACRO COSMOS
DARK REVELATION VOL. 4:
$35-$75
DUEL TERMINAL 6B: $10-$30

MERMAIL ABYSSMEGALO
ABYSS RISING: $30-$75
WAR OF THE GIANTS: $10-$30

MONSTER REBORN
THE LOST ART PROMO: $25-$75
RETRO PACK: $25-$100

MORPHING JAR
TOURNAMENT PACK 2ND
SEASON: $350-$500
TOURNAMENT PACK 4: $50-$100

NEEDLE WORM
TOURNAMENT PACK 3RD
SEASON: $200-$300
TOURNAMENT PACK 5: $15-$30

POT OF AVARICE
ELEMENTAL ENERGY: $15-$50
DARK REVELATION VOL. 4:
$15-$30

POWER BOND
DARK REVELATION VOL. 4:
$25-$50
CYBERNETIC REV.: $10-$25

RAIGEKI
RETRO PACK: $100-$200
DARK LEGENDS: $30-$50

RED-EYES BLACK DRAGON
LEGEND OF BLUE-EYES: $50-$150
ANNIVERSARY PACK: $25-$75

ROYAL DECREE
TOURNAMENT PACK 4: $50-$125
YUGI'S WORLD MEGA PACK:
$2-$10

SARYUJA SKULL DREAD
EXTREME FORCE: $50-$100

SCAPEGOAT
RETRO PACK: $200-$350
JOEY'S WORLD MEGA PACK:
$10-$25

SOLEMN JUDGMENT
RETRO PACK: $40-$100
METAL RAIDERS: $20-$40

TOON CANNON SOLDIER
TOURNAMENT PACK 6: $300-$400
DARK BEGINNING 2: $5-$15

URIA, LORD OF SEARING FLAMES
DARK REVELATION VOL. 4:
$150-$400

VICE DRAGON
DUEL DISK- YUSEI: $500-$800
GOLD SERIES 3: $2-$10

WIDESPREAD RUIN
DAWN OF DESTINY PROMO:
$200-$300
MILLENNIUM PACK: $1-$5

OTHER COLLECTIBLE CARD GAMES

Collectible card games may not have truly arrived until the early 1990s, but since the debut of *Magic: The Gathering*, the style of game has been adapted to numerous kinds of properties. The instantaneous success of *Magic* created an entirely new market of games and led to the creation of a number of other CCGs. While many of these faded pretty quickly, some have remained worthy of attention.

Vampire: The Masquerade inspired *Vampire: The Eternal Struggle*, which originally released in 1994 as *Jyhad*. The game was designed by Richard Garfield, the creator of *Magic: The Gathering*, and is based in the RPG's setting of the World of Darkness. *The Eternal Struggle* can actually be played with up to five players simultaneously, which makes it somewhat of a standout within CCGs; most card games are aimed at one-on-one battles. The game puts players in the role of an ancient vampire called a Methuselah, who wants to eliminate their opponents by sending minions out to do their bidding.

The Eternal Struggle managed to carve a niche for itself by focusing more on larger group play, which created a unique gameplay style that allowed for team-ups and political dealings that aren't typically present in most other popular CCGs. After the game's 1994 debut, it saw a number of different expansions until White Wolf Productions ended publication of the game in early 2010. However, in April 2018, Black Chantry Productions announced plans to return the game to print beginning with reprints of earlier sets.

Most products from *Vampire: The Eternal Struggle* are easily found in online auctions at a low price for those looking to start playing the game. Both individual cards and unopened boosters can be found cheaply, with the most expensive products tending to be unopened starter decks, which generally run about $40 or $50. Full boxes of unopened boosters can be found for anywhere between $100 and $200, depending on the expansion the boosters are from.

Another long-running collectible card game is *Legend of the Five Rings*, which first debuted in late 1995 after having been previewed at that year's Gen Con. The game was passed through a few different companies within its first few years, having been created by the Alderac Entertainment

Group, published by Isomedia, bought out by Wizards of the Coast in 1997, and then sold back off to Alderac in 2001 after Hasbro sold off the IP rights.

Unlike many card games, which have a loose framework of a story that the gameplay mechanics are based around, *Legend of the Five Rings* is incredibly story-focused. Every expansion sees a massive update to the storyline with new releases, and a quarterly publication, *The Imperial Herald*, also helps to advance the plot. The outcome of game tournaments can and has impacted how the story plays out.

Legend of the Five Rings is generally played with two to four people, but can accommodate up to eight players in a single match. The game actually features several possible ways to win a match beyond simply eliminating the opponents – though even that process can be achieved through different methods. A player can win by having their "Honor Score" reach 40, which grants them an "Honor Victory," or by playing all of the titular Five Rings, which grants an "Enlightenment Victory." There's also the more straightforward method of victory, which is to be the last person standing,

by destroying all of another's provinces (a "Military Victory"), or by reducing their Honor Score to at least -20 (a "Dishonor Victory").

The game is fairly easy to find at a reasonable price point, though there are a handful of cards – usually convention exclusive releases or other promotional cards – that tend to run about $25 or so in online auctions. It should also be noted that, as of 2017, the original *Legend of the Five Rings* has been discontinued in favor of a successor game that is part of Fantasy Flight's "Living Card Game" lineup. This new version of the game is incompatible with the original version, and is meant for two-person gameplay only. However, its nature as a "Living" card game still places the emphasis on the plot, which will continue to see effects based on how the game itself gets played.

The *BattleTech* universe is massive, having encompassed wargaming, video games, more than 100 novels, a television series, comic books and much more. In 1996, Wizards of the Coast published the *BattleTech Collectible Card Game*, which was designed by Richard Garfield – noted for his creation of *Magic: The Gathering*.

BattleTech as a CCG played in a similar fashion to *Magic*, though the goal of the game is to cause the opponent to run out of cards from their deck rather than eliminating life points. Players attack each other's stockpile with various units in order to deplete the deck. The *BattleTech* CCG was in print for five years until it was discontinued in 2001, but saw a pair of expansions in that time.

Those looking to collect the *BattleTech Collectible Card Game* are likely going to be fans of the franchise as a whole, and thankfully can pick up the cards at a fairly cheap price. Individual cards only run a few dollars at the absolute most, and the most expensive items related to the game are most often going to be unopened, factory-sealed sets of cards – and even those will only run up to about $50-$100. For existing fans of the *BattleTech* franchise, the card game is an easy addition to make to a collection.

Besides *Magic: The Gathering* and his work designing *BattleTech* and *Vampire: The Eternal Struggle*, Richard Garfield was responsible for a handful of successful card games in the late 1990s, including *Netrunner* and *The Great Dalmuti*. Garfield also designed *Star Wars: The Trading Card Game*, produced by Wizards of the Coast in 2002.

Designed for two

players, the *Star Wars Trading Card Game*'s goal is to take control of the in-game arenas. Players control various units to battle for the arenas, and units can only be placed in certain arenas based on what type of card they are (Character, Ground or Space). From 2002 to 2005, Wizards produced various sets and expansions for the game: *Attack of the Clones, Sith Rising, A New Hope, Battle of Yavin, Jedi Guardians, The Empire Strikes Back, Rogues and Scoundrels, The Phantom Menace, Return of the Jedi*, and *Revenge of the Sith*. In 2005, the company put the game on an indefinite hiatus, and they have not produced any further sets since; however, a group of fans, the *Star Wars Trading Card Game* Independent Development Committee, has developed new sets of cards in the years since, and has made them available for free online for fans to continue to play with.

This wasn't the first CCG based on *Star Wars*, though – there was also the *Star Wars: Customizable Card Game*, published from 1995 to 2001 by Decipher, Inc. A unique aspect of this game was that one player *must* play with a Light Side deck, while the other plays with a Dark Side deck. The "Premiere" set for this game debuted in 1995, and was followed by numerous expansions, including *Hoth, Dagobah, Cloud City, Jabba's Palace, Tatooine,*

Coruscant, and more. Like its successor, the *Customizable Card Game* had a strong fanbase that has continued to produce free online expansions following its discontinuation.

Both of these discontinued games can still be found online fairly cheaply (or, in the case of the fan-made expansions, for free). The more expensive products tend to be booster boxes or deck releases, and those can run anywhere from $100 to $300 or more depending on if they're still factory sealed and on the exact set expansion involved.

More recently, Fantasy Flight Games has released *Star Wars Destiny*, which involves both cards and dice to play. The game has already proven popular with the fanbase within its first few years of release, and is easily found at any local game store or online.

Star Wars is hardly the only licensed property to have a collectible card game released for it, though. There are card games based on films, such as *The Crow, Austin Powers, James Bond,* and *Pirates of the Caribbean*; games based on anime and manga such as *One Piece, Dragon Ball Z, Naruto, Bleach, Sailor Moon,* and *Gundam*; card games based on video games like *Kingdom Hearts, Sonic the Hedgehog, Tomb Raider* and

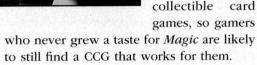

Mortal Kombat; and card games based on television shows like *The Simpsons, Buffy the Vampire Slayer, Avatar: The Last Airbender,* and even *SpongeBob SquarePants*. Chances are, if a property has become a multimedia franchise, a card game has likely been a part of that multimedia.

The card game formula has also successfully been applied to online video games, creating an entire community of digital collectible card games. *Hearthstone*, developed by Blizzard, might be the single most successful example of this, but there's dozens of others, such as *The Elder Scrolls: Legends, Gwent: The Witcher Card Game,* and *Phantom Dust*. The most successful physical collectible card games have also largely gone digital in their own ways, with *Magic: The Gathering, Pokémon* and *Yu-Gi-Oh!* all having online play available.

Though a few have stood out above the rest, there's a collectible card game out there to suit just about everyone's taste. The rise of crowdfunding has also enabled new card games to be produced and sent to market. A quick online search can yield tons of results for collectible card games, so gamers who never grew a taste for *Magic* are likely to still find a CCG that works for them.

CROWDFUNDING: ALTERING THE LANDSCAPE OF TABLETOP GAMING

One of the driving forces of the recent tabletop renaissance has been the concept of crowdfunding. Websites such as Kickstarter and Indiegogo have allowed for a huge boom in creativity in the tabletop industry, with projects that wouldn't necessarily appeal to a wide, mass-market audience getting funded and finding success.

In order to understand how crowdfunding sites have shaped the industry, it's important to understand what it actually is. Crowdfunding is essentially a means of circumventing traditional investment models by appealing directly to the potential audience of a given product and gathering small amounts of money from those larger amounts of people in order to fund the product.

"Traditionally, if you wanted to make a small number of things, you would handcraft it in a shop and sell it to a customer. You would take a limited risk on the materials in the hopes you would sell out of those items," Daniel Zayas, U.S. Sales Manager for LongPack Games, said. "Now let's say you have an idea and want to make 1,000 things or more. You would need thousands of dollars to do this efficiently: manufacturing in China, setting up worldwide distribution channels, and ensure your marketing engine was helping sell those products.

That is a substantial financial risk to you, the creator. You could take out a loan or sell the idea to the highest bidder. Now let's say you could flip that model in reverse, where you had 1,000 customers waiting to buy your product, and were willing to wait for you to manufacture it with their money and receive it six to 12 months after purchase. You immediately transfer the risk to the customer, but the risk per person is minimal."

Typically, the crowdfunding platform itself (Kickstarter, Indiegogo, or any other company) will charge a fee for the sake of using it. Indiegogo and Kickstarter both apply 5 percent fees on contributions raised, and the processor of credit card payments also ends up taking a fee of anywhere from 3-5 percent as well. It's important for anyone trying to use the platform to be aware of these fees and how they'll impact the bottom line once any crowdfunding campaign comes to a conclusion.

Besides simply raising money, though, crowdfunding sites allow for their users to gauge interest in a wide number of things related to the final product, according to game designer Elisa Teague.

"Kickstarter allows you to gauge how well your product is going to be received before production, and it allows you not only to crowdfund but also to crowdsource: packaging design opinions, component choices, rules questions, and more," Teague said. "Not to be ignored is the tremendous effect Kickstarter has had on game marketing, as running a campaign is basically free advertising for your product, if you know how to manage your social media correctly."

Between the relatively low risk to consumers on the money front as well as their ability to potentially have an impact on the game that they're backing, it should come as no surprise that tabletop gaming has seen such a boom on crowdfunding platforms. On Kickstarter alone, tabletop gaming has been one of the leading success stories overall; since that site's 2009 launch, tabletop projects on the site have received pledges totaling more than $200 million total. Tabletop also continues to trend upwards, while their digital counterparts in video gaming have started to fall off on pledges.

The rise of crowdfunding has, according to Zayas, totally "changed the landscape of board games."

"Now, at trade shows, there's a 50-50 split on games you can buy now, versus support on Kickstarter to receive later. Where only a handful of publishers exist-

ed before Kickstarter, now you have thousands," he said. "I am not even saying that traditional publishers are being left behind. Where crowdfunded games may introduce thousands of people to the hobby, traditional publishers are picking up new customers when those crowdfunders go on to look for more games to play."

Druid City Games' James Hudson primarily utilizes Kickstarter to launch game projects and credits the platform with ushering in the revitalization happening in the industry today.

"The board game industry is in the middle of a Golden Era! You can draw a lot of correlations between this massive comeback and Kickstarter," he said. "The platform gives anyone a chance to put their ideas out in the world and the market responds to those. *Kingdom Death Monster* is a great example of someone chasing their dreams with a niche product that hit it big!"

Kingdom Death Monster is certainly a success story

Lantern Festival Expansion - Unlocked

Major Expansion Special • $45 to Pledge (MSRP $45)
New Monsters, New Story Events, Greatly Extends the Campaign!

The Twilight Cloak
A mysterious relic crafted from a fallen Watcher

for Kickstarter, having raised $2 million on the platform. Other major successes have included *Zombicide: Black Plague*, which raised $4.1 million (with *Zombicide: Season 2* and *Zombicide: Season 3* also raising $2.3 million and $2.8 million, respectively), *Conan*, which raised $3.3 million, and *Exploding Kittens*, which raised an astounding $8.8 million.

With these kind of big-dollar figures, it's no shock that plenty of up-and-coming devel-opers have flocked to crowdfunding. But that's where things start to get tricky.

"The biggest pitfall about Kickstarter is that people see huge successes on the platform, dollar signs and all, but they don't under-stand that raising the money is the easiest step," Teague said. "I've spoken with doz-ens of people who have run a Kickstarter, met their funding goal, and then had no idea what to do next. Unfortunately, they got to me too late, and many of the first blunders have been setting the funding goal too low, account-ing only for production and no money for logistics, testing, ship-ping, or basic overhead. This results in failure to deliver on time, if at all, and it is the reason why so many campaigns have raised hundreds of thousands of dollars, yet profited barely anything. All in all, making a game is starting a business, and if you don't have the basic struc-ture and background of running a business, it is going to be a much bigger challenge than most people anticipate. Most of these campaigns result in failure, but the huge successes are blinding aspiring designers to all of the risks involved."

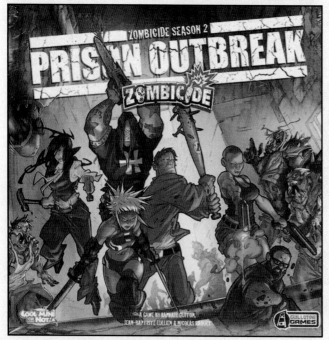

Besides incompetent developers, there's some far more malicious and unsavory types who use the platform as well.

"The downfall [for crowdfund-ing] is the chance for scams. Right this moment there are some Kickstarter campaigns which may never be fulfilled. That means backers are out of that money with little to no retribution to be had," Zayas said. "Per Kickstarter's Terms of Service, as long as a company has made every effort to fulfill a project, but failed, they are legal-ly in the clear. But that doesn't solve for underestimating costs

ing successful Kickstarter campaigns for his games, he made his own mistakes, especially early on.

"Shipping product all over the world and not having a clue about some of the laws of certain countries really cost me on my first campaign," he said. "We also missed on a lot of different marketing strategies, but you can't worry about those too much. With big risk comes big reward."

Zayas also quickly learned the ups and downs of crowdfunding – as well as social media and marketing – in one of his early campaigns.

"One of the first things I ever did in the board gaming world was to launch what I soon learned was a very tone-deaf and insensitive campaign on Kickstarter called *Antichrist*. It was marketed as a horror card game and featured demons on it. I genuinely thought nothing of the theme, as plenty of Hollywood movies share this horror genre with much worse content," Zayas said. "In any case, I quickly realized the error based on the outcry, canceled the campaign within 48 hours and moved on. The funny part of this is that people still bring up this campaign whenever I am mentioned in blogs. To me, it is fascinating that 48 hours of a viral campaign always follows me. It stands as is an excellent example of capturing mindshare, which I similarly strive to create for my clients, but maybe in a not-so-divisive way."

or sheer incompetence. One way creators have managed to combat this is to quote with manufacturers and other partners early and often, then to announce in the campaign with whom all the partners they are working. Similar to game reviews, this gives backers a little more to lean on in the trust department."

Hudson also admitted that, despite hav-

Consumers themselves also have a tendency to have some serious misconceptions about crowdfunding and how it functions, as well, according to Zayas.

"They think they are buying a product similar to how you might find on Amazon. At least on Kickstarter, that is not the case. You as a backer are helping a company or project come into existence," he said. "You want this person to succeed because you believe in the mission and products they provide the world. The reward you receive as part of that support is never guaranteed. If the company fails, they will have no money to fulfill your order."

Ultimately, though, when things come together correctly – a good idea with a good gameplay mechanic, a good theme, and a solid marketing angle – Kickstarter and similar websites have been a huge boon to the industry.

"I still consider my first game project my biggest success, even though it pales in comparison number-wise to other projects. It raised $17,000, but it was my first game design and our first project on Kickstarter," Hudson said. "In today's climate, it is very hard to get noticed and even harder to get a family game noticed, but we funded and got to make our first successful project. It was our first step to becoming a successful board gaming company and that is something I can never replace with another project.

Thanks to the ability to appeal directly to a niche consumer base, crowdfunding has been able to jump start a huge variety of different games that might not have ever ended up on shelves otherwise. With seemingly millions of dollars up for grabs, crowdfunding is likely to remain a significant driving force in the tabletop industry for years to come.

ELISA TEAGUE

Elisa Teague is a game designer who has worked on the Apocrypha Adventure Card Game *as well as the smash-hit* Betrayal at House on the Hill: Widow's Walk. *She also authored the book,* Girls on Games: A Look at the Fairer Side of the Tabletop Industry *which she successfully funded via Kickstarter, bringing in nearly $20,000 against a goal of just $2,500. We chatted about the status of the board game industry today as well as about the struggle against the perception of gaming as a "boy's club."*

Overstreet: First, could you tell us a little bit about yourself?

Elisa Teague (ET): I'm a game designer in the tabletop board game industry with several games currently on the market. However, over the last 18 years, I have worked on well over 100 titles from nearly every segment of game production, from design and development to art direction and graphic design, pre-production management, costing and sourcing, content generation and more. I love games and gaming, and I enjoy all of it.

Overstreet: What was your first experience with tabletop gaming? What about it drew you in?

ET: I've been gaming my whole life, as far back as I remember. My parents both pushed games on us early on, and I was playing chess and *Scrabble* at five. My earliest strategy board gaming memory is playing Avalon Hill's *Gettysburg* with my dad when I was about eight. By the time I was an early teen, I was playing *Dungeons and Dragons* and *Cyberpunk 2020*, as well as buying up board games to play with my friends at my local game shops. So I guess it has just always been a huge part of who I am.

Overstreet: The realm of tabletop has historically been seen as somewhat of a "boys' club." Do you think that's still true today?

ET: I do think it is still true, but that being said, things are moving forward with positive change. We are currently in the phase of progression where these issues are being called out and spoken about openly, which is a very good thing. I published a book called *Girls on Games: A Look at the Fairer Side of the Tabletop Industry* two years ago, in which over a dozen women in the industry wrote their perspectives on this issue. Over the last few years, "Women in Gaming" panels and articles are happening more frequently, which is bringing light and voice to the subject, but I don't think the "boys' club" will be officially gone until women in the industry are asked to speak their voice without having their gender pointed out first.

Overstreet: What, if anything, has changed recently to make the hobby more appealing or welcoming to women or other minorities?

ET: In addition to conventions making a point to put more women on panels, as mentioned above, I think that more game stores and game community groups are starting to learn to cater towards women and other minorities by promoting an atmosphere of inclusiveness. This is a great start, but I believe that the way to accomplish true inclusivity is for the game manufacturers to lead the trend, which will cause a trickle-down effect.

If game manufacturers start producing games with true and broad representation, making games with playable characters and themes that are relatable to everyone, and force zero-tolerance policies about harassment and exclusive behaviors/talk in their organized play programs, the systemic notions that games are for the white male community only will finally be broken. It will take time, but it is worth doing our best to set this in motion now. There are many companies starting to make this part of their mission statements, and I encourage others to follow suit. I know that I person-

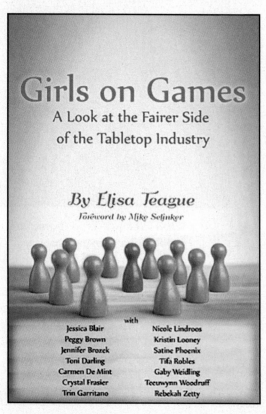

Girls on Games
A Look at the Fairer Side
of the Tabletop Industry

By Elisa Teague
Foreword by Mike Selinker

with

Jessica Blair
Peggy Brown
Jennifer Brozek
Toni Darling
Carmen De Mint
Crystal Frasier
Trin Garritano

Nicole Lindroos
Kristin Looney
Satine Phoenix
Tifa Robles
Gaby Weidling
Teeuwynn Woodruff
Rebekah Zetty

ally choose to work with companies that have adopted these ideals.

Overstreet: There's clearly been a huge resurgence with board gaming within the last few years. What would you attribute that sudden rise in popularity to?

ET: I think it is a combination of a number of factors, but one of the biggest is the economy. A $50 board game will supply an average of 2-3 hours of fun for 2-8 people, and once finished, it can be played countless more times. It costs about $50 (without snacks) for a family of four people to go to the movies just once, and then the movie is over. Tabletop also provides a much needed dose of fun social interaction that so many of us desperately need in today's world of fast-paced work environments and solitary digital communication. Sitting down at a table with friends – or even strangers! – and having a fun time while engaging in an activity like a board game allows for socialization and entertainment to happen at the same time. That's just another bonus versus the movie example I gave.

Funny enough, I think that movies themselves have also contributed to the so-called board game renaissance. We've had a huge influx of what would have been considered "geeky" movies in the last several years, thanks to new *Star Wars* films, the MCU, and more. Hollywood leads trends, and all things geek are now cool, tabletop gaming being high on that list. With game cafes opening everywhere, YouTube and Twitch channels dedicated to tabletop gaming, and people able to carry mobile versions of board games around with them in their pockets, it is easy to see how accessible games are now over just a few years ago.

Overstreet: What do you think it is about the modern board game industry that differentiates it from how the industry was even 10 or 15 years ago?

ET: I could go a lot of ways with this question. First of all, the industry is producing exponen-

tially more games each year. Just 15 years ago, there were a few dozen game companies that were producing more than a title per year, and I could name all of them for the most part. Now, there are hundreds of little companies, and the larger ones are producing more games per year as well. With Kickstarter and other crowd-funding platforms, anybody can try their hand at producing a game, and though many fail (even when funded), that doesn't seem to be discouraging people from trying. Because of this, there is a huge effect on game sales in general. The industry is generating more money than ever before but the number of sales per game is going down, simply due to the fact that retailers and consumers cannot buy everything that is being generated.

Unfortunately, a huge side-effect of this is that the general quality of games is being watered down quite a bit. It used to be that if a game didn't play very well, it was culled from a line or never picked up by a publisher in the first place. Now, if a designer cannot license their game to a publisher, many will just publish on their own. All this being said, I do believe that if you take the top 100 games each year, the overall quality and depth of those games has increased many-fold over those being produced 15-20 years ago. Because gamers have so many choices and a limited amount of dollars to allocate to their new games, the ones rising to the top in quality of game play are truly inspired, with original mechanics and brilliant design.

Overstreet: Do you happen to collect anything related to board gaming or other tabletop games? If so, what's in your collection and why?

ET: Aside from games themselves? I do have well over 1,000 games in my personal collection, which I guess nowadays isn't all that many, given what I've said about how many are produced. While I do also have a ridiculous amount of dice, stored in multiple gallon-sized storage boxes, I don't think that is all that odd for gamers either! So I guess I'd say my favorite "collection" are the copies of games and RPG books that are personalized and signed by my friends in the industry. I have some really funny inscriptions on many games that I treasure deeply. I love supporting my friends, and being in such a tightly-knit industry with such awesome people makes that really easy!

GEN CON

Having long been referred to as "the best four days in gaming," Gen Con is the largest and likely best-known of the tabletop conventions around the world. These days the show is held annually in Indianapolis, where it draws more than 50,000 attendees for a celebration of all things tabletop – but like many shows, it had quite humble beginnings.

Gen Con was founded in 1968 by Gary Gygax – of course, known best as the creator of *Dungeons & Dragons*. The show was actually formed as a wargaming event and was spun out of other similar events that had been held previously by the International Federation of Wargaming. Gygax rented out a hall in Lake Geneva, Wisconsin, and the first Gen Con drew about 100 people. The name of "Gen Con" is derived from "Geneva Convention" due to the show's original location in Lake Geneva; the actual Geneva Conventions are trea-

ties regarding wartime, and the original show's focus on wargaming also made for somewhat of a pun.

The show was taken over by TSR, Inc. (the original publisher of *D&D*) beginning in 1975. Throughout the late '70s and into the '80s, the main show continued to be hosted in various locations in Wisconsin, while spinoff shows – Gen Con West, Gen Con South, and Gen Con East – also began. These shows, held in California, Florida, New Jersey and Pennsylvania, only lasted for a few years each, with the most successful being the South show, which ran from '78 to '84.

Beginning in 1985, the show was held at the Milwaukee Exposition and Convention Center and Arena in order to have more space. Within the next decade, the attendance rose exponentially, going from about 5,000 to 30,000. Worth noting is how, in 1988, Gen Con and Origins Game Fair joined

up as a single event; that happened again in 1992, but has not happened since. Thanks largely in part to a collectible card gaming craze headed by *Magic: The Gathering*, more interest in tabletop games and related conventions exploded in the 1990s and was a huge factor in the attendance boom.

TSR was bought out by Wizards of the Coast in 1997, and Wizards was then bought out by Hasbro two years later. In 2002, Peter Adkison, Wizards of the Coast founder, bought Gen Con from Hasbro and founded Gen Con LLC in order to run the show. A year later, the convention was moved to Indianapolis in order to have more space, and it's been there ever since – in fact, the convention center itself expanded in 2011 largely due to a desire to hold larger Gen Con events.

Other conventions under the banner of Gen Con have also been held since the '90s, including Gen Con SoCal (Southern California), European Gen Con, Gen Con Barcelona, Benelux Gen Con (Netherlands), Gen Con UK, and Gen Con Australia.

Events at Gen Con typically involve the showcasing and playing of board games, tabletop role-playing adventures, and card games. Many games have held their championship tournaments at Gen Con over the years, including *Magic: The Gathering*. The *D&D* Championship Series has also been held at the show, going back to 1977. The main draw for many attendees remains the showcase of numerous products in the expo hall – it has become a common practice for new games to be launched at Gen Con, or for established games to have a convention exclusive product or tie-in available only at that year's show.

Gen Con celebrated its 50th anniversary in August 2017, when it packed the show floor with more than 60,000 gamers of all ages. From a small wargaming get-together to a four-day celebration of all things tabletop, Gen Con has come a long way – and fortunately shows absolutely no signs of slowing down.

ORIGINS GAME FAIR

Since 1975, the Origins Game Fair has been held annually in celebration of all things tabletop. The show was founded in Baltimore, Maryland, as a collaboration between game publisher Avalon Hill and a local wargaming club in the area.

The show, which was originally known as the Origins International Game Expo, was run by both Avalon Hill and Simulations Publications, Inc. (SPI), another wargame publisher, for the first few years. Since 1978, the show has been run by the Game Manufacturers Organization (GAMA).

GAMA is a non-profit organization focused on the advancement of the tabletop gaming hobby, and was actually formed in 1977 in order to run and protect the interests of Origins. GAMA also runs the GAMA Trade Show (GTS) in Las Vegas every year – that show is aimed more at professionals and retailers in the hobby, where Origins is instead aimed at the consumers and game-players themselves. According to the GAMA website, the show's mission is "to promote the general interest of all persons engaged in the buying, selling, licensing, and manufacturing of hobby game prod-

ucts. To that end, GAMA provides member affinity programs such as handbooks, trade and consumer shows, and education programs."

For the first 20 years of Origins Game Fair, the show bounced around to various locations around the country, not settling in one place for too terribly long. Origins locales included Baltimore, Dallas, Detroit, Ann Arbor, Milwaukee, Atlanta, Fort Worth, San Jose, and Philadelphia, among others. In 1988 and 1992, Origins was held in conjunction with Gen Con, and in 1990, it was held alongside DragonCon.

Beginning in 1996, the show has been held annually in Columbus, Ohio, where it's been ever since. Since settling down in that location, attendance has steadily climbed over the years to eventually start drawing gamers in excess of 15,000, a feat reached in 2015.

Events typically held at Origins include collectible card game tournaments, live-action role-playing events, role-playing game demonstrations, and much more. Many game publishers will debut new content at the show, making it a highly desirable destination for fans in order to get that first look at what's about to hit store shelves.

The Origins Awards are also presented at the show every year, recognizing and rewarding excellence in game design. The Awards are presented by the Academy of Adventure Gaming Arts and Design and categories for the awards include excellence in Card Games, Miniature Games, Collectible Games, Family Games, Role-Playing Games, Gaming Accessories, and Board Games, among others. A Game of the Year is also presented.

For any convention to run for more than 40 years is certainly a triumph, but for Origins, it stands as a testament to the longevity of tabletop gaming. With attendance continuing to grow as the industry enjoys this most recent renaissance period, Origins continues to have nowhere to go but up.

UNPUB

THE UNPUBLISHED GAMES NETWORK

For games that are finished and ready to hit store shelves, a convention like Gen Con or Origins is likely the place to be. But for games still in development, Unpub is where games can be highlighted and workshopped.

Unpub is the event held by The Unpublished Games Network, founded in 2010. The first Unpub event took place in a small hall in rural Delaware, after its founder, John Moller, saw a need in the board game community for quality play testing. The network itself is a community of game designers, publishers and players that get together in order to work towards the creation of new tabletop games of all kinds. The main, weekend-long Unpub event has been held just north of Baltimore, Maryland, where it fills its convention space with game developers and players of all ages for three days of gaming and feedback.

Unpub has been able to thrive as a low or no-cost program that instead relies on participation from its attendees. Developers spend the event time demonstrating and showing off the games that they've been working on, and gamers are able to play the game and give constructive feedback on the game itself.

"Our mission, essentially, is to get game designers together with game players, or play testers, in order to help the designers get feedback on their games. These games have to be in some form of development to be part of an Unpub event," Brad Smoley,

"The lifeblood of Unpub is feedback. When a designer registers their game with Unpub, not only are they able to sign up for events, but they also have access to great feedback input directly by the play testers," Smoley said. "As a play tester, all you need to do is show up with a desire to play games and tell the designers exactly what you think."

The main event is "Unpub Prime" or The Unpublished Games Expo, which takes place annually every March in Maryland. In addition to that, there's also Unpub ProtoAlleys, which take place in several of the major gaming conventions that happen across the U.S. all year long, including at Origins, PAX, and BGGcon. There's also a number of Unpub Mini events that take place at local game stores, libraries, schools, or wherever gamers gather to play.

Assistant Director of the Unpub Network, said. "Getting games and gamers together is managed through our website where designers can register their prototypes and individuals can set up their own, local Unpub events."

Perhaps the most intriguing thing about Unpub is that all of the games being presented are in widely different stages of development. There are plenty of games that are nearly-finished, with full-color artwork and a professional-looking setup that look just about ready for mass production. On the other hand, there are just as many games that are fresh off the initial idea-building stage, with home-printed materials often in black-and-white.

However, the goal across the board (so to speak) is to get feedback on games, regardless of how far along it technically is in production. Every game designer presenting at an Unpub event is looking to hear what people liked and disliked about the game, and everyone is open to suggestions as to what could be improved.

Those looking to get involved with Unpub as a designer can register their games on the website (Unpub.net) and check for an Unpub event near them. The website also provides opportunities to get involved with hosting an event. Whether as a designer or as a gamer, Unpub is an event worth paying attention to in order to potentially get the first look at the next must-have board game.

THE ART OF THE GAMES

Many tabletop games rely on the players' and game runners' creativity and imagination to create and build a setting, characters, and storyline. Accordingly, the artwork seen within books and instruction manuals and even on the covers of boxes have proven to be a valuable touchstone for many role-players and gamers across generations.

The artwork seen in the likes of *Dungeons & Dragons* handbooks or on the covers of even the most classic of board games such as *Clue* allow the players to better immerse themselves in the stories that the games' creators aim to tell – especially when the game itself is being played with simple colored plastic or wooden pieces, or is only played with paper and dice rolls. Because of how the artwork is able to help gamers create the worlds that they play in, original pieces of art are a valuable commodity all on their own.

CLERICS OF MAGIC BY MICHAEL DUBISCH - SOLD FOR $418.25

TOP: *GOLGARI GRAVE TROLL* BY GREG HILDEBRANDT - SOLD FOR $418

Dungeons & Dragons, being one of the longest-running tabletop RPGs out there, has a rich history of artwork that can be seen in every book, module and resource ever published within the system. A number of artists have contributed to *D&D* artwork since the earliest iterations and continue to do so today, such as Larry Elmore, Jeff Easley, Clyde Caldwell, Erol Otus, Keith Parkinson, Wayne Reynolds, Todd Lockwood, and many more. Worth noting is how several of these artists also contributed to *Magic: The Gathering* artwork as well (TSR, the original publisher of *D&D*, was bought out by Wizards of the Coast, the publisher of *MTG*, in the late '90s).

Because of how much artwork has been made for *Dungeons & Dragons* and for related publications (such as official and unofficial magazines, comics, and so on) over the years, there's actually a significant amount of it on the market – and for a wide range in price, as well. For a full original color painting, collectors can expect to pay well into four figures or more, depending on the artist and subject matter involved.

Original pages from the *Dungeons & Dragons* comic books can fairly easily be found online in auctions or via comic art dealers, and many times can be found for under $100. This makes them a more affordable alternative to the full-color paintings for fans of the RPG that are looking to include something original within their collection.

Many *D&D* artists have continued to work both on the game and outside of it throughout their careers, and have websites or online stores from which fans can either purchase original pieces, commission an original piece, or simply buy a print. Generally speaking, prints can be found

DragonLance: Dragon's Rest by Fred Fields - Sold for $1135.25

from anywhere between $20 and $100 depending on the size, if the print is limited, and if the print is signed – but it provides yet another way for fans to showcase their favorite realms from the *D&D* world.

There have also been a number of artbooks released over the years, either focusing on *Dungeons & Dragons* overall or on a specific artist. Generally coming in at under $100, these are a solid way for a role-player on a budget to include artwork within their collection.

HORROR OF HORRORS TRADING CARD ART BY SIMON BISLEY
SOLD FOR $1135.25

Card games, too, often feature intricately detailed artwork that lead many to collect certain cards just for how they look, rather than for what they actually do in-game. *Magic the Gathering* is absolutely at the head of the pack in this regard; due to its long history and popularity, artwork from the game is particularly desirable to fans and collectors. Fortunately for potential buyers, there's a lot of resources available online to do so, with multiple online shops (such as the Vintage Magic and Original Magic Art websites) offering original artwork for sale, often directly from the artists themselves.

Most original art pieces for *Magic: The Gathering* fall within the $1,000 to $2,500 range, though there are some high-dollar outliers – some pieces listed at $10,000 or more – as well as some pieces that ask for just a few hundred. The final dollar amount

TSR WORLDS ANNUAL #1 COVER BY LARRY ELMORE
SOLD FOR $9560

MAGIC THE GATHERING NIGHTMARE #1 COMIC BOOK ART
SOLD FOR $42

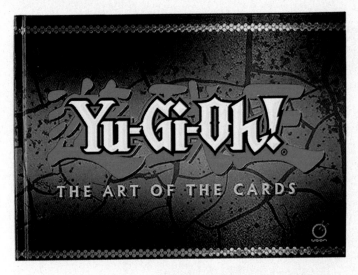

limited framed prints of his work for about $250 a piece.

Of course, there are plenty of other RPGs, board games, and card games out there, and it's fairly easy to do a little bit of research to figure out who exactly is providing the artwork. Many artists attend conventions around the world, and even more provide an online store to order originals or prints directly. Much like with original comic art, the prices will continue to see a significant range from the hundreds well into the thousands (or tens of thousands) of dollars, but that comes with the territory; original art is just that – an original, one-of-a-kind piece. Collecting original artwork requires a level of patience (and funding) often far above collecting just the games themselves, so those looking to expand their collection to include artwork should be prepared for what lies ahead. However, the payoff is absolutely worth it.

largely depends on the artist themselves, the set the card was featured in, what the card depicts, and the popularity of the card in-game.

Fortunately, for the more casual *Magic* fan, many artists offer prints of their work online for just about $20 or so. While prints like these don't have much collectible value, they do present a way for fans of the game to display a high-resolution print of their favorite card artwork.

When it comes to *Pokémon* and *Yu-Gi-Oh!*, though, there's next to no original artwork from the cards available on the market. Fans of the card art from *Yu-Gi-Oh!* can, however, find a collection of it in a hardcover book released in 2017 – *Yu-Gi-Oh! The Art of the Cards*. The book features more than 800 cards from the game and is currently one of the only ways for fans of the game's artwork to get a better look at it. On the *Pokémon* end of things, Ken Sugimori, one of the main artists for the card game and for the franchise at large, has released artbooks in Japan that can easily be imported. The Pokémon website also sells

LARRY ELMORE

Larry Elmore has been creating fantasy and science-fiction artwork for more than four decades, and has contributed artwork to games including Magic: The Gathering, EverQuest *and, perhaps most notably,* Dungeons & Dragons. *Elmore set the standard for fantasy gaming artwork during his time working for TSR, where he worked on covers for* D&D *as well as on* Dragon *magazine. He also dabbled in comics for many years with his classic* SnarfQuest.
We chatted with Elmore about his history in the tabletop world, his own fandom for the games he worked on, and his current and future projects.

Overstreet: How did you come to work on *Dungeons & Dragons* in those early days of the game?

Larry Elmore (LE): Shortly after I got out of college, like many other guys my age, I was drafted into the army. I did two years in the military – I actually lived close to Fort Knox at the time. I went to Germany, and then I got stationed at Fort Knox for a year. There, I was working as an illustrator, and they liked my work, so when I got out, they hired me as a civilian. I also started freelancing around that time, and I got some work at *National Lampoon* magazine, which at that time was pretty popular, and also at *Heavy Metal*.

A friend of mine, when I was working at Fort Knox, he played *Dungeons & Dragons*. This was in 1979, probably, so it hadn't been out a long time yet. And he told me, "Your work would look good for this, you should work for *Dungeons & Dragons*." So I tried to get a freelance job with them – my friend actually sent the samples in. They gave me a call back to do a freelance job, so I did that for them, and they liked that so much that they wanted to hire me.

I was in Kentucky, and I had a home there, and my wife and I both had pretty good jobs. I was making about $20,000 a year – which was really good at the time! And I was freelancing on the side, so I was pretty happy. All my family had lived in Kentucky for going on 200 years or so at that point, so I knew that area pretty well! So, they wanted to hire me and that would require my wife and I to move up to Wisconsin. Some of the people [at TSR] were in their 30s, but everybody else was 18 or 19, maybe 21 years old. And I didn't want to work at a place with a bunch of kids! So I told them no, I'll just freelance for you.

Then I got a call at work, and it was them, and they told me, "the president of the company is flying down, he wants to talk to you." And I'm like – oh *crap*, okay. But I picked him up at the airport and brought him home, fixed him a nice supper, and then we talked business. He asked me what I made, and I told him. And he said, "I'll double it." I'm like, well, God, my wife also works, and she made about $12,000 or so a year, not too bad, and he said, "We'll double that, too." So at that point I'm just like, "Well God, that's $64,000 a year." Today that'd be like $150,000 a year! But there was the issue of the house, too, which we had been making payments on, and he said, "We'll sell it for you, so you don't have to worry about it." And at that point I looked at my wife, and looked back at him, and said, "Well, I guess you've bought yourself an artist!" Right off

the bat, they put me to work, and I did a bunch of different covers. They were also putting out a little board game for kids, which I also worked on – that was called *Fantasy Forest*.

At that time, I knew Jeff Easley – I knew he was working freelance for them at the time. But I called him up and he asked me if I thought they'd hire him, and I said, "Oh, hell yeah!" So he sent his samples in, and he got hired. And then Clyde Caldwell came in and he got hired, so we had a core crew. But anyway, I was there about two years and they decided to have me do the covers for *Basic, Expert* and *Companion D&D*. They said my art looked more ready for mass-market audiences, while Jeff's art looked better for the hobby market, so Jeff did *AD&D* and all those books. I wanted to do the *AD&D* stuff, because we were running a campaign at the time and we ran it on *AD&D*. We all worked in one big room together so it was easy to play a game right in the middle of the room!

Overstreet: So you played the game a lot?
LE: Oh yeah, we campaigned. We played it at lunch, sometimes we'd go to someone's house and play all night. We were all real into it.

I had played *D&D* once before going to Fort Knox, a guy got us all to play a game. I

had no idea what the game was like, so we took like a week for us to all roll up characters! We were all just like, "What kind of a game *is* this?" Finally, he got us all sitting together and the game officially begins – he tells us it's night, and we're camped by a big river, and asks what we're all doing. And he comes to me first, and I'm thinking, "Well, I'm a fighter, and we've got a thief with us... I'm gonna kill the thief!" So I grabbed the dice and started rolling, and the thief started fighting back, and we had a wizard in there, so he casts some sort of spell to stop us, and the guy running the game is just yelling "Stop, stop! This is not how you play!" And he told us that we were a team and we needed to be working together. So we were all kind of just like, oh... we'd never played a game like that before! All the games I'd ever played in my life were either you against an opponent or you against the board. There was only ever one winner. We didn't comprehend it, playing against whatever he dreamed up and playing as a group.

I realized that everything was important in a game like that, all the little details in a setting that creates a mental picture. So I told the other guys working on the art to work in the land, the nature, the seasons, all of that was important. It's gotta be real. You're taking an imaginary scene and making it real.

Overstreet: When you were working on the art at the time, were you drawing from your experiences as a player?

LE: Yeah, once we started playing and had the full crew. Around '81 or '82, Keith Parkinson – we hired him, and he was young, but he was a DM. By this time, a lot of people were playing it. Keith wanted to paint like I did, anyway – drawing the whole scene – and I thought the best thing to do was to get everyone else to go along with that. Most fantasy art was just one major figure and not hardly any background – that was the style at the time. And I said, "We've got to change this." We figured if we could get the other artists playing the game, they'd get on board with that.

The cool thing was that we were customers of our own products. So we knew what we wanted, and luckily all the other people playing liked it. The higher-ups for the most part just kind of let us go and do what we wanted. One rule came down one time, though, which was "If you paint blood on a cover, it's got to be green. It can't be red." And we all thought that was stupid. I think we did that for one or two paintings and then we went back to painting it red.

We mostly just did the paintings our way, and I think because of that, they got better paintings from us. But at the same time, all of the paintings had deadlines. Most of us, pretty much, if they gave us two weeks to do something, that was great. Sometimes they'd want an oil painting in an afternoon. And Jeff Easley would do it – he could do a complete oil painting in about four hours. The rest of us, we busted Jeff – we said, "Don't do that! If you start doing that, they'll be asking for that all the time!" We couldn't keep up with that, especially on oils. But most of the time they gave us a schedule with decent enough time – enough time to get one done.

Overstreet: Tell us a little bit about *SnarfQuest*. What drove you to do a comic?
LE: Well, back when I was working at Fort Knox, I think I had more time then to buy more comics and more art books. There was another guy who worked there, a friend of mine, and he enjoyed thinking up fantasy worlds and little critters and whatnot – and actually it was more steampunk then, before steampunk ever became popular. So I thought that I wanted to do that too, but I couldn't make it like his world, and I had some ideas – one of the little black-and-white stories I did ended up posted in *Heavy Metal*.

I wanted to have different kinds of characters. Little critters where you didn't really know what they were, but you knew they were intelligent. Humans, dragons, anything could be in this world. So I had thought about it for two or three years, doing sketching and whatnot. When I went to TSR, I was pretty busy there, but one day the editor of *Dragon* magazine came in and wanted to run a three-page comic strip. He said it could be anything we wanted, and to make up five pages, and then they'd choose one.

My question was if TSR owned the rights to it – because they owned the rights to our paintings. And he said, "No, *Dragon* magazine is work-for-hire, so you retain the rights to your work." And it would be $100 a page – so an extra $300 a month, which was pretty good! I sat down and did five pages, and I had no clue where I was going with it, but I submitted it. Three months go by, and I don't hear anything about it, but then they call me in one day and tell me that they liked it and wanted to run with it.

It seemed like the characters took over, and I just followed what they did. The only rule I had was that something sort of funny had to be happening in each episode – a little payoff. So I continued moving the characters to different places and following what they did. In Snarf's case, nothing went hardly to plan. But that was the funny part – he would make a plan that was pretty simple and things would go wrong. He had bad luck, but he always persisted. Or somehow, through luck and effort, he'd achieve his goal.

I didn't know it until years later, but I picked up a book of old *SnarfQuest* stories and started reading it, and I thought – my God, *I was Snarf!* And Telerie was my wife! Even their relationship at times was just like me and my wife. Why couldn't I see it then? In the story, the old king died under unknown circumstances, and all you had to do was go out in the world and make enough money and make the biggest name for yourself, and you'd get to be king. Well, when I left home here, my goal was to try and get a name for myself, so I could make enough money, so one day I could just freelance for myself and support my family. So I was out for money and fame! And my wife was more grounded, like Telerie was more grounded than Snarf. It just hit me then – man, that was my life's story right there!

Overstreet: You fairly recently did a Kickstarter for more *SnarfQuest* content. Were you at all surprised that fans were still demanding more stories 30 years later? **LE:** Yes! Over the years, people have always asked me at conventions, "When are you going to do more *SnarfQuest?*" And I always told them that I didn't have the time to do it – at *Dragon* magazine I was getting paid to do it, and magazines like that slowly disappeared. So there wasn't really a market for me to put it in. I couldn't figure out a way to do new *SnarfQuest* and get paid for it.

I did my first Kickstarter, which was a big artbook – it was super successful. So I thought, well, I had started a little story for a magazine, but the magazine folded after a few issues. I had a whole story in mind before the magazine quit. But I thought, well, I've got black-and-whites for 15 pages or so already done. I'll need to do another 25 or 30 pages for a full story... if I do a Kickstarter, by the time I fulfill it, I would have had time to do those other pages, and if the Kickstarter went well, I'd get paid. So this was a new story, basically, where the first 15-20 pages had been published in a magazine that saw very low circulation, so I figured most of the fans hadn't seen those yet. So we Kickstarted that book, and it made good money – more than I thought it would make – so I got paid and covered all my expenses and managed to fulfill the promise I made when I told people that

one day I'd do some more *SnarfQuest*. I finally did it.

Overstreet: After you left TSR you obviously continued to produce fantasy art for a bunch of other games – *Magic: The Gathering* and *Everquest* and whatnot. All of these games generally fall under what would be considered "high fantasy" but all of them have a distinct feel to them. How difficult is it to give a piece a specific feel for the game it's from?
LE: Well, for *D&D*, we mostly just painted the way we painted. We had hardly any art direction, so it was mostly our own painting style. We played the game, we knew what we were painting for, so we didn't need someone to tell us what to do. And that went pretty smoothly for us. After I started freelancing, a lot of game companies contacted me for art, so I just did the same thing I always did!

Basically, I always just wanted to get better... my whole career, I've just wanted to paint better and learn more. I'd ask what the flavor or feel of the game was, and if it was just typical fantasy role-playing, then that was fine by me. It wasn't ever that difficult, because I worked at TSR about eight years before I went freelance, and I knew what roleplaying companies were out there and what they did. Doing stuff

for other game companies became pretty easy. I did a lot of different things – I did toy packaging for *ThunderCats*, I did model car boxes, I did all sorts of stuff.

I stayed busy, and I was working, on average, about 14 hours a day. I'd go to bed around 3 AM, got up about 9... I lived on about five hours of sleep for 20 years or so! But I enjoyed it, and I was making good money, but I was painting myself to death. It finally caught up with me when I had a light stroke, and then I had a heart attack almost three years in a row. I lived off of caffeine, nicotine and junk food for all those years. So I had to change a lot of habits, but as long as I can stay healthy, I'm going to continue painting – it's what I love to do.

Overstreet: What are you up to these days?
LE: I'm glad you asked that, because I've talked to a lot of illustrators, and most of them, by the time they get to be about 45 years old, they burn out. You've painted your whole career, and hope-fully you've gotten better as an artist, but you've always been painting someone else's work or someone's scene. It was always art-directed, especially after I went freelance. When you do an illustration, that's what the client wants. And so I didn't argue with art directors much, I'd do what they told me – now I wish I had asserted myself more.

Most artists, by the time they've been painting for 20, 25 years, they want to do their own work. The only chance I had to totally do my own work was when I was doing *Dragon* magazine covers. They'd give us a topic – "This month we're talking about clerics, so paint

something with a cleric in it" – and that was so good! I did about 14 covers or so, because while they didn't pay as much, I was more free to do what I wanted to do. Most of my better paintings were for *Dragon* magazine.

All of my life, I want-ed to paint my own stuff, and *finally*, when I did my Kickstarter, I realized then that I could paint my own work and sell origi-nal paintings. I've been selling a lot of things over the years. When I paint what I want to paint, there's no deadline, and it's 10 times more fun than illustration for other folks. I did the Kickstarters, and then I got caught up on everything that I owed people – com-missions and other things – and it took two years to get that all done. So I finally got even with the world. I've got three paint-ings on boards ready to paint, and I've got other drawings around, and I'm as happy as I've ever been.

My goal right now is just to make it to 80 while keeping my brains, because that would give me another 10 years of painting my own work. And these are some of the best paintings I've ever done.

All these old *D&D* fans are now older and richer, and while I've always sold original *D&D* stuff pretty quickly, now, there's fewer and fewer to buy. So I've been catering to that market more. Original art will always find a place in a home someplace. There will always be a market for original paint-ings – and I did the right thing, because there's a bigger demand for my stuff than ever. So, I'm pretty happy right now! I collect a little social security and my wife collects retirement, so with selling paintings, we're doing pretty good. I'm so happy these days, it scares me.

GRADING

For card collectors of all kinds, grading services have long been favored in order to assess and preserve value. Though this practice started with baseball and other kinds of sports cards, it has also extended to collectible card games like *Magic, Pokémon* and many others. Most grading services that were formed around sports memorabilia, such as Professional Sports Authenticator (PSA) and Beckett Media, have been able to apply the approach they formed for sports cards to CCGs of all kinds.

Many graded cards can be found in online auctions, and graded cards are favored by many collectors for a number of reasons. It all boils down to the process used by the services, which starts with verifying authenticity of the card itself – with the amount of counterfeit cards having been produced over the years for CCGs, this might be the single most important step. Any professional grading service likely won't even bother with the grading process itself if an authenticator determines that the card submitted to them is a counterfeit.

Even cards determined to be authentic are going to be examined for doctoring of some sort. For CCGs, this might include evidence of trimmed edges or restored artwork. While doctored or restored cards might still receive a grade, they'll probably be categorized into a different kind of grading scale in order to differentiate it from an untouched card. Due to how CCGs have really only been a mass market item for the last 25 years or so, it's unlikely that a *Pokémon* or *Yu-Gi-Oh* card would have been subjected to any kind of serious restoration in the same fashion that an

80-year-old comic book or baseball card might have seen – but it's still something that the grading services look out for, and something that serious collectors need to keep in mind.

Once a card has been authenticated, it's given a grade – usually on a 10-point scale, with 10 being the highest possible grade – and placed in a case. The case provided is generally designed to be tamper-proof (or at the very least tamper-evident) and, most importantly, designed to prevent any sort of further wear, damage or aging to the card itself. The case will also have a label on it of some sort, showing the grade given to the card, details about the card itself (such as its name, manufacturer, or set it belongs to), a unique bar code and number for verification, and a security label of some sort that provides proof of the grading service itself.

So, what determines the grade itself? For the industry leaders in card grading, it tends to boil down to the condition of the corners and edges, the centering of the image, and the condition of the surface of the card itself. (In fact, Beckett Grading Services gives a final overall grade based on four sub-grades on centering, corners, edges, and surface.)

When it comes to the grading scale itself, a card graded at a 10 is considered a virtually perfect, almost untouched card. It would be as if a pack was opened very carefully and the card was taken directly out of the pack and then immediately graded and slabbed. A 10 card is also going to be called a "mint" card, and will feature sharp edges, bright colors, no staining or damage of any kind and a perfectly-centered image. Even the slightest amount of fraying on an edge or minor printing issue can take an otherwise perfect card down to an 8 on many grading scales, which would qualify it as "near-mint."

As more damage to edges, corners and the overall surface of the card becomes apparent, it puts that card in a lower and lower grade. Off-color images and general wear and tear (often coming as a result of the actual playing of the cards themselves in CCGs) can quickly take a card down to a grade of 5 or below. Cards that feature visible creases of any sort will also generally be graded pretty low. Many grading services have half-grades (8.5, 7.5, et cetera) within the scale that they use to allow for a more gradual stepping down of the scale.

Having a card graded will cost money to do, but that cost is considered worth it by many collectors for the preservation aspect of the card – as well as for how much more a graded card can command in an auction or online sale over a raw, ungraded one. A quick search through eBay auctions can show anyone the price disparity between a graded card and a raw card, and generally speaking a graded card (particularly one receiving a grade of 8 or better from Beckett or PSA) will command a price of three, sometimes four times higher than that of its ungraded example.

For those looking to invest in cards for future sale, getting top-dollar cards graded is an absolute no-brainer. And even for those just looking to preserve their collection so that it doesn't deteriorate any further, having cards graded means that they'll be slabbed and protected from any further wear. The nature of paper products is, unfortunately, somewhat delicate – simply leaving cards in a shoebox isn't going to do much to protect them from the elements over the course of decades. Those looking to have their most prized cards graded should check out the variety of services available to them and seek out what kind will work for them.

PRESERVATION & STORAGE

The best thing to do in order to preserve the value and longevity of any sort of game item is to make sure that it's being stored properly. But with the wide variety of tabletop gaming materials, there's really no one single proven method that's been accepted across the hobby.

STORING BOARD GAMES

Board game collectors might have the hardest time of all when it comes to finding a storage solution, given the significant size of many contemporary board games. Many classic board games typically came in a long, somewhat-flat box that contained all of the necessary pieces to play, and could easily be stacked sideways on a shelf. Today, board games often come in a stouter, thicker box that is more of a square than a rectangle in terms of its footprint. A board game today often takes up the same amount of physical space as several books,

leading to some obvious and some less-obvious solutions.

Many board game aficionados have taken a shine to cube-based shelving units, which can often fit a handful of games in each individual cube. These can be purchased at nearly any department or furniture store and usually come in a variety of colors to suit whatever interior design someone already has going on. This style of shelving usually tends to be deeper to accommodate drawers of some sort, making it a top choice for many collectors. Cube organizers can also usually be bought somewhat à la carte, which allows collectors to essentially just buy additional cubes to add to a stack or unit as they need them.

Others take a more traditional route, simply by having board games stacked on a regular bookshelf. The downside to standard

bookshelves, though, is that many of them are not going to be deep enough for a lot of more modern board games to fit appropriately. Having part of the box hanging off the side of a shelf causes the possibility of being knocked off by a passerby, which can lead to the box being damaged – which will reduce its value in a collector's market. The bottom of the box can also be dented where it hangs off if there's too much weight (such as other board games) on top of it.

On top of the "what to use" question here, there's also the "where to store" one. For collectors who have a selection of games they play on a regular basis with friends or family, many will keep a number of them in a main living area of their home. While there's certainly nothing inherently wrong with this, a concern in regards to preserving games is exposure to sunlight.

Ultraviolet rays will cause the color to fade on just about anything that gets consistent exposure to sunlight. Color gets faded or "sun-bleached" – also known as photodegradation – due to how UV rays interact with inks and dyes. Essentially, after extended exposure to UV radiation (as well as to the heat that usually accompanies sunlight), the dyes will begin to break down and fade away, causing the sun-bleached effect.

Accordingly, a lot of collectors will store their more valuable games out of the sunlight, leading to many opting to store their collectibles in a basement. Which leads to another key factor to keep in mind – humidity. Many older houses tend to have damp basements, and storing games in such an atmosphere can be tricky. To counteract this, many gamers will store games in an airtight plastic container if they choose to keep them in a basement – and usually that container will be see-through for easy identification of which games are where. Many will also simply invest in a heavy-duty dehumidifier to help stave off the effects of moisture.

Storing Miniatures
Despite their name, miniatures can take up a pretty significant amount of space. Lots of different styles of games make use of miniature figures, and there's just as many ways to store them as there are to play with them.

For large wargames that use an equally-large amount of miniatures (such as *Warhammer*), storage solutions are a must. Plenty of people take a lot of pride in their custom-painted armies – rightly so – and will display at least part of their collection in a glass display case of some sort. Like with board games, though, exposure to UV rays can cause the paint to eventually start to fade after prolonged exposure, so it's best to make sure that any piece being displayed out in the open is not in direct sunlight.

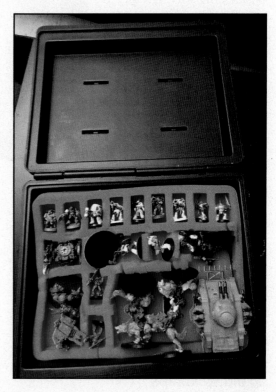

For large quantities of minis, though, many have used foam of some sort in order to store them in layers in a large plastic bin of some sort. Egg crate foam is a favorite of many, due to how the bumps and ridges on the foam create natural pockets that most standard miniatures can fit right into. Certain kinds of egg crate foam can be pretty expensive, with the heavy-duty stuff designed for soundproofing being at the top of the list.

Some folks on a tighter budget have sometimes taken a cheap foam mattress topper produced in an egg crate style and cut it up into smaller pieces on their own.

For larger minis, sometimes egg crate foam isn't going to cut it. Instead, many wargaming fans have protected their bigger pieces by buying a thick sheet of flat foam (which can be found in varying quantities from any major craft store) and custom-cutting it to fit a specific miniature with a precision knife or similar tool. While this may result in some trial-and-error situations, the value of the larger figures should be protected just as much as that of smaller ones.

Besides the varying types of foam, some mini collectors have taken to using magnets in order to secure the figures in a storage container. For those who need to transport a large amount of minis at once, this helps keep everything in its place for travel and can also make sure things stay organized within a large container.

The ultimate goal when storing minis is to make sure that the paint on them stays as pristine as possible. This means making sure that they're not being stored in direct sunlight (to prevent the paint from fading) as well as making sure that they're not being stored where they can knock into each other at all (to prevent the paint from chipping off).

STORING CARDS

Thanks to how long card collecting has been a passionate hobby, there's been a few proven methods to storing and preserving cards that are affordable and easy to find. For most, the choice boils down to two main options – boxes or binders.

Boxes specifically designed for cards are made by a number of different companies and can generally be found very cheaply at your local comic or game shop. These boxes are generally made out of cardboard, though there are also plastic and even metal card boxes made as well – cardboard has long been the go-to for many collectors, though, due to its relatively inexpensive price point compared to other materials. Many collectors will use these boxes to sort their cards in a number of ways, usually either alphabetically or by set.

Within boxes, it's common to see toploader sleeves used for individual card storage. Toploaders are plastic sleeves designed to keep out dust and moisture and keep the card clean and protected (they're called "toploaders" because the sleeves are loaded from the top). Several companies make toploaders in varying sizes and thicknesses, so it's very easy to find what works best for your own collecting habits and your budget.

Many collectors will use toploaders only for their most valuable cards, or to have one full complete set, and will have the excess common (and less valuable) cards stored outside of the sleeves. It's not uncommon to see longtime collectors have a complete, pristine set in toploaders and then have what they consider to be essentially excess cards (or ones that have seen a lot of wear-and-tear from play) stored without sleeves.

For those who enjoy playing the game as well as collecting the cards, there's a number of companies that produce what are colloquially referred to as "deck protectors" – thin plastic sleeves that encase cards in a similar fashion to a toploader without taking up as much space. While these will not provide the same level of protection as a rigid toploader, these thin plastic sleeves will at the very least keep the cards clean of the sweat off a player's hands, and are recommended for anyone who enjoys playing these games. Deck protector sleeves usually come in packs of 60 (the standard size deck for a number of different card

games) and generally don't cost more than a few dollars. Some are totally transparent on both sides, while others have a color or design on the back to give the deck some flair during gameplay.

A key thing to keep in mind when storing cards in boxes, even with toploaders, is to make sure that there's some breathing room in the box. You don't want to pack cards in a box so tightly that they cannot be flipped through, as pressure can cause damage to cards over long periods of time.

The downside to having things in boxes is that the cards aren't really on display if they're being stored in an opaque box. For those who have cards that they want to show off, binders might provide a better storage solution. Many of the same companies that sell boxes and toploaders also sell binders and pages for those binders. Most card binders have pages with 3-by-3 sleeves

in them, to display nine cards per page. This is a good solution for many, as the sleeves will generally protect the cards from wear and tear, and it's easy to lay out an entire set of cards within a single binder in order to keep a large collection organized.

The best protection of a card investment, though, is to get it graded – a process discussed at length earlier in this book.

Much like with board games, the biggest factors to keep in mind with cards is to make sure that they are not being stored in direct sunlight or in a hot or damp environment. Moisture, heat and UV rays can do a lot of damage to cards over long exposures to those elements, so to protect a collection, cards should be stored in sleeves whenever possible and in a cool, dry place.

Regardless of what you happen to be collecting and playing, storing those games and accessories properly is the key to making sure that those games can be enjoyed for years to come. As tabletop gaming continues to boom as a hobby, it's entirely possible that new methods will become available as new storage products start to hit the market. The best thing you can do is simply head to your friendly local game store and see what they have available to suit your needs.